St. Louis Community College

Library

5801 Wilson Avenue
St. Louis, Missouri 63110

WILLIAM PENN'S
"HOLY EXPERIMENT"

THE FOUNDING OF PENNSYLVANIA

1681–1701

WILLIAM PENN'S
"HOLY EXPERIMENT"

THE FOUNDING OF PENNSYLVANIA

1681–1701

EDWIN B. BRONNER

GREENWOOD PRESS, PUBLISHERS
WESTPORT, CONNECTICUT

Library of Congress Cataloging in Publication Data

Bronner, Edwin B   , 1920-
    William Penn's "holy experiment."

    Reprint of the ed. published by Temple University
Publications, New York.
    Bibliography: p.
    Includes index.
    1. Pennsylvania--History--Colonial period, ca. 1600-
1775. 2. Friends, Society of--Pennsylvania.
3. Penn, William, 1644-1718. I. Title.
[F152.B84 1978]   974.8'02   78-5882
ISBN 0-313-20432-2

Reprinted in 1978 by Greenwood Press, Inc.
51 Riverside Avenue, Westport, CT. 06880

Printed in the United States of America

10 9 8 7 6 5 4 3 21

FOR ANNE

and

our four daughters

ACKNOWLEDGMENTS

A substantial amount of my research was undertaken in the dignified and friendly atmosphere of the Historical Society of Pennsylvania. I am greatly indebted to the members of the staff for their guidance and assistance. In addition, I have been extended every courtesy by the personnel of the following institutions: the American Philosophical Society, the Free Library of Philadelphia, the Library of Haverford College, the Library Company of Philadelphia, the Library of Congress, the New York Public Library, the Pennsylvania Historical and Museum Commission, the Department of Records of Philadelphia Yearly Meeting, the Friends Library of Swarthmore College, and the Temple University Library.

It has been a pleasant and profitable experience to discuss this subject with several scholars who are interested in the period; especially the late Albert Cook Myers and Henry J. Cadbury. I am deeply grateful to Professor Leonidas Dodson and Dean Roy F. Nichols of the University of Pennsylvania for criticism, encouragement, and guidance while preparing this manuscript. S. W. Higginbotham, formerly of the Pennsylvania Historical and Museum Commission, has made many helpful suggestions. Joan Teitel, Assistant Editor of the Columbia University Press, has given invaluable editorial guidance to me in preparing the final draft. Any attempt to express my gratitude to my wife would sound trite, and so I will say nothing.

Philadelphia, Pennsylvania   E. B. B.
December, 1961

CONTENTS

INTRODUCTION

THE BOOKS WRITTEN about colonial Pennsylvania would fill many shelves, and it is pertinent to ask why another study of the same old subject? The writer naturally has an answer to that question. He would not have taken the trouble to produce a re-study of the significant first twenty years of Pennsylvania's history under William Penn, if he had not considered it a highly worthwhile project.

There is no thorough, well-documented, chronological study of Pennsylvania for the years 1681 to 1701. The books which are valuable for the later period are scanty during the first twenty years.

This contribution to bookshelves already full of Pennsylvania material is a chronological narrative, primarily political, written to clarify and explain Pennsylvania history between the years 1681 and 1701. Because political history is no longer confined to the study of elections, political parties, assemblies, and governors, these chapters contain material about the religion, the philosophy, the economic life, and the social life of the people in Pennsylvania.

The plantation was founded as a "holy experiment" by William Penn and his fellow Quakers. It was hoped that virtuous men, laboring under divine guidance, might establish a virtuous government and society as an example to all mankind. During the eventful first two years of its history the little Quaker colony grew rapidly, and William Penn's "holy experiment" was firmly planted.

After Penn returned to England in 1684, the idealism which permeated the first years was replaced by a spirit which boded ill for Penn's utopian dreams. Pennsylvania had been planted as an exception to a new colonial policy, and was forced to struggle to maintain her integrity. Economic pressures both within the colony and from the outside severely marred her tranquillity. There were groups in Pennsylvania which attempted to secure political domination over the remaining freemen, and, on occasion, all the provincials joined to oppose the governor and proprietor. Fundamental differences of opinion existed in religion, and the main religious stream was divided by a schism which had political overtones. As an absentee Governor, William Penn could exert little control over the government or the citizens of his plantation. He was forced to sit helplessly by in England and watch the "holy experiment" slowly fade in the colony.

Nevertheless, the people in Pennsylvania felt that it was an exciting time in which to live. They believed that there were other things in the world besides "holy experiments," for the colony grew and prospered. During his second visit, beginning in 1699, Penn established a vigorous government, granted a liberal constitution, joined the Friends in worship, and realized, when he returned to England in 1701, that he had planted a successful colony, though the "holy experiment" was nearly forgotten. Fortunately, a residue remained from the idealism of the early years, a residue that leavened the society as well as the government of Pennsylvania during the remainder of the colonial period.

In this study of Pennsylvania, the writer has concentrated his efforts on understanding the struggle for politico-economic-religious self-realization by the dominant element of society, the English-speaking people. That has meant that several aspects of Pennsylvania, the Indians, the Germans, or Delaware society, have not been fully treated. Where these groups have noticeably influenced the dominant group, or where they have fitted naturally into the general narrative, they have been introduced in brief summaries. This is not an attempt to amass between two covers everything that is known about Pennsylvania between the years 1681 and 1701.

CHRONOLOGY FOR PENNSYLVANIA

1681 TO 1701

1681	March 4	William Penn obtained the Charter for Pennsylvania from Charles II
	April 8	Penn addressed a letter to the inhabitants of Pennsylvania
1682	April 25	First Frame of government completed
	August 24	James, Duke of York, granted Delaware to Penn
	October 27	Penn landed at New Castle, Delaware
	December 4–7	First session of the Assembly at Chester
1683	April 2	The Charter of Liberties, or Second Frame, adopted
1684	August 12	Penn returned to England
1684–1687		Provincial Council placed in charge of the government
1685		James II succeeded Charles II as king
1687	February 1	Commissioners of state named to control government
1688	September 25	John Blackwell named lieutenant governor
	December	Glorious Revolution. William and Mary succeeded James II
	December 10	Penn first arrested as a Jacobite (Under suspicion until November, 1693)
	December 17	Lieutenant governor Blackwell arrived in Philadelphia
1689–1697		King William's War
1689	April 9	Blackwell sent his resignation to William Penn
1690	January 1	Provincial Council again in control of Pennsylvania
1691	April	Pennsylvania and Delaware separated. Thomas Lloyd deputy governor in Pennsylvania, and William Markham deputy governor in Delaware
		Beginning of Keithian Schism in the Society of Friends
1692	October 21	Benjamin Fletcher commissioned royal governor of Pennsylvania and Delaware
1693	April 26	Fletcher arrived in Philadelphia to take over government

1694	August 9	Crown returned Pennsylvania to William Penn
1695	March 26	William Markham assumed control of Pennsylvania in Penn's name
1696		Board of Trade replaced Lords of Trade
	November 7	Markham's Frame of government replaced earlier charters
1699	December 2	Penn landed at Philadelphia on his return to Pennsylvania
1700	June	Both the Charter of Liberties, 1683, and Markham's Frame, 1696, laid aside
	November	Laws of Pennsylvania completely revised
1701	October 28	Charter of Privileges adopted
	November	Penn sailed for England. Andrew Hamilton to serve as lieutenant governor

Chronology can be troublesome in a study of this kind. The English used the Julian (Old Style) Calendar instead of the Gregorian (New Style) Calendar until 1752. This meant that the year began on March 25, and that dates from January 1 until that time were indicated by a double numeral, as 1688/89. Furthermore, the Julian Calendar was ten days behind the Gregorian Calendar until 1700, and eleven days behind it after that date.

To make matters worse, the Quakers did not use the "heathen" names for the months, but instead wrote "First Month" for March; "Second Month" for April, "Sixth Month" for August, and "Tenth Month" for December. This made February "Twelfth Month."

In this study all dates are given as in the New Style Calendar, but without adding the ten or eleven days.

CHAPTER ONE

THE BACKGROUND OF THE

"HOLY EXPERIMENT"

FOR MY COUNTRY, I eyed the Lord, in obtaining it; and more was I drawn inward to look to him, and to owe it to his hand and power, *than to any other way; I have so obtained it, and desire to keep it;* that I may not be unworthy of his love; but do that, which may answer his kind Providence, and serve his truth and people: *that an example may be set up to the nations:* there may be room there, though not here, for such an *holy experiment.*[1]

In this, William Penn stated in simple fashion his deepest feelings in regard to Pennsylvania. First, he believed that God had been instrumental in granting him the magnificent province in the New World. Secondly, and growing naturally out of his gratitude, he desired to use the gift from above to the glory of God. Finally, he hoped that the operation of his colony in accordance with the highest Christian ethic might serve as a model for mankind, to indicate by example what men may achieve on earth if they will but put themselves into the hands of God.

Thus to William Penn, the word "holy" was the more important word of the two. He expected the "experiment" to be permeated with the spirit of God. He was certain that if the province were filled with virtuous persons, who not only knew God's will, but who lived according to His Light, his "holy experiment" could not fail. Penn expected Pennsylvania to be largely peopled with such persons, his fellow religionists in the group called the Religious Society of Friends.

The Friends, or Quakers as they were nicknamed in derision, were a new sect which grew largely from the vision of George

Fox. Dissatisfied with conventional beliefs, and yearning for answers to all of his internal doubts and questions, Fox searched for a revelation of God's will for three years before it suddenly came to him in 1647: "When all my hopes in them and in all men was gone, so that I had nothing outwardly to help me, nor could tell what to do, then, O then I heard a voice which said, 'There is one, even Christ Jesus, that can speak to thy condition.' and when I heard it, my heart did leap for joy." [2] The faith in the inner voice of Christ, and the realization that no outward thing can help man achieve peace with God, are at the core of Quakerism. Fox began to preach the inward Christ, and gathered a great following, perhaps as many as 60,000 persons by 1682.

The followers of George Fox believed that the teachings of Christ were meant to be obeyed, not just discussed or agreed to in a passive manner. The Sermon on the Mount was not an ideal towards which a person might gaze, but an actuality to be achieved. Furthermore, Quakers were filled with the conviction that God still spoke to them and that they were to be constantly in communion with divine authority. These were people on fire with a divine spark. Is it any wonder that Penn believed his "holy experiment" would be a success?

The concrete manifestations of the spirit which motivated the "holy experiment," such as religious liberty, political freedom, or pacifism, were all founded in a deep spirituality. To William Penn this spiritual quality was fundamental to all else. He frequently implored his colonists to regain the spirit which had been the foundation stone of the "holy experiment." For example, in February, 1687, when he sent instructions regarding a change in the government from rule by the Council to rule by Commissioners of State, he closed his words of advice with this plea: [3]

Be most just, as in the sight of the *all-seeing, all-searching* God; and before you let your spirits into an affair, retire to him (who is not far away from every one of you; by whom Kings reign, and princes decree justice) that he may give you a good understanding, and government of your selves, in the management thereof; which is that which truly crowns public actions, and dignifies those, that perform them . . . Love, forgive, help and serve one another; and let the people learn by your example, as well as by your power, the happy life of concord.

To William Penn the "holy experiment" was a community populated by virtuous people who were motivated by an all-pervasive love of God.

Once it has been agreed that all of life in the "holy experiment" will have a spiritual basis, it is not difficult to discover the proper pathway to follow. It is only necessary to ask of an idea, a practice, a theory, "is it in accordance with the Will of God?" If the answer is "no," it must be discarded, and if "yes," it must be adopted. This measure would be used in relation to such an important concept as religious liberty, and such a practical matter as people living in caves along the bank of the Delaware because they were too lazy to build houses. The Quakers believed that perfection was possible, and anything less than perfection was a failing.

William Penn had long been an advocate of religious liberty, although his efforts in that direction were not successful in England. Edward C. O. Beatty, in his excellent study, *William Penn as Social Philosopher,* stated that Penn considered religious liberty "the cornerstone of the ideal political edifice." [4] The first law passed by the Assembly which met in Chester, Pennsylvania, in December, 1682, guaranteed religious toleration to anyone who "shall confess and acknowledge one Almighty God to be the Creator, Upholder and Ruler of the world." This concept continued to be a part of the fundamental law of Pennsylvania until Penn transferred it to the Charter of Privileges of 1701 with the proviso that it could never be amended. Thus, it was hoped that Pennsylvania would not be solely a retreat for Friends, but that it would also be a haven for the religiously oppressed everywhere. Advertising was carried out in the Rhine Valley and elsewhere in the Germanic states where persecution was rife.

William Penn was born in London in 1644, son of Captain William Penn, a naval officer, and Margaret Jasper van de Schuren. The nation was embroiled in a Civil War at the time of his birth, and his father rose to the rank of admiral in the navy which Parliament pitted against the forces of Charles I. While Admiral Penn was given high honors and substantial gifts of property at one point during the Interregnum, he later incurred the disfavor of Oliver Cromwell and retired to live quietly on his Irish estates. After Cromwell's death, Penn participated in the intrigue to bring Charles II to the throne of England. The new monarch, son of Charles I who had been beheaded, knighted the Admiral, and Penn, now serving under the new Lord High Admiral, the King's brother the Duke of York, won more glory and honor.

Young William Penn, a member of a family which had risen to great prominence in one generation, was ready to enter Oxford at the age of sixteen. He became involved with a group of religious nonconformists, and was expelled from Christ Church during his second year. His father was deeply disturbed by this, for he wanted his son to become one of the gay, sophisticated courtiers of Restoration England. He sent young Penn to the continent, hoping to make him forget somber religious ideas. While Penn spent some of his time in France attending a Huguenot college at Saumur on the banks of the Loire, he also toured Europe with young aristocrats, was introduced at the court of Louis XIV, and returned home with the manners and appearance of a courtier.

Penn began to study law at Lincoln's Inn in 1665, but this training was cut short because of the plague which desolated London that year. Penn then went to Ireland to manage his father's estates, and served briefly in a military capacity. He fell under the influence of Irish Quakers, and to the despair of his father, remained faithful to this hated sect for the rest of his life. He spent many months traveling and preaching, both in England and on the continent, was jailed many times as a Quaker, and married Gulielma Springett, the step-daughter of an important Quaker leader, Isaac Penington. The doughty old Admiral threatened to disinherit his Quaker son, but was reconciled to him before his death in 1670, and left him the major share of his estate.

It is evident that Penn was a most unusual man. He had the background, wealth and station of the aristocracy, and the religious convictions of a member of a lowly nonconformist sect. His political loyalties were influenced more by his religious beliefs than by his station in life. He was a strong Whig despite his friendship for the royal family of England. During the political campaign of 1679, he wrote a broadside to advance the candidacy of Algernon Sydney, who was striving for a seat in the House of Commons. The title briefly was *England's Great Interest in the Choice of this New Parliament* in which he enunciated many of his political beliefs. He wrote that there are three fundamentals of government: property, legislation, and trial by jury. He stated: "the Power of *England* is a *Legal* Power, which truly merits the Name of *Government:* that which is not Legal, is a *Tyranny,* and not properly a *Government . . . No law can be made, no Money levied, nor not a Penny legally demanded* (even to defray Charges of the Government) *without your own Consent: . . .* There is nothing more to your Interest, then for you to understand your *Right* in the *Government,* and to be constantly Jealous over it; for your *Well-being* depends upon its Preservation." [5]

William Penn intended to include these Whiggish beliefs in the "holy experiment." In 1687 he sent to Pennsylvania for publication, a small volume entitled *The Excellent Priviledge of Liberty and Property* which included many of the fine old cornerstones of the liberty of Englishmen, such as Magna Charta, Edward I's Confirmation of the Charters, and the statute, *De tallagio non concedendo.* Penn introduced the documents with a brief essay which reiterated his beliefs of 1679. He reminded the people of Pennsylvania of the inheritance that every free-born subject of England was heir to by birthright, "I mean that unparalell'd Priviledge of *Liberty and Property,*" which could not be taken from him "but by the tryal and judgement of *Twelve* of his *Equals,* or *Law of the Land,*" upon the penalty of the bitter Curses of the whole People." [6]

While William Penn was a Whig, and expected those in his colony to defend their freedom as Englishmen, his ideas about the government in his "holy experiment" cannot be completely described by calling them the ideas of a Whig.

In the preface of the First Frame of the government, prepared in England before he came to Pennsylvania in 1682, Penn enunciated his ideas about government in the "holy experiment." [7] He suggested that at the beginning of the world men did the will of God, and obeyed His laws without compulsion. However, man began to do evil, and laws and government were established to constrain him. He quoted the apostle who said: "The powers that be are ordained of God. Whosoever therefore resisteth the power, resisteth the ordinance of God." [8] Penn continued: "This settles the divine right of government beyond exception, and that for two ends; first, to terrify evildoers; secondly, to cherish those that do well; which gives a government a life beyond corruption, and makes it as durable in the world, as good men shall be. So that government seems to me a part of religion itself, a thing sacred in its institution and end."

He added that the government which crushes evil is "an emanation of the same Divine Power, that is both author and object of pure religion." Penn stated that government spent most of its time regulating the ordinary affairs of man, and only a fraction of its energy was taken with punishing evildoers.

However, Penn did not subscribe to the belief that government should be autocratic because it was ordained of God. After mentioning several types of government, he concluded: "Any government is free to the people under it (whatever be the frame) where the laws rule, and the people are a party to those laws, and more than this is tyranny, oligarchy, and confusion."

The proprietor reiterated the initial point made in this chapter, that the "holy experiment" rested on virtuous men who followed the Will of God. He wrote,

Governments, like clocks, go from the motion men give them, and as governments are made and moved by men, so by them they are ruined too. . . . Let men be good, and the government cannot be bad; if it be ill, they will cure it. That therefore, which makes a good constitution, must keep it, viz: men of wisdom and virtue.

He continued by emphasizing that the government must be supported by the people "in reverence," while the authority of the government should be limited "to secure the people from the abuse of power," and magistrates would be needed who would be honorable in administering justice. Thus the people would be made "free by their just obedience, . . . for liberty without obedience is confusion, and obedience without liberty is slavery." William Penn not only guaranteed freedom, but he also expressed his belief that good government carried with it certain responsibilities for the citizens. He expected the freemen to share in the government, and to give their time, energy, and thought to make it work.

The early Friends did not feel that they were a chosen people set apart from mankind. They completely accepted the concept that all people are the children of God. They did not stop with the conventional Christian attitude, but added that there is "that of God in every man." They believed in a brotherhood, a spiritual kinship, of all mankind. From this enlightened concept of humanity many of the testimonies of Quakers grew in the centuries which followed, such as the attitudes toward slavery, Indians, prisoners, and the mentally ill.

The first outgrowth of this belief was an opposition to war. It began slowly during the troubled years preceding the Restoration in 1660, and was widely accepted among Friends in 1682. It was not just a negative attitude to war, but included a positive approach to problems of society. George Fox expressed the Quaker peace testimony when he said that he "lived in the virtue of that life and power that took away the occasion of all wars." [9] Pacifism was unpopular in the seventeenth century and Friends had considerable difficulty with the government because of their peace testimony.

When the "holy experiment" was contemplated, William Penn hoped to establish in Pennsylvania a government which would not engage in warfare. He believed that with virtuous people and a virtuous government there should be no trouble with Indian or white neighbors, and that perhaps the colony would be an "example to the nations" of the way pacifism could be practiced.

The attitude of Penn and the other Quakers towards the Indians grew naturally out of their belief in the brotherhood of all men. There were some early attempts to Christianize the Indians, without much satisfaction to either side. More successful was the policy of recognizing the Indians as equals, not only in drawing up treaties, but also in the punishment of crimes perpetrated by members of one group against the members of the other.

In addition to these concrete manifestations of the spiritual quality of the "holy experiment," there were other expressions which are almost mystical in nature. The Friends expected to live in accordance with the teachings found in the Sermon on the Mount. It was hoped that they would live peaceably with one another, that they would be meek, merciful, pure in heart, and peaceful. This was no Bible Commonwealth, but the highest ethical teachings of the scriptures were known and held up as the yardstick against which life would be measured.

Quakers were not Calvinists in their theology, but they were strongly influenced by some of John Calvin's teachings, and were as puritanical as his staunchest followers. The stern moral code which they followed rejected all forms of amusement. They maintained a strict attitude in regard to sex morals, and lived a rigorous, plain life.

But, these are mere manifestations of something deeper and less tangible. The people of Pennsylvania were to be filled with the same spirit of love and Christian fellowship which motivated Christians in the days of the Apostolic Church. That William Penn considered Quakers to be in the tradition of the early Church is clearly indicated in the tract which he wrote in 1696, *Primitive Christianity Revived in the Faith and Practice of the People Called Quakers*. That spirit was the very substance of the "holy experiment."

THE BACKGROUND OF THE QUAKER COLONISTS

While the members of the Religious Society of Friends measured up to the expectations of William Penn in many respects, they possessed characteristics which did not aid the success of the "holy experiment." As aspects of the background of this project are examined a gap is apparent between utopian dreams and the actual situation.

For example, a student of the economic motivation for the actions of men would discover such a stimulus in Pennsylvania. A desire for financial betterment was in the minds of many of the colonists, especially those who came with practically nothing, and this might interfere with the success of the "holy experiment." Certainly William Penn entered the enterprise with the hope that he would establish a substantial income for his old age, and an inheritance for his children. The desire for material comforts and security was eventually satisfied in the colony even though the first years were difficult. Many who were motivated by the desire for the riches of this world were undoubtedly gratified.

However, a desire for economic betterment was not the primary reason for settling Pennsylvania. Those who had money would have gone to a colony where the pecuniary possibilities were well known, such as an island in the West Indies, if dividends had been their chief aspiration. They might have settled in established colonies on the mainland, rather than face the hazardous life on the frontier along the shores of the Delaware and Schuylkill. If Penn's principal aim had been monetary gain, he would have accepted the offer of £6,000 for a monopoly of the Indian trade in the new province. Instead he wrote to Robert Turner: "I did refuse a great temptation last 2d day, which was 6000 pounds . . . I would not abuse his love, nor act unworthy of his providence, and so defile what came to me clean. No; lett the Lord guide me by his wisdom, and preserve me to honour his name and serve his truth and people.[10]

It could be argued with some justice that the founding of Pennsylvania was motivated by other things in addition to the desire to found a "holy experiment." But it would be impossible to discredit the tradition that William Penn and his friends were primarily interested in planting a utopian community, based on the beliefs of the Society of Friends. The search for a suitable site for a colony, planted according to Quaker principles, had been in progress for two decades, and Penn had shared that concern for many of those years.

We must go back to the beginning of the Quaker movement if we are to have a clear picture of what led to the establishment of the Quaker commonwealth in Pennsylvania in 1682. The founding of the Religious Society of Friends was part of a religious movement which was shaking all of England. Troublesome times vexed the country in the 1640s with Charles I nearing his end and the Interregnum about to begin. The land was full of new religious sects: Fifth Monarchy Men, Muggletonians, Ranters, Familists, Seekers, and others. The Anglican Church was split asunder with the Puritan movement rising against the authorities appointed by the king. Presbyterians were urgently pressing into England from Scotland, and the Independents, a religious-political-military movement, was taking form. The country was in the midst of a religious ferment.

It is axiomatic in history that religious minorities tend to become political minorities. In France, the Huguenots under the House of Navarre had been in opposition to the king. In England, the Catholics engaged in plots against Elizabeth. Charles V found his German Protestant subjects banded together against him.

The Quakers and other religious minorities were suspected by the party in power, which assumed that they had political aspirations. This was especially true after the uprising of Fifth Monarchy Men early in 1661, which resulted in the arrest of 4,230 Friends.[11] Even before the Restoration more than a thousand followers of Fox were imprisoned for such offenses as failure to pay tithes, failure to show proper respect for authorities, or refusal to take an oath.[12] From the beginning, the Quakers suffered severely for their faith.

Accurate figures for the imprisonments in the years 1661 to 1685, when large-scale persecution came to an end, are difficult to secure. William C. Braithwaite indicated in his studies that considerably more than 15,000 were imprisoned, and that at least 450 died as a result of their sufferings. Other estimates range as high as 60,000 incarcerations and 5,000 martyred dead for all dissenters in the period, with the Friends a majority of that group.[13]

Friends were deprived of their liberty and of their worldly goods through fines. They were forced to pay fines in money, such as the £16,000 fine levied upon Quakers in Bristol in 1682 for violating the statutes against recusancy, or non-attendance at Anglican services, but they were also frequently deprived of their means of livelihood by the representatives of the law. In the four years before John Simcock came to Pennsylvania, he lost eight cows and eleven heifers, and other goods valued at £140. Others lost the implements of their trade, such as looms and tools.[14]

These savage attacks upon their personal liberty and property undoubtedly played a part in influencing Friends to look for a spot in the New World where they could control their own destinies. However, Frederick B. Tolles, in his book *Meeting House and Counting House,* suggested that there was considerable opposition to the colonization of Friends, where the sole reason was a desire to escape persecution.[15] Friends were anxious, however, to find a spot where their children could be reared in a more favorable atmosphere.

George Fox was early interested in the New World, and extensive missionary efforts were carried on in Barbados, New England, and on to the south among the English colonies. There was also interest in preaching to the Indians and converting them to Christianity. As early as 1660 Josiah Coale worked among the Indians and at the same time unsuccessfully attempted to purchase land from them along the Susquehanna.[16]

Quakers were welcome in Rhode Island and missionaries soon found many converts in the colony founded by Roger Williams. Eventually the Friends became prominent in the life of the colony, not only religiously, but politically and economically. However, just to the north, the commonwealth of Massachusetts persecuted the Quakers, imprisoned many, and took the lives of four Friends, including a woman, Mary Dyer.[17]

The year 1671 saw a large missionary movement to the New World, headed by George Fox himself. The Friends first went to Barbados, then to Jamaica, recently taken from the Spanish by Admiral William Penn, and on to Maryland. Fox moved overland to New England, through New Jersey and New York, and traveled in the Chesapeake Bay area and as far south as Albemarle Sound in North Carolina, before returning to England.[18] When he landed at Bristol in June, 1673, William Penn and his bride Gulielma were there to greet him, and entertained Fox and his wife Margaret, several days.[19]

In the early years Friends were positive that they had a message which would sweep across the colonies in the New World and carry all before it. They were convinced that they had but to spread the Word among the dissenters, the Puritans, and even members of the Church of England where they were far away from the home influence, and a great change would be wrought. It is true that the Friends of New England, New York, Maryland, and North Carolina were largely converts among those who had already colonized, and not Quakers who came over from England. Quakerism grew in these places at the same time that it developed in England, and the first Yearly Meeting which came into existence was that of New England, not the venerable London Yearly Meeting.

While Friends had considerable influence in these colonies, and became numerous, they were always set apart from the others in the community. The Quakers in England felt a continued desire to have a colony for themselves, or at least one which would be in their hands. The opportunity came in the year 1674. The land now called New Jersey was taken from the Dutch in the Second Dutch War, and shortly thereafter was given to John, Lord Berkeley, and Sir George Carteret. In 1674 the territory had been divided between them into East Jersey, in the hands of Carteret, and West Jersey, which Berkeley controlled. Berkeley was an old man who grew tired of dealing with the colony, and sold it to John Fenwick, a yeoman from Buckinghamshire, and Edward Byllynge, a London merchant, for £1,000. These men were both Quakers, and James Bowden wrote in 1850: "There is good reason to believe that the property was acquired by them for the advantage of the Society at large." [20] Whether Bowden was correct or not, Fenwick and Byllynge soon fell to quarreling about the new colony. Friends believed that differences should be settled among themselves, rather than taken to court, and William Penn was chosen as an arbitrator between them. A settlement was accepted, in which Fenwick received a sizable sum of money and one-tenth of the land, and Byllynge received the other nine-tenths. Fenwick eventually assigned his land to cover a sum of money which he had borrowed, and then came to New Jersey and settled on the land anyhow, which created more difficulties. [21]

Byllynge also was embarrassed in his circumstances, and assigned his right to the land to three trustees to protect his creditors and Friends' interest in the project. William Penn, Gawen Lawrie, and Nicholas Lucas were the trustees, and they soon found themselves involved in selling land to pay the indebtedness, in sending settlers to populate the area, and in establishing a government. Penn not only shared in the direction of West Jersey, but in April, 1681, joined with eleven other Friends to purchase East Jersey from the estate of Carteret, who had just died. Thus in the very months when Penn was drawing up plans for Pennsylvania, he was forced to give some attention to East and West Jersey. Penn also had the advantage of experience in such an enterprise, upon which he drew in establishing his own province. The West Jersey venture was successful, and encouraged him to enter into the great project on which his fame lies. Obviously, the fact that several hundred Quakers were living across the Delaware from his new province was an encouragement to Friends who were thinking of colonizing in the vast American forests.

It is evident that there was a good deal of interest in the New World, both as an area to evangelize and as a place to practice Quaker beliefs.

Perhaps it will be easier to understand why Quakers behaved as they did in Pennsylvania, if the Quaker philosophy of government is understood. Actually there was no philosophy of government for all Friends, but the beliefs of some leading Quakers can be examined, and perhaps the opinions of some of the authorities on the history of the society will prove useful.

One of the early writers was Edward Burrough, who, in his tract, *To the Present Distracted and Broken Nation of England*, written in 1659, said: "For what is a King, and what is a Parliament, what is a Protector, and what is a Council, while the presence of the Lord is not with them? And we are not for names, nor men, nor titles of Government, but we are for justice, and mercy and truth and peace, and true freedom, that these may be exalted in our nation, and that goodness, righteousness, meekness, temperance, peace, and unity with God and with one another, that these things may abound." He called for the day "when tyranny and oppression shall be clean removed, strife and contention and self-seeking utterly abandoned." Braithwaite made the following comment: "This fine passage admirably expresses the political standpoint of the early Friends alike in their intense interest in righteous government, their peaceable submission to the existing authorities, their want of sympathy with any of the influential parties, and their somewhat exaggerated claim to know the Divine mind." [22]

In another part of his study, Braithwaite wrote that Quakers "were at this period indifferent to the form of government. Their point of view was theocratic rather than democratic on the one hand, or royalist on the other." [23] He added later that Friends did not believe in the conventional theocratic state of the seventeenth century, where chosen people enforced their views on others, but rather in a freedom of choice. They stressed that each person in the government, and under it, should be full of the same power of God, and theocratic in that sense. [24] The belief in the Inner Light, the Spirit of God within the life of all, which made all men equal before God, was fundamental in Quakerism. This faith in their ability to know the will of God enabled them to withstand all earthly pressures against their consciences.

Philip S. Belasco, in writing about Quaker political beliefs, said: "The first great attack on behalf of the individual against The Sovereign State came from the Quakers in the seventeenth century." They believed in the sovereignty of God, and in the realization of His sovereignty through the Inner Light. Thus, "The highest judgement of men could be pitted against the sovereign will of the state." He wrote further: "The sovereignty of God therefore involved a continuous evaluation of the acts of the legislator; no morality inhered in legislation by the mere enunciation." He quoted William Smith, who wrote in 1668: "No temporal power of law, can maintain your proceedings against the law of the spirit of Jesus Christ, for it is He alone that hath power and authority to rule and govern the conscience." [25]

Most of the Quakers who arrived in Pennsylvania in the early years had had no experience in government because of regulations at home. Those who qualified voted, but they were not eligible to hold office because of their testimony against taking oaths. They had participated in a negative way by challenging the laws in court, and Arnold Lloyd suggested that they spent rather large sums of money in that manner.[26] Friends did some campaigning in the parliamentary elections of 1679 and 1680, only to see their candidates defeated and the winners begin persecution anew. After Penn began his quest for Pennsylvania, Quaker leaders advocated keeping out of English politics to prevent hurting his chances of obtaining the charter.[27]

The Quakers in Ireland held office, and George Fox wrote to them in 1687 urging "that they keep to truth." He reminded them to refrain from taking or giving oaths, from wearing fancy clothing such as officials donned, and from attending feasts and banquets. He continued: "In their places they should do justice to all men, and be a terror to them that do evil and a praise to them that do well; and preserve every man both in his natural rights and properties as in his Divine rights and liberty, according to the righteous law of God." [28]

To sum up these comments: Friends generally arrived in Pennsylvania with no previous political experience. They were somewhat skeptical of governments, and had no fear of opposing a state which they believed was in the wrong. As it turned out, they soon learned to act as political creatures, and it was not long before Penn was calling on them not to be so "governmentish." [29]

CHAPTER TWO

PRELIMINARIES OF COLONIZING

ON THE NORTH AMERICAN continent, only one uninhabited area remained in the English territory. The entire coastline was occupied from Maine to Carolina, but in the middle, behind East and West New Jersey, below New York, above Maryland and beyond the Delaware Bay and River, lay an area which was scarcely touched.

This Delaware Valley had been the site of a long struggle between the Dutch and the Swedes, who wrested it from one another during the first half of the seventeenth century. Such names as John Printz, Peter Minuit, and Peter Stuyvesant would never be forgotten in the area. However, during the Dutch Wars, James, Duke of York, seized all of the territory between Maryland and Connecticut formerly held by the House of Orange, and made it securely English. Despite the early settlements which could be traced back to 1619, there were probably less than 2,000 white persons in 1681 living in what now are Delaware and Pennsylvania, and three-fourths of them were in Delaware.

The fact that this area was relatively unoccupied made it a likely place for Quakers to settle, if they could gain control over the region. This was the area which Josiah Coale had attempted to purchase for Friends in 1660, and the Quakers may have retained some interest in the intervening years. Furthermore, William Penn, one of the leading figures in the Quaker community, was a close friend of James, Duke of York. This friendship has always puzzled historians. It is true that Admiral Penn and the Duke of York had been closely associated for many years. However, that is not enough to explain why a man eleven years older than the Admiral's son would feel a strong attachment for him. It seems even more unlikely when it is remembered that James was an ardent Roman Catholic, while Penn had become a Quaker. The warm feeling was no less real because it is not clearly understood, and it endured through the strain of the abdication of James II in 1688. James had given New Jersey to two of his friends, and it seemed Penn might receive a similar grant through his intervention.[1]

In addition, Charles II owed William Penn a considerable sum of money, an indebtedness which Penn had inherited from his father. The sum may have been £11,000 in the beginning, with interest augmenting the figure until it reached £16,000, or perhaps it was always the latter amount. It had been incurred when Admiral Penn outfitted his fleet on one occasion at his own expense, during his years of active service. Charles was not one to lose sleep over his debts, and it is possible that he would never have reached a financial settlement with the younger Penn if this inexpensive method of canceling the indebtedness had not been suggested. However, the unoccupied land was there, it nominally belonged to James, and if he was willing that it be granted to William Penn, there was no reason to object.

Penn made application to Charles for the land on June 24, 1680, by presenting a petition to the committee of the Privy Council for the Affairs of Trade and Plantation, commonly called the Lords of Trade. The agents of Lord Baltimore and the Duke of York were immediately notified of the petition. Sir John Werden, who represented James, claimed the territory for his lord, and William Penn went to his friend to obtain a release of the land so that the King might grant it to him. Barnaby Dunch and Richard Burk, agents for Lord Baltimore claimed all land as far north as Susquehanna Fort, a Maryland outpost on the Susquehanna River. Arguments continued for nearly a year over the boundaries of the proposed grant, and finally the Attorney General, Sir William Jones, approved of the petition; further meetings were held, and a seemingly just and permanent settlement was reached. Actually the conflict over the boundary continued well into the eighteenth century. The charter was signed by the King, March 4, 1681.[2]

William Penn was granted a charter which gave him almost complete control over his province.[3] He was to rule with the consent of the freemen, but might govern without that consent in an emergency. He was to submit his laws to the Privy Council for approval; appeals might be made to England from his courts, and he was to maintain an agent in London, but otherwise he had an absolute proprietary. His control over the land was more arbitrary than over government. William Penn, the Quaker believer in equality, the Whig advocate of self-government was the near-absolute ruler of a province in the New World.

Charles M. Andrews has pointed out that the charter contained three factors which were in opposition to one another. The document was drawn up as a proprietary grant, which gave Penn the prerogatives of a medieval proprietor, for the officials knew of no other way to grant the land, and followed the pattern which had been established during previous decades. But as the English government had incorporated into its colonial policy a decision to control the provinces firmly in the future, Penn's medieval charter was encompassed with many more restrictions than had been customary in former years. Finally, in addition to these contradictory pressures and perhaps superimposed on them were "the idealistic purposes of a man who wished to found a state based upon the most honorable principles of toleration, morals, justice, and brotherly love." [4] It is seen that the charter, which represented an attempt to reach an equitable balance in regard to three concepts which had little in common, contained "seeds of troubles to come."

Fortunately, Penn was unaware of the heartaches his colony would bring him, and he did not worry about the attitude of the civil servants who disapproved of his grant. His great friend was heir to the throne, and there was no reason to suspect that all would not be well. With friends at court, virtuous people in the colony, and the hand of God over all, the province should prove to be a blessing.[5]

Thus with the Charter in his hand, William Penn began the eighteen months of planning and preparing which were necessary before he could set sail for his new province. He wrote the good news to his fellow religionists, suggesting that they begin to make plans for joining him in the venture. To Robert Turner he wrote: "Thou mayest communicate my grant to friends, and expect shortly my proposals. It is a clear and just thing, and my God, that has given it me through many difficulties, will, I believe, bless and make it the seed of a nation. I shall have a tender care to the government, that it will be well laid at first." [6]

Planting a colony was not simple, and Penn was busy with a multitude of details. He obtained a letter from Charles II addressed to the inhabitants of the new land, wrote one himself, and sent them both off in the hands of his cousin, William Markham, who served as Penn's deputy in Pennsylvania during the ensuing months. He wrote a series of advertisements calculated to attract colonists to the new province. Penn and his friends labored over a Frame of Government which might serve as the constitution of Pennsylvania. Just before he set sail, William Penn persuaded the Duke of York to grant him Delaware, thereby guaranteeing an outlet to the sea for the new colony.

The King's letter said in part: "His majesty doth, therefore, hereby publish and declare his royal will and pleasure, that all persons settled or inhabiting within the limits of the said province, do yield all due obedience to the said William Penn, his heirs and assigns, as absolute proprietaries and governors thereof . . . as they tender his majesty's displeasure." [7] Penn wrote a friendly and generous letter "for the inhabitants of Pennsylvania, to be read by my deputy." He told the settlers "that it hath pleased god In his providence, to cast you within my lott and care." He said that he believed that God would give him guidance in the new task, adding: "I hope you will not be troubled at yr change, & the kings choice, for you are now fixt at ye mercy of no Governour yt comes to make his fortune great, you shall be govern'd by law of yr own makeing. . . .

In Short, wtever sober & free men can reasonably desire for ye security & improvement of their own happiness, I shall heartely comply wth, & in five months resolve, if it please god, to See you." He ordered the colonists to submit to his deputy, in so far as his commands were consistent "wth ye law, & pay him thos dues, (yt formerly you paid to ye order of the Governour of new york.)" [8]

Penn prepared a commission for Markham which authorized him "to act and perform what may be fully needful to the peace and safety thereof, till I myself shall arrive." [9] The Deputy Governor was to convene a council of nine men, himself presiding, and read the letters from Charles II and Penn. In return, he was to receive from them, as delegates from the inhabitants, an acknowledgement of the new authority. Further, the commission called upon Markham to settle the boundaries between Pennsylvania and her neighbors, and to "set out, rent, or sell lands, according to instructions." He was granted all the powers necessary to establish law and order, in a word, all "the power granted to me in the letters-patent, calling assemblies to make laws only excepted."

With Markham on his way to occupy the province, Penn prepared advertisements which would attract colonists to his new land. At least eleven publications were released before Penn arrived in Pennsylvania, beginning with *Some Account of the Province of Pennsilvania*, which was published in April, 1681. [10] A brief summary of this brochure will give some idea of the type of advertising and promotional work which Penn contemplated.

With deliberate understatement, he described the location in these words: "I shall say little in its praise, to excite desires in any, . . . as to the Soil, Air and Water: This shall satisfie me, that by the Blessing of God, and the honesty and industry of Man, it may be a good and fruitful land." He described what the land would produce without cultivation, and what settlers could raise by tilling the soil.

Of the government he wrote, "For the Constitutions of the Country, the Patent shows, first, That the People and Governour have a Legislative Power, so that no Law can be made, nor Money raised, but by the Peoples Consent. 2dly. That the Rights and Freedoms of England (the best and largest in Europe) shall be in force there." He added that the people could make any laws they liked, so long as they were not repugnant to the laws of England. His fourth point in regard to the government promised, "That so soon as any are ingaged with me, we shall begin a Scheam or Draught together, such as shall give ample Testimony of my sincere Inclinations to encourage Planters, and settle a free, just and industrious Colony there."

After discussing the conditions for taking up land, mentioning quitrents, city lots and dividends, he turned to a description of the types of persons who would be best fitted for the colony. He listed "Industrious Husbandmen and Day-Labourers" first, and craftsmen second. His next classification was more vague: "A Plantation seems a fit place for those Ingenious Spirits that being low in the world, are much clogg'd and oppress'd about a Livelyhood, for the means of subsisting being easie there, they may have time and opportunity to gratify their inclinations, and thereby improve Science and help Nurseries of people." He encouraged younger sons without too much money to turn to the New World. Lastly, turning over in his mind his dream of the "holy experiment," he called to join him, "Men of universal Spirits, that have an eye to the Good of Posterity, . . . such persons may find Room in Colonies for their good Counsel and Contrivance, who are shut out from being of much use or service to great Nations under settl'd Customs."

Penn discussed the cost of going to Pennsylvania, carefully described the goods which would be needed during the journey across the ocean, and listed some of the things which the colonists would require on arrival. After publishing an abstract of his charter from Charles II, Penn closed with a paragraph in which he reminded his readers of the hardships which would face them. He expressed the hope that they would only go with the consent of their families, and called for God's blessing on their endeavor.

Penn not only published pamphlets to advertise the new colony, he also carried on an extensive correspondence. He wrote to Robert Barclay about Scottish settlers going to Pennsylvania. Although Barclay could not buy property himself, he offered to outfit an establishment if Penn wanted to give him some land, and thus encourage others in Scotland to go to the new settlement.[11] Barclay was the leading Scottish Quaker, distantly related to the Stuart family, and author of the famous *Apology*. The proprietor wrote to Thomas Janney suggesting that people buy immediately if they wished the best land. He added, "Mine eye is to a blessed governmt, & a virtuous ingenious & industrious society, so as people may live well & have more time to give ye L[or]d then in this Crowded land. God will plant Americka & it shall have its day in ye Kingdom." [12]

Penn sometimes mixed spiritual admonition with business, as in a letter to James Harrison: "first my Soul is affected wth ye sense of yr Sense of ye breaking powr & presence of ye lord yt was among you. O let my Soul dwell there. & so lett my Country prosper, or not at all. the Acres are Statute measure." [13]

Friends and non-Friends responded in large numbers and purchased approximately 875,000 acres by the time that Penn landed in Pennsylvania.[14] Some individuals purchased 10,000 acres or more. The Free Society of Traders purchased 20,000 acres. In addition, there were many persons who purchased at least 5,000 acres, some of them unknown in provincial annals, and others who were to play important parts in the development of the new country. Apparently many purchasers bought as an investment, with no idea of coming to the New World.[15] Penn not only found persons interested in migrating to his colony from the British Isles, including Ireland, Wales, and Scotland, but other people came from the Continent in response to advertisements published in Dutch and German. Many deserted the older colonies and went to Pennsylvania from New England, New York, Barbados, and other English possessions.[16]

William Penn however, was not solely interested in numbers and in material success. He constantly thought of the "holy experiment" which he hoped would be planted, and wrote feelingly of God's hand on the establishment of Pennsylvania. To Thomas Janney he wrote, "And as to my Country it is the Effect of much patience & faith as well as cost & Charges for in no outward thing have I knowne a greater exercise, & my mind more inwardly resigned to foolo [follow] the L[or]ds hand to bring it to pass & truly I owne it." He mentioned that there had been "opposition of envious gr[ea]t men, & since I have been maid to look to ye Ld & believe in him, as to ye obtaining of it, more than ever as to any outward substance, it comforts me & I am firme in my faith yt the Ld will prosper it, if . . . [we] do not grieve him by an unworthy use of it" [17]

The charter received from the king could have served as the constitution of Pennsylvania, as the charter held by the founders of Massachusetts had filled their needs. In fact, during a part of 1700 and 1701, it was the constitution. However, Penn desired something more specific, a document which expressed in concrete terms what he and his enterprisers planned. While the other activities were moving forward, Penn was also thinking about his frame of government. In April, 1681, he wrote to Turner, "For the matters of liberty and privilege, I purpose that which is extraordinary, and to leave myself and successors no power of doeing mischief; that the will of one man may not hinder the good of an whole country; but to publish those things now, and here[,] as matters stand, would not be wise, and I was advised to reserve that till I came there." [18]

Drawing up a Frame of Government was a laborious task. The sheaf of discarded frames gathered in the manuscript collection of the Historical Society of Pennsylvania bears testimony to the mental struggle which went into the First Frame. For example, at one time a two-house Parliament plus a Council was contemplated for Pennsylvania; the House of Proprietors to consist of those owning 5,000 acres or more, and the Assembly to be elected by those owning fifty acres or more, plus townsmen paying scot and lot. Another draft provided for the initiation of money bills by the Assembly.[19] Even after the First Frame had been completed, it was altered as soon as the colonists had the time and the courage to question it. Much has been written about the First Frame of Government which need not be repeated here.[20]

Not only was Penn influenced by conservative forces, hinted at in his letter to Turner, but he also was influenced by liberalizing advice. The biographer of Algernon Sydney leaves the reader with the feeling that Sydney was virtually the author of the First Frame.[21] Penn credited Sydney with exerting influence on it, but the extent to which his ideas permeated the new document has remained a mystery. Benjamin Furley, at Rotterdam, criticized the final product as dangerously inconsistent with public safety.[22]

The First Frame was signed April 25, 1682. Penn followed the long preamble with an introduction, and finally the constitution which was composed of twenty-three chapters.[23] It provided for a Provincial Council of seventy-two persons, to serve for three years, which would have considerable power. The Council would advise the Governor about most matters of government, and would propose all bills which were to be considered for enactment into law. A second house, the 200 man Assembly, elected annually, would approve or reject proposed legislation. Both bodies would be elected by the freemen of the colony. Other officials of the colony and the methods of choosing them were described, and provisions were made for various other matters in the colony.

In closing, Penn promised: "neither I, my heirs nor assigns shall procure or do any thing or things, whereby the liberties in this charter contained and expressed, shall be infringed or broken; and if any thing be procured by any person or persons contrary to these premises, it shall be held of no force or effect."

Penn was still not ready to sail for Pennsylvania. Although he owned that province, and had taken steps to occupy it, to colonize it, and to govern it, he believed that all this would come to nothing if he did not also obtain Delaware, also called the three lower counties, which would give him access to the Atlantic. He persuaded the Duke of York to grant this region to him, and deeds were drawn up August 24, 1682, a few days before Penn set sail. Penn was given the land around New

Castle in one deed, within a circle of a twelve mile radius, and was given the two lower counties in the second deed. He paid ten shillings for each of these grants.

It is significant, in view of what happened in the following years, that in both deeds the Duke of York promised within the next seven years, to draw up whatever further documents to convey title to Penn which his lawyers might feel to be necessary to protect Penn's interest in the land, with the further provision that Penn should pay the cost of obtaining a new deed.[24] If these deeds had been adequate, this sentence would have been unnecessary. Further, there is no mention of government, or the granting to Penn of government in these documents. However, if Penn worried about this, he left no written record, and no mention was made of it for several years.

Penn explained to James Harrison in August 19, 1681, why he was not going to Pennsylvania that year, writing that people were buying land and sending servants to clear it and build houses, but that landowners would not go until 1682. "When they goe I goe; [but] my going with Servants will not [settle] a Government[,] the great end of my going." [25] With the deeds from James, Duke of York, in his hands, Penn felt that his departure need be postponed no longer. He had made adequate preparations for nearly every eventuality, and he was ready to embark for Pennsylvania.

CHAPTER THREE

THE BIRTH OF THE
"HOLY EXPERIMENT"

WILLIAM PENN set sail for Pennsylvania from the port of Deal, just north of Dover, on August 30, 1682, aboard the *Welcome*. Crossing the Atlantic in a 300 ton vessel would have been unpleasant at best, but this voyage was made especially burdensome by a severe epidemic of smallpox which killed nearly thirty persons. Penn, who had lived through an attack of the dread disease in childhood, moved among the stricken, giving them aid and care. The sailing time was good for those days, and in less than eight weeks the ship's master, Robert Greenway, sighted the Capes. The ship anchored off New Castle, the old Dutch settlement, on October 27.

Penn produced the papers which he had only recently obtained from the Duke of York, giving him possession of the Lower Counties or Delaware, and the inhabitants of New Castle offered their allegiance to the new proprietor. On October 29 he journeyed to Upland, an old Swedish settlement, which he renamed Chester, and it was there that Penn first touched the soil of his famous commonwealth. The proprietor soon moved up the river to the present site of Philadelphia and confirmed the location of his "Greene Country Towne" where Thomas Holme, Surveyor General, and William Markham, Deputy Governor, and others had planted it.

The *Welcome* was one of many vessels which sailed up the Delaware that year. A letter written in March, 1683, by Friends in East and West Jersey and Pennsylvania to their fellow religionists in England reported that "2000 people came into this river Last yeare." [1] Apparently the year 1683 saw a great exodus to the new province as well. In letters which Penn wrote during the summer to prominent men in England, he reported that sixty ships came into the colony during the year, and that 300 farmers had established themselves since the previous fall. He wrote of the prosperity of the colony, and boasted that Philadelphia was already larger than any town of the Carolinas, Virginia or Maryland.[2] He reported the town numbered eighty houses, and " a fair we have had, and weekly markett, to which the ancient lowly inhabitants come to sell their produce to their profit and our accomodation." [3]

Penn was not the only one writing letters. The colonists wrote back to their families and friends about conditions in the New World, which encouraged others to follow. In October, 1683, Phineas Pemberton received a missive from Henry Baker, which read in part: "very glad am I to hear of yor well faire & likeing of the Country: & now am a litle trobled yt I had not sent money by thee to buy lands." [4] Ships and people poured in, and Penn reported at the end of 1683 that 4,000 persons had come to the colony by that time, that Philadelphia had grown to 150 houses, and that there were 400 farmers settled in the country.[5]

Just as conditions had been very severe on the *Welcome,* the passengers suffered great hardships on other vessels, but no ships were lost during the early months. Epidemics were likely to break out aboard ship, food to become scarce or unfit for human consumption, and water or other drinks to run short. Living conditions were poor by modern standards, and sometimes the captain and crew of a ship imposed upon the passengers. For example, the Provincial Council heard complaints by the passengers against James Kilner, master of the *Levee* from Liverpool. Hugh March testified that Kilner stepped on him, whereupon March cried out, "Dam it, cannot the man see! for which ye M[aste]r beat him and made his mouth bleed." John Fox complained that the captain bade him clean the deck, and when he answered that it was clean already, he was beaten. Because Kilner thought Edward Jones had wasted water, he beat Jones with a staff, made his nose bleed, pulled him by the hair, kicked him in the side, "and run his fingers up his nose." The passengers claimed that the seamen drank all the ship's beer and water, and then drank up what the passengers had brought as well. Master Kilner denied everything, but as a sop to their indignation admitted kicking a maid, "and that for Spilling a Chamber Pott upon ye Deck; otherways he was Very Kind to them." Governor Penn reprimanded the Master, and ordered him to make his peace with the passengers, which he did.[6]

THE ASSEMBLY AT CHESTER, DECEMBER, 1682

While the arrival of the colonists to participate in the "holy experiment" was vital, it was also important that a government be established which would be favorable to the utopian ideals. Penn was concerned about law and order in Pennsylvania, and in his charge to Markham in April, 1681, and later in the orders given to his land commissioners in September, he issued direct instructions to be followed by his subordinates until a government was organized formally.[7]

It has already been seen that a First Frame of Government was prepared in England. In addition, Penn supervised the compilation of laws which were to serve the new colony. The Governor wanted these submitted to representatives of the inhabitants as soon as possible, to give them added legality and stature. Three weeks after he set foot on Pennsylvania soil, Penn issued writs calling for an election November 20 to choose representatives to meet him at Chester on December 6. The men actually gathered on Monday, December 4.[8] Little is known about the membership of this Assembly, for there was no list of the members at the beginning of the records, as became the custom in later years. The names of seventeen persons are mentioned in connection with committee appointments and such matters. Even the name of the Speaker is unknown, although many students have assumed that Nicholas More, president of the Free Society of Traders, held the chair.[9]

This was a peculiar legislative session, for the Council did not yet exist, the laws were not promulgated ahead of time as the First Frame required, and the Assembly certainly did not include as many persons as called for under that document. The first meeting of the General Assembly, that is of both a Council and an Assembly as provided for in the First Frame of government, took place in March, 1683. This group met a second time in October. The following year, 1684, the General Assembly met in May as provided for in the Second Frame or Charter of Liberties.

The short, extra-legal session was left to its own devices when it first gathered because Penn had not finished drawing up bills to submit to the Assembly. Several committees were named; one for elections and privileges, another for justice and grievances, and a third, a "Committee of Foresight, for the Preparation of Provincial Bills." Considerable time was taken in reaching agreement on rules of procedure for the House. Among the rules agreed on was one which was proposed, "That any Member may offer any Bill, publick or private, tending to the publick Good, except in Case of levying Taxes." In establishing a committee to prepare bills and in agreeing that any member could introduce bills, the Assembly took for granted that it had a right to initiate legislation and to discuss and amend bills freely. This attitude of the Assembly was in keeping with the legislative precedents of England, but counter to the provisions of the First Frame. William Penn conceived of his Council as the body which would draw up proposed legislation. This group of men would agree on proposed legislation and promulgate it throughout the colony several weeks before the Assembly met. When the latter body gathered it would discuss the proposed legislation and then only express its approval or disapproval. The Assembly never fully accepted Penn's theory, and this difference of opinion was the subject of severe debate and argument during the first two decades of the colony's history.

A petition was received from the Lower Counties calling for an Act of Union, in order that the citizens of New Castle, Jones

(Kent), and New Deal (Sussex) counties "may be endowed with the same Privileges of Law and Government" as those of the province. A second petition, from the Swedes, Finns, and Dutch of Pennsylvania and adjacent counties, asked that they might be naturalized to "make them as free as other Members of this Province." In answer to these petitions two laws were drawn up with the approval of the Governor, the Act of Union and the Naturalization Act.

Penn presented to the Assembly the collection of laws drawn up in England before his coming to Pennsylvania, commonly called The Laws Agreed Upon in England, and published under that title, May 5, 1682. He had appended written laws, that is, those added since the printing of the first group. The minutes of the Assembly indicate that there were ninety laws proposed, and that the Assembly passed all but twelve. However, only sixty-one titles were listed in the record at the end of the proceedings while seventy-one were actually passed.[10] There was no mention of the First Frame of Government in the minutes of the session.

On Thursday, December 7, Penn presided over the Assembly and signed the bills for naturalization and for union, as well as the other laws accepted by the Assembly. Nicholas More took this occasion to question the Governor about some matters of a material nature, following which Penn gave the Assembly religious counsel. Shortly afterwards, with the Governor's consent, the Speaker adjourned the body.

The laws enacted at Chester were at the center of the legislation which Penn believed was necessary to implement the "holy experiment." Actually the laws passed in all four of the legislative sessions held during Penn's sojourn in the colony should be considered together. It will then be possible to see how Penn's understanding of suitable laws for a holy community was modified by the beliefs and opinions of the representatives of the people.

It is difficult to know how many laws were passed during the two years Penn lived in Pennsylvania. The *Charter and Laws of Pennsylvania* lists 174 laws enacted, but compiles only sixty-two for the sessions at Chester in 1682. Marvin W. Schlegel, who has proved that seventy-one laws were passed in that session, wrote that most of those he discovered were re-enacted in 1683. Some other laws were duplications as well. It can be said with assurance that more than 150 laws were passed during the two year period. If the colonists are to be understood some knowledge of the laws they lived by and the laws they enacted will be necessary. Some of the more important and interesting laws must be examined.

The legislature itself left a record of the laws which it considered most important, for in the law numbered 141 in the *Charter and Laws of Pennsylvania* a list of fifteen laws was drawn up as "Fundamental in the government of this Province and territories." These were not to be changed or repealed without the consent of the governor and six-sevenths of the freemen in Council and Assembly.[11] This list was headed by Penn's law protecting liberty of conscience, and included laws which established various procedures for the colony. These laws strengthened the "holy experiment" for they were consistent with the high idealism which Penn hoped to achieve in Pennsylvania. Most of them were solid guarantees of Anglo-Saxon liberties, but a few grew out of the peculiar beliefs of Friends, such as the one regulating marriages. This, however, was soon repealed.

There were other laws which were important in the colony and important to one's understanding of the colony. The second law prescribed that all officers and commissioners should profess a belief in Jesus Christ as the Son of God and the Savior of the World, a profession which would exclude Jews but not Catholics. The death penalty was required for those found guilty of premeditated killing, but for nothing else. In keeping with the "holy experiment" were laws such as that which called for the appointment of three persons in every precinct as "Common peacemakers . . . and their Arbitrations may be as Valid as the judgements of the Courts of Justice." Another attempted to lessen lawsuits by providing that those judged Common Barrators, that is those bringing about frequent and unjust lawsuits, should be punished by fine and imprisonment.

Penn's enlightenment could be seen clearly in the law which stipulated that all children should be given the opportunity to learn to write and to read the Scriptures by the time they became twelve years of age, and that both rich and poor be taught some trade, "that the poor may work to live, and the rich, if they become poor may not want." Another law called for the printing of all of the laws, "that every person may have the knowledge thereof; And they shall be one of the Books taught in the Schooles of this Province, and territorys thereof." This law was never fulfilled, probably because there was fear in some circles that if the liberality of Pennsylvania laws was known reprisals would come from England. But the provision for schools was soon put into effect, for the Governor and Council set up a school with Enoch Flower as schoolmaster. Rates were set as follows: "to Learne to read English 4 s[hillings] by the Quarter, to Learne to read and write 6 s by ye Quarter, to learne read, Write and Cast acco[un]t[s] 8 s by ye Quarter; for Boarding a Scholler, that is to say, dyet, Washing, Lodging, & Scooling, Tenn pounds for one whole year." [12]

Two laws were passed to assess duties on trade. One placed a fee of two pence per gallon on strong liquor and one penny on cider, plus a duty of twenty shillings on every 100 pounds worth of goods, molasses excepted. The other laid an export duty on hides and pelts. Both of these were to aid in the support of the government. On July 2, 1683, a proclamation was sent out in the name of Governor Penn but signed by Nicholas More, newly named secretary of the Council, which set aside all duties and customs for one year as an encouragement to the settlers. [13] Another law granted to the magistrates of the counties power to collect a land tax, and a poll tax on men between the ages of sixteen and sixty. In 1684 there was again talk of a bill to provide Penn with income from imposts and other duties, but at the last minute the bill was laid aside. A group of prominent men in the government felt that the colony would progress more rapidly if there were no taxes to hinder trade, and they promised to collect at least £500 for Penn in voluntary subscriptions, in exchange for dropping the money bill. The signers made this promise, we "doe freely & with willing hearts & Minds, offer to raise by a Voluntary Subscription five hundred pounds at Least." [14] The offer was accepted, but Penn never received all of this money.

Many other matters were covered by the laws. The fees for all services by office holders were listed, and provisions were made for the care of indentured servants. Prices were fixed for beer and ale and for food and lodging in taverns. One law stated that the days of the week and months of the year were to be called as in Scripture, "and not by Heathen names." First month and Second month meant March and April, and First day and Second day meant Sunday and Monday. One is reminded of loyalty oaths by Chapter 115, which demanded of all landowners a promise of "Allegiance to the King and fidelity and obedience to Wm Penn Proprietary and Governor." The following year a law was enacted to protect Penn from bodily harm and from revolution by writing, printing, speaking or acting. It was to prevent persons from advisedly writing, publishing, or uttering contemptuous or malicious things to stir up hatred or dislike of the Governor, or things which tended to the subversion of the government.

Punishment was provided for those guilty of swearing and cursing, of sexual crimes, for those who sold liquor to Indians, engaged in dueling, drank healths, or who were "Clamorous, Scolding & Railing with their tounges." The puritanical strain of these Quakers is further evidenced in the laws which forbade all sorts of creaturely enjoyment, as "Prizes, Stage-plays, Masques, Revels, Bull-baitings, Cock-fightings, . . . Cards, Dice, Lotteries, or such like enticing, vain, and evil Sports and Games."

The legislation enacted during the two years which Penn spent in Pennsylvania laid the foundations for a good life for the colonists. Religious toleration was guaranteed, the liberties of Englishmen were carefully guarded and extended to all European inhabitants, taxes were virtually non-existent, and adequate provision had been made to punish vice and cherish virtue. The Quakers had been free to write into the statute books those laws which would further the ideals of the "holy experiment."

THE CHARTER OF LIBERTIES, 1683

The second legislative session, which convened March 12, 1683, was also of doubtful legality. The First Frame stated that the Council should consist of seventy-two persons, and the Assembly of a number not to exceed 200. Penn realized that it would be impossible to find such a large number of able persons for the General Assembly, and in a letter to William Markham on February 5, 1683, agreed to some modification.[15] Thus, when the freemen who met February 20 to choose their representatives in the Council petitioned that the twelve men chosen from each county should serve for both the Council and the Assembly in the 1683 session, Penn readily agreed.

When the Council met March 10, 1683, members were apprehensive lest the change would harm the colony, and one person proposed a motion "that the Governr may be desired that this alteration may not hinder ye people from the benefit of this Charter, because it seems thereby to be returned to him again by not being accepted as largely as Granted." Penn answered these misgivings with the statement, "they might amend, alter, or add for the Publick good, and that he was ready to Settle such Foundations as might be for their happiness and the good of their Posterities, according to ye powers vested in him."[16]

With this assurance from William Penn the Council adjourned, to meet again March 12 with only eighteen members. The other fifty-four chosen representatives met separately as the Assembly. Both houses met daily for the next three weeks, Sunday excepted, until the Assembly adjourned April 3 and the Council adjourned the following morning. The Governor generally presided over the Council, and Thomas Wynne was chosen Speaker of the Assembly.

While great care had been taken in England in preparing a constitution for Pennsylvania, Penn had scarcely arrived in his new province before he realized that changes would be necessary. A committee was named in the March session to discuss changes and bring proposals to the Governor.[17] Little is known about the deliberations of this committee, except as the results were apparent in the new document. There is record however that the committee members from the Assembly demanded that the lower house be allowed to initiate legislation. Penn refused to allow such a change, and gave as his reason that they might "forfeit his Patent by enacting such Laws as are contrary to the Grant and Tenure thereof." [18] Obviously, he had more faith in the small Council than in the larger and more unwieldy Assembly.

The new constitution, generally called the Second Frame or the Charter of Liberties, was accepted by both houses and engrossed upon parchment April 2, 1683. In the presence of both houses Penn stated, "That what was inserted in that Charter, was solely by him intended for the Good and Benefit of the Freemen of the Province, and prosecuted with much Earnestness in his Spirit towards God at the Time of its Composure." [19] The evening of the same day, in the presence of the General Assembly, William Penn affixed his signature and seal to the document and handed it to James Harrison and Thomas Wynne, who represented the freemen of the province and territories. They in turn restored the original charter to the Governor. The Charter of Liberties was then endorsed by all the members of the Council and the Assembly who were present, and by some inhabitants of Philadelphia who were in attendance at the session.[20]

This constitution remained in force at least until Governor Benjamin Fletcher of New York came down in 1693 to become royal governor of Pennsylvania as well. William Penn recognized it as the charter of Pennsylvania until it was returned into his hands in 1700. The document contained an introduction or preamble and twenty-five chapters.[21] The long preamble to the First Frame was omitted, and the new charter be-

gan with the same introduction as had appeared in the earlier
one, except that mention was made in appropriate places of the
territories which the Duke of York had deeded to Penn in the
interim.[22]

The Second Frame stated that the Provincial Council would
consist of eighteen members and the Assembly of thirty-six.
The date of elections was changed to March 10, and a new date
for the meeting of the Assembly, May 10, was established.
Chapter Six of the First Frame, which provided for the treble
vote of the proprietor, was omitted.[23] The twelfth chapter
stated that the governor or his deputy should preside in the
Provincial Council, and "hee shall att no time therein perform
anie publick act of State whatsoever that shall or may relate
unto the Justice, Trade, Treasurie or Safetie of the Province
and Territories aforesaid, but by and with the advice and consent of the Provinciall Council thereof."

In a chapter related to the taking of ballots, the Second
Frame stated, "all things relating to the preparing and passing
of Bills into Laws, shall be openlie declared and resolved by
the vote." The twenty-third chapter confirmed the land of the
freemen into their own hands, and the Charter of Liberties
ended with the same guarantee as the former one.

Much has been made of the fact that Penn's treble vote in
the Council was lost in the new constitution. Certainly three
votes in a body of eighteen men would have been more deci-
sive than three votes in a group of seventy-two men. If Penn
had reserved a veto power however, the number of votes he
held in the Council would have been immaterial. Apparently
he did not consider himself to be in possession of that power,
for if he had he would not have expressed fear that the Assembly would enact legislation which would endanger his
patent.

More important than the loss of the treble vote, was Penn's
acquiescence to Chapter Twelve, in which he surrendered his
right to perform any public act of state, "but by and with the
advice and consent of the Provinciall Council thereof." When
the effect of this chapter is added to the apparent lack of veto

power, it appears that William Penn placed himself in a position of subservience to the Provincial Council. Whether the proprietor at this rosy period of the "holy experiment" really contemplated surrendering his executive supremacy in the government is not known. In the next chapter of this study there is a description of the Quaker philosophy of government for the business meetings of the Society of Friends. When it is remembered that Penn may have considered operating the Council in the same way, it is easier to believe that he did disavow superiority in the government under the Charter of Liberties. Certainly as long as he was present, the Governor's personality and spiritual leadership gave him the power to guide and direct the Council.

However, Penn did exercise the right of veto in later years. The most notable occasion was his disallowance of a law passed in 1698, entitled, "An Act for Preventing Frauds & Regulating Abuses in Trade . . ." at the insistence of the Board of Trade. Furthermore, when one reads the instructions given to John Blackwell, who was named Lieutenant Governor in 1688, there is no indication that Penn considered his executive powers merged with the powers of the Council. In 1689 he made specific mention of his veto power when he returned the government to the freemen.

Perhaps the answer to these complex questions lies in the following surmise. In 1683 William Penn seriously considered abdicating his supremacy, and felt that the colony would be well cared for and protected by a Council of virtuous men. However, even before 1688, he began to realize that the "holy experiment" did not rest on the spiritual qualities which he had expected and he determined to restore to himself certain governmental powers granted under the patent from the king, despite promises made in the Charter of Liberties. It is an understatement to say that one can only wish that more was known about Penn's intentions under this document.

If William Penn had wanted evidence that the "holy experiment" would have difficulties, he had only to watch the Assembly in the spring of 1683. Practically the only power delegated to the Assembly was the right to discuss proposed laws and vote its negative or affirmative. Since the Council convened on the same date, the Assembly was left waiting for bills to discuss.

The first day one member suggested that the Assembly be allowed to propose to the governor and Council "such Things as might tend to the Benefit of the Province, &c. which possibly the Governor and Council might not think of, nor of very long Time remember, which might, in the Interim, tend to the great Detriment of the Province." [24] The following day, March 13, a member suggested that the Assembly should debate matters introduced to it, which brought a reply that such action was infringing upon the Governor's privileges and royalties and seemed "to render him Ingratitude for his Goodness towards the People." Several persons came to Penn's defense. Later the same day, when the Governor and Council sent for the Assembly to come for a conference, a vote was held on whether they would accede to the invitation. They voted by placing beans in a balloting box and while the vote carried, there was no indication of unanimity. When the Assembly was sent a test requiring fidelity and lawful obedience from the members to the governor, the members refused to sign it at first and only acquiesced after learning that the Council had already done so. On Wednesday, March 15, one member expressed his resentment at "undeserving Reflections and Aspersions cast upon the Governor." The following day, when the Assembly was asked to vote on granting the governor a veto power in the Council, it was approved unanimously, but the lower house rejected granting the governor the same power over itself.

The struggle for more power and recognition for the Assembly continued for many years. The spirit exhibited bore little resemblance to the spirit Penn hoped would be typified in the "holy experiment." Perhaps the non-Quakers were resentful of the power of Penn and the Council and took these opportunities to show their feelings. Penn indicated in a letter written in February, 1683, that there had been a struggle between the Quakers and others for the choice of a Speaker of the Assembly at Chester. The contest between the two groups, which became so pronounced in later years, was somewhat in evidence even in the beginning.[25]

Outside the legislative halls a non-Quaker, Nicholas More, stirred up trouble during the opening days of the session by condemning the change in size of the two houses of the General Assembly. He was heard to remark in a public house that these modifications of the First Frame, "have this day broken the Charter, & therefore all that you [the legislators] do will come to Nothing, & that hundreds in England will curse you for what you have done, & their children after them, and that you may hereafter be impeacht for Treason for what you do." [26] When the Council called upon More to explain himself he denied that he had made such utterances, but said rather he had been making queries. In 1684, while he was Speaker of the Assembly, More was quoted as saying that the "Proposed Laws Were Cursed Laws . . . hang it, Damn them all." [27] Until his death four years later More was constantly in the center of turmoil.

Another episode in the minutes of the Assembly during this two year period minimizes the importance of the differences during the spring session of 1683. In the fall of the same year, after the laws had been enacted, Speaker Thomas Wynne told the Assembly that Penn granted them the liberty to discuss any proposals to the governor and Council which "might tend to the Benefit of the Province." A writ was drawn up to express the thanks of the Assembly, signed by the members, and presented to Penn by the Speaker and others, but there is no record of anything being discussed.[28] This suggests that there were times of good feeling between the Assembly and the Governor and Council, and makes impossible a dogmatic statement that the "holy experiment" was proving either successful or unsuccessful during Penn's sojourn in the colony. The Governor expected some friction during the infancy of the province, and there is no indication that he was apprehensive about the future when he made his plans to return to England.

While the sessions of the General Assembly where laws were made and constitutions rewritten were an important part of the government of colonial Pennsylvania, there were other important branches of the government as well.

The Council, serving as an advisory group to the Governor and meeting frequently with him, was a vital organ in the effective operation of the province. Penn believed that the Council should meet twice a week, but it seldom did. Sometimes it met weekly, but more often there was an interval of two or three weeks between sessions. At first the Governor had hoped that all the Council would meet with him, but he soon forgot that idea, and named six men to attend him in the months between sessions of the General Assembly.[29]

These meetings were often cluttered with petitions for justice which belonged in the county courts. Difficulties between neighbors over boundaries were brought before them. Complaints were made which the Council eventually learned to shunt to the courts. But throughout this period the Council remained the highest court of appeal in the colony. Even after the provincial court was established in 1684 appeals were made to the Council, and it held a judicial position in Pennsylvania patterned on that of the House of Lords in England.

As has been mentioned before, the Council was the source of all laws. Until 1693, when Benjamin Fletcher changed things considerably, no bill was ever introduced except by the Council. Weeks of debate preceded each meeting of the General Assembly, while the Council decided which proposals advanced either by citizens or members of the Council should be accepted and promulgated for the consideration of the Assembly. Many of the proposed laws were useful, but others were poor and needed to be amended or dropped.[30] The reconsideration of old laws also rested with this body.

The Council was an advisory group to the Governor. He turned to it when he received letters from England or the other colonies, when he was contemplating cooperation with West Jersey, and when he was deciding the boundary disputes with Maryland. The Council was also responsible for the enforcement of laws enacted in the General Assembly. This organ of the government was a very powerful body even before William

Penn put the executive power into its hands when he returned to England.

Of the third branch of government, the judiciary, W. R. Shepherd wrote, "It was not until after the passage of the law of 1701 that the provincial court and the other tribunals were firmly established, and their jurisdiction defined." [31] This meets with general agreement, although the county courts operated in a fairly satisfactory and stable manner during the twenty years. Those tribunals were patterned on the same courts in England, and thus there was less need for experimentation and less likelihood of failure in their operation.

Penn was given wide privileges under his Letters Patent to establish courts of justice, in a phrase which granted him the power "to doe all and every other thing and things which unto the compleate establishment of Justice unto Courts and Tribunals, formes of Judicature and manner of proceedings doe belong, altho' in these presents expresse mencon bee not made thereof." [32] As the Proprietor he was also given express permission to establish courts baron.

There were already county courts in the area when Penn arrived and he continued them, taking for himself the power of appointment. Laws were enacted throughout the period to direct the justices of the peace who presided over the courts of common pleas and quarter sessions. These laws culminated in the law of 1701, apparently drawn up by David Lloyd. These same justices held orphan's courts and courts of equity, although the right to hold the latter was under question at times. While Penn had the power of appointment by law, when he was not in the colony existing executive authority made appointments with the consent of the Council, and for more than three years the Council carried the executive power in itself.

To serve as an intermediate court and to save the Council from expending much of its time in listening to legal questions, a provincial court was established by law in 1684. It provided for five judges appointed by the Governor, of whom three were to hold a provincial court in Philadelphia twice a year. In addition, at least two judges were to go on circuit and visit each county seat in the spring and fall. The court was to have the power of "hearing and Determining of all Appealls from inferior Courts. Also, all trialls of Titles of Land, and all Causes as well Criminall as Civill both in Law and Equity, not Determinable by the respective County Courts." [33] The first judges were commissioned by Penn August 4, 1684.[34]

The men who filled the offices of justice and judge had little or no legal training. In fact, there were very few men in the colony during the twenty years under study who had legal backgrounds. David Lloyd, John Moore, Thomas Story, James Logan, and Penn himself are the only ones who are known to have had a preparation for the law. Penn never practiced law in the colony, while Story and Logan did not arrive until 1699. Moore apparently did not practice much law before the establishment by the crown of the new admiralty court in 1697. Only Lloyd was in the colony for any length of time, for he arrived in 1686.

It was expected that the members of the county courts should be men of prestige in the county, sturdy, respected men, but not necessarily trained in the law. However, the provincial court which should have included persons acquainted with the fine points of justice never did. Penn once wrote to James Harrison, while he was one of the provincial judges, of the surprise which would be expressed in England if it were known that a man who wrote such poor letters as Harrison did was one of the chief justices of Pennsylvania.

In addition to the lack of legally trained men, there was sometimes a lack of men of any sort for the courts. The men were paid very little, and frequently felt that they could not give up their living to serve in a judicial capacity. John Blackwell wrote to Penn on January 25, 1689, while he was Lieutenant Governor, "Some have had the confidence with more than becoming heat to say openly in Councill to my face, without blushing that they will not act unless they be compelled by Law . . . Some Glory in their not taking the wages by law allowed them and conceive your Laws compell them not to hould, but that you are beholden to them for the necessary support of your Governmt." [35] He added that the justices of the peace did more than those in England for they are "Judges of Assize, Oyer terminer & Goale delivery." He suggested that Penn find two or three "Grave & prudent pious persons" to go on circuit twice a year, "to inspect the manners, Conversations & professions of the Looser sort principally but punishing also all evill & corrupt communication even in the justices themselves whom they shall find faulty." He believed that Penn should find some way to pay able men to serve in that capacity. Laws were enacted to provide fines for the justices and jurymen who failed to appear for service, but still justice did not proceed smoothly.

All of this was a severe disappointment to William Penn. He did not feel that virtuous men would need courts of law except in most unusual cases, and he believed that virtuous men would gladly serve the government and their fellow citizens in every necessary way, including the conduct of courts.

In defense of the men it should be added that the establishment of justice was not always an easy matter to accomplish. Roads were very bad, the weather sometimes made travel difficult, and in winter ice in the river hindered the progress of the judges. The provincial court on circuit traveled entirely by water, since the county seats, beginning with Buckingham or Bristol at the north, and going south all the way to Lewes in Sussex County, lay along the Delaware River. In fact most early travel was by the river, although roads were under construction.[36]

There was eventually a regular schedule for the sitting of the county courts which met every March, June, September and December. In the province of Pennsylvania they met the second Wednesday in Bucks; the first Tuesday in Philadelphia; and the second Tuesday in Chester counties. The same men sat as the orphan's court to probate wills and handle other legal matters on the first Tuesday in March and October in all counties. The existence of rules for the regulation of the operation of the courts, even though these rules were unpublished, indicates that progress was being made.[37]

During the first decade there was not much need for judicial machinery, especially in the province, for Friends settled most of their problems themselves through the Monthly Meeting. When others began to enter the colony, especially in the last five years of the century, it became apparent that more efficient and better regulated methods of settling disputes and maintaining law and order were needed. The law of 1701 made provisions for those needs.

There were other officials at the provincial and county levels of the government. The provincial officials included a secretary of the Council, treasurer, register, and master of the rolls. The county officers included a sheriff, coroner, clerk of the courts, register, and master of the rolls in each county.

It should not be forgotten that William Penn expected the government and each official of the government to further the "holy experiment." When the General Assembly convened in New Castle May 10, 1684, Penn addressed the freemen, "in the Way of Christian Council and Exhortation, advising the Members of Assembly to look unto 'God, in all their Proceedings, and to act in every Thing, not with any unadvised Rashness, but with serious Consideration.' " [38] It is worthwhile to repeat what Penn wrote into the Preface of the First Frame: "Governments, like clocks, go from the motion men give them . . . Let men be good, and the government cannot be bad . . . But if men be bad, let the government be never so good, they will endeavour to warp and spoil to their turn." [39]

CHAPTER FOUR

THE COLONISTS AND THE LAND

WILLIAM PENN placed his ultimate hope for the "holy experiment" in the Quaker community, that gathering of kindred spirits drawn together in worship, fellowship, and loving care for one another. Because the Quaker community was the most important segment of Pennsylvania society in the first twenty years of its existence, and was essential to the success of the "holy experiment," an attempt at definition and description must be made. The organization of the Quaker community can be easily described, as can the activities of the organization. Difficulty comes when an attempt is made to portray the spirit which motivated the Quaker community.

Friends might be called a congregational group. That is, the center of authority for their organization was in the hands of each small group of fellow worshippers. The Quakers who gathered together to wait on God on First Day, and at least once during the week, also met each month to discuss business matters. At first they met in a home, and later in an unpretentious building called a meetinghouse. [1] These business meetings took place once each month, hence the name Monthly Meeting.

The Monthly Meetings in an area sent representatives to one meetinghouse four times a year to hold the Quarterly Meeting. The friends of Pennsylvania, Delaware, and the Jerseys combined for a Yearly Meeting, which met in alternate years at Philadelphia and Burlington, West Jersey. Although Quarterly Meetings exerted some control over Monthly Meetings and the Yearly Meeting exerted control over both, those at the larger gatherings were appointed by the local group. Authority did not come down from above in the usually accepted sense. There were no permanent officials at either the Quarterly or Yearly Meeting level.

There was a strong democratic spirit in the Society of Friends, and it was apparent in the meeting for worship and in the business meeting. However, it was not called "democratic," and it was not transferred from the religious sphere into the political. In meetings for worship, there was no minister or leader, and all waited before the Lord for His divine leading. Anyone in the gathering might feel the Spirit move him to speak or pray. There were laymen, called Public Friends whose gift in the ministry was recognized, but Quakers strongly denounced the "hireling clergy."

In meeting for business, Friends never made decisions by a majority vote, but rather waited until there was a "sense of the meeting" that action should be taken. It was felt that business meetings should be under the guiding hand of God as were meetings for worship, and that if all who were in attendance listened to the voice of God a spirit of unanimity would be reached. The presiding officer of a business meeting was called the Clerk, for his prime duty was to record the "sense of the meeting." If agreement could not be reached by those in attendance, the matter under discussion was tabled until a later time. Sometimes action was postponed for a number of years, but more often, if all were willing to sit in silence to listen to the Inward Christ, a sense of agreement swept over the body.

To illustrate the divine compulsion under which these people lay and their refusal to be deterred from doing God's will, an incident from the epistle sent to London Yearly Meeting in 1696 may be repeated. The Yearly Meeting was in session, holding a meeting for worship, when it was interrupted by George Hutchinson, a Keithian, and Henry Barnard Coster and other German pietists, who began to berate Friends for their unorthodox views and accused them of denying the divinity of Christ. Friends ignored the intruders, and some even rose to speak. The epistle reported that although the invaders shouted the louder to drown out the Quakers, "the Lords

Power Weighed & Chained them down & they left us, after which we had in the Close of our Meeting, a Sweet & Quiet Time in which Friends were much blessed & United in the Love & Life of Truth." [2]

While Friends were democratic in their relations to one another and believed that all persons were equal before God, logic forced them to admit that some men and women seemed to be nearer Truth than others. A person who had ministered to his fellow men for decades, who had suffered imprisonment for his convictions, whose devout life had been an example to his coreligionists, was recognized as a spiritual leader and was referred to as a "weighty" Friend. Although the assumption was logical, it was an exception to the fundamental beliefs of the Society of Friends, and eventually proved dangerous. Once the Society admitted that some were set apart and had greater wisdom, the spontaneity of the movement began to suffer. The time came when persons were recognized as "weighty" Friends because they were old, revered, and experienced, and it was forgotten that they had also become conservative and were no longer fit to be the bellwethers of a vigorous society. When the Quakers lived at their highest spiritual level they did not allow themselves to be bound by tradition, but waited expectantly for their Heavenly Father to open up new avenues to them.

The Quaker community was composed of all the Quakers in Pennsylvania, and there was a unanimity of spirit throughout the province. But the real functioning of the Quaker community was at the Monthly Meeting level. The Monthly Meeting was in part a social agency. It cared for widows, saw that their children were apprenticed, and it watched over the aged and indigent. It supervised marriages, investigated both parties, and made certain that both the man and the woman were "clear" before giving approval. [3]

The Monthly Meeting was also a court of arbitration and settlement. Quakers seldom became involved in court because their differences were settled in the meeting. For example, Edward Penington, Penn's brother-in-law, appeared against William Say in 1701, with the following statement: "I am sorry I am forced to complain to you against a troublesome Neighbour, who wearing the mark of a Quaker (though I fear little in reality) while that continues on, I cannot take those Legal courses, whereby I could soon bring him to a just compliance with my reasonable demands; and the breach being lately widened between us, so that it seems not likely to be made up by ourselves, I intreat this meeting to take cognisance of the things in difference." [4] Say had allowed his cattle to break down a fence, tampered with a well, and thrown planks into it. Say was also involved in a misunderstanding with his mother-in-law, Alice Guest. Thomas Story, Casper Hoodt, David Lloyd, Isaac Norris, William Hudson, Henry Willis, and Anthony Morris, or any four of them, were named by Philadelphia Monthly Meeting to attempt a peaceful settlement between Say, and Penington and Alice Guest. Later the Monthly Meeting called for reports from the committee until all attempts at agreement had been made.[5] This committee included two of the three Quaker lawyers in the colony, as well as three other men who were prominent in the government. The peaceful settlement of disputes was considered an important matter by Friends. As another aspect of its legal work, the Monthly Meeting cared for the settling of wills and the estates of the deceased.

The Monthly Meeting was also a disciplinary body. When Friends were found guilty of various offenses they were forced to appear before their fellow religionists and confess guilt. Sometimes they were disowned by the body, but more often they were duly forgiven and told to sin no more. Some lurid crimes were mentioned in Monthly Meeting records, but two examples of a less sensational nature will illustrate the point. In 1686 Griffith Jones confessed to the sin of drunkenness in a letter to Philadelphia Monthly Meeting.[6] Thomas Davis apologized in 1700 for saying that "there was nott an honest man in the province Except Governour penn and that they would goe down in the bottomless pitt." [7]

On rare occasions the Yearly Meeting handed down opinions on morality. In 1700 it stated that proposals and acceptances for a second marriage which came before nine or ten months had elapsed since the death of the first spouse, were an indication of being "over hasty, and Indecent." [8] In 1694 directions were drawn up for parents in regard to their children. It was decided that children should not challenge one another to races, engage in wrestling, lay wagers, "pitch barrs," drink healths to one another, engage in idle talk, nor dally with the affections of several persons of the opposite sex. Children were to be obedient to their parents, and keep away from the "Worlds corrupt Language, manners, & Vain needless Things & Fashions, in apparel." The youth were to renounce immoderate and indecent smoking, especially while riding in the streets. Parents and masters of apprentices were to be good examples to children and servants.[9]

These Quaker communities were tightly knit organizations where the people were interested in one another. They were willing to lend a helping hand, and willing to use corporate strength to maintain discipline. It must not be forgotten that the meeting for worship was at the center of these communities.

This feeling of companionship and fellowship for fellow Quakers was not entirely localized. Friends had a concern for inter-visitation and took long journeys to preach the Word. Robert Proud compiled a list of twenty-eight Friends from foreign parts, all but three of them from England, who visited in the Yearly Meeting between 1684 and 1701.[10] One, Roger Gill, died during the great epidemic of 1699 while carrying out his ministry. Proud also listed twenty-six visitations by people from Pennsylvania in the years 1690 to 1701.[11] The majority of these persons remained on the North American continent, visiting in New England or the south. Eight of them returned to the British Isles or Europe for ministry. Those who traveled did so with the prayerful approval of Friends where they worshipped. Sometimes a man or a woman waited for months until the "call" which he or she felt was also recognized by the group. William Biles, of Bucks County, felt a leading which was not shared by the group, although the ministers were willing to recognize the call of his wife Jane. She waited until his call was also recognized. There was no reluctance to tell a man that he had weaknesses, as the following quote indicates: "Joseph Paul proposed to this Meeting his inclination to visit New England, wch friends here do assent to, provided he have a good stayed Companion & keep low in himself to his own Gift." [12]

Traveling in the ministry was considered of utmost importance. Thomas Story, a visiting Friend who was persuaded by William Penn to remain in the colony for a time, was given several positions of trust in the government. His journal listed every meeting for worship which he attended, and recorded his personal feelings about the spirit of the meetings. He found space for just one paragraph on his political activities. These had lasted for two years, and had taken a good deal of time, as indicated by his regular attendance at meetings of the Council, and by other records.[13]

The place of the Quaker community in the society of the colony should be mentioned to evaluate its importance to this study. The inhabitants of the three counties of Pennsylvania were overwhelmingly Quaker in the first twenty years of William Penn's control over it. In Bucks and Chester counties a non-Quaker was an oddity, although there were many in Philadelphia County. The counties of Delaware were largely peopled with those of other faiths, with a strong sprinkling of Friends. Some Quakers were always sent to the Council and Assembly from those counties, although they were in the minority. We are primarily concerned with the upper counties.

The Quaker community and the government were very closely allied. The legal provisions in regard to marriage, or the requirement that the names for the days of the week and months of the year should be after the manner of Friends indicates this. The provision for arbitrators or common peacemakers to be attached to the courts of justice, the establishment of affirmation and attests in place of oaths, and the failure to provide a militia all testify to the close relationship between church and state.

Two incidents from Quaker records illustrate the connection. In March, 1685, John Eckley and James Claypoole were appointed by Philadelphia Quarterly Meeting to request the magistrates of the county not to hold court on the day set aside for mid-week meeting for worship.[14] Fifteen years later Friends were not quite as presumptuous, but still showed an awareness of government: "The youths Meeting falling out on ye Election day Its thought Convenient, that it be defered till the Second day following." [15]

William Penn felt strongly that government and religion were closely related, although he did not believe in a legal attachment. He could never understand why the Quakers could not get along together in government, nor why their Friendly spirits could not overcome their political adversaries in a peaceful manner. He wrote, "For as Government is an Ordinance of God, so most assuredly, the conscientious discharge of our Duty therein shall not be left out of the number of those good Deeds that God will recompense at the last," and added, let all be "weighty, serious and deligent, least men profane Government by an unhallowed use of it." [16] He even believed that God had a place in the taverns of the day, and told the magistrates to continue such drinking houses as "are most tender of gods glory & ye reputation of the governmt." [17] At the same time he was tolerant of those who were not Quakers, and he frequently enjoined the Friends to fill offices with persons of ability, no matter what their persuasion: "Employ the sober yt are not Friends as well as those yt are." [18]

Most of the Quakers were from the British Isles, and the great majority were English. A few Scottish settlers, some Irish, and more Welsh came. Some Friends came from the continent, and many people became Quakers after they arrived. The Welsh, the Dutch and the Germans tended to withdraw into their own sections. In fact, they had purchased land before coming with the intention of living separately.

There were some among the settlers who were not Friends. Many of the German or Dutch people, such as the Mennonites, brought faith and loyalty to their own denomination with them and maintained a separate existence. In the last years of the century there were some Baptists, Presbyterians, and Anglicans in the colony, mostly among those from the British Isles.[19] Penn was not interested in an exclusively Quaker community. He circulated pamphlets and other printed material on the continent, and was pleased to see other groups find religious freedom under his protection. When Louis XIV intensified his persecution of the Huguenots in France, Penn immediately offered a haven in Pennsylvania. In October, 1685 he sent Charles de la Nowe to Pennsylvania and asked the Quakers to be kind to him. "It will be of good savour. For a lettr is come over from a great professr there to some well inclined here, telling them, that there is no room for any but Quakers." [20] There are several indications in correspondence of the period that not all Friends shared Penn's openmindedness in regard to non-Quaker groups settling in Pennsylvania. The Governor frequently mentioned the situation in France in his letters to colonial leaders, and once wrote of the "great cruelty there, to ye Protest[ants,] many comeing to you." [21] John Bellers was also interested in the French, and sent several persons to settle his 5,000 acres.[22]

There was one other small minority group in the colony, the Negroes. There were some Negroes among the Dutch and Swedes, and more were brought in by the Quakers, although some Friends elsewhere had already begun to protest against the enslavement of human. beings.[23] The story of the protest against slaveholding which originated in Germantown in 1688 is a familiar one. Although the response of other Friends was slow at first, the Yearly Meeting decided in 1696 that additional importations of Negroes should be discouraged. Further, it was agreed that those in the colony should be given every opportunity to develop spiritually, especially by attendance at Friends meeting or through instruction at home. In addition, Friends were asked to "Restrain them from Loose & Lewd Living as much as in them lies, & from Rambling abroad on First Days or other Times." [24] When Penn returned in 1699, he carried a concern for the religious and educational development of the Indians and Negroes. It should not be forgotten that the Negroes were a small fraction of the population during the twenty years. To explain this Edward R. Turner, wrote, "Before 1700 Pennsylvania was all frontier; hence it had very few negroes." [25]

Surely William Penn had every reason to believe that the Quaker community would be a source of strength to the "holy experiment." If the people gathered together in religiously-centered groups where the highest Christian ethic would be constantly before them, how could they wander far from Truth. Should one Monthly Meeting be led astray, there was the influence of the larger groups at the Quarterly Meeting and Yearly Meeting levels to give guidance and encouragement. Perhaps more important, there were frequent visits from Public Friends of other Yearly Meetings, who would bring spiritual bread.

Throughout the years covered by this study there was a strong religious spirit in the Quaker community which strengthened the "holy experiment." To be sure there was a split in the Society of Friends in the 1690s when some members joined a Scottish schoolmaster named George Keith in denouncing the main body of Friends. The schismatic group claimed that Friends denied the divinity of Christ, and criticized them for refusing to adopt a creedal statement and for participating in the government. This split lasted for a few years, but the wound was largely healed by the end of the century.

The difficulty was that Friends developed a dualism. They followed the beliefs of Quakerism in the meeting and within the Quaker community, but lived in accordance with the practices of the world in their financial affairs and in their government. While Friends practiced scrupulous honesty in their dealings with one another, they were not completely honest in their financial responsibilities to William Penn and the government. They continued to plead an inability to pay taxes long after they had money available for other things. There was evidence in this period of their inordinate desire to accumulate money, which was another heritage from their Calvinistic background and certainly not in keeping with the ideals of the "holy experiment." Further, once they became politicians they put aside the spirit which Penn had proclaimed so necessary in government.

John Blackwell, who was lieutenant governor during 1689, was deeply angered and frustrated by the Quaker politicians, and after he retired he denounced them in vigorous language in a letter to Penn. Of the quarrels in the colony he wrote, "The Principles whence these things flow, and what countenance you give by the continuance of your favours on such persons, who have made, & are thereby incouraged to make more divisions amongst your people of different persuasions (Especially sober Christian people not coming up with them) and what unrighteousnesse abounds in all your Courts towards such, your Contrey will be an entire stand, as to farther peopling, & becomes fitt for none but such as love to live in the fire of contention, and are fore-ordayned to a being amongst hipochrites & un believers etc. I hope Sr better things of you: Look to it that you be not held in this Error, etc." [26]

The truth is that despite its weaknesses, the Quaker community was one of the strongest forces working for the success of the "holy experiment" in the entire colony.

THE LAND POLICY

William Penn was a forward-looking person, especially in his religious beliefs and political philosophy. Yet he maintained a feudal arrangement between himself and the freemen of Pennsylvania in regard to land, through the proviso that those who purchased land from him would owe annual quitrents. In medieval times, under feudalism, all men held their land from a lord and owed him certain goods and services each year. In the dawn of modern times, in the fourteenth and fifteenth centuries, there were many changes in society. Men began to exchange annual financial payments called quitrents for the old obligations of goods and services. By the payment of money, a man was able to quit himself from all other feudal responsibilities.

When the crown granted land in America to men of the nobility or to other prominent persons, the letters patent were in the form of proprietary grants. It was either stated or understood that though the colonists purchased land from the proprietor, they would still owe an annual quitrent. These fees were generally nominal. For example, William Penn charged a quitrent of one shilling for each 100 acres. However, the income from an entire colony held in this fashion might be considerable.

The letters patent which granted Pennsylvania to William Penn stated that he held the province "in free and comon Socage by fealty only," not directly from the king, that is *in Capite*, but of the Castle of Windsor.[27] He was to pay the king at Windsor two beaver skins annually, plus one-fifth of all gold or silver found within the bounds of the grant. Penn did not own Pennsylvania in the usual sense of the word, he did not have an allodial claim to it, but he held it from the king under feudal tenure.

William Penn contemplated selling his land in blocks of 10,000 acres. However, he realized that few persons would purchase an entire block, and he made provision for purchase of much smaller parcels. The land was sold at the rate of 500 acres for ten pounds, plus the annual quitrent forever.

John E. Pomfret, in a recent article about the "First Purchasers in Pennsylvania," shows that 155,000 acres were bought by 392 colonists in parcels of 125–675 acres; while 254,000 acres were obtained by 196 persons in estates of 750–3,000 acres; and 380,000 acres were absorbed by only 69 colonists who bought 5,000 acres or more. His figures indicate that there were many more small purchasers than large purchasers, and that more colonists (235), bought 500 acres than any other amount.[28]

There were exceptions to the rule of one shilling quitrent for each 100 acres. A purchaser could obtain a commutation of his quitrents by paying a lump sum of eighteen shillings for each 100 acres. Some persons could not purchase land, and Penn provided that such settlers could rent land at the rate of one penny an acre per annum, to a limit of 200 acres. Penn agreed to grant fifty acres of land to purchasers who brought indentured servants to the colony, and he promised to grant fifty acres to such servants when they had served their time and gained their freedom. In such cases the master owed four shillings a year for his land, and the servant owed a quitrent of two shillings a year.

Penn's plans for developing the sale of land included a proposal to build a large town in the province, and provided that each purchaser of land would receive two per cent of his total purchase in the town. That is, a man who bought 5,000 acres, would receive 100 acres in the new town. It was rightly presumed that the land in the town would be much more valuable than the rural property.

This offer and all of his land policies were contained in a document entitled, "Certain CONDITIONS or CONCESSIONS agreed upon by *William Penn,* Proprietary and Governor of the Province of *Pennsylvania,* and those who are the Adventurers and Purchasers in the same Province." This brochure also established rules to be followed until a government was established such as those in Chapter XVI which stated, "That the Laws, as to Slanders, Drunkenness, Swearing, Cursing, Pride in Apparel, Trespasses, Distresses, Replevins, Weights and Measures, shall be the same as in *England,* till altered by Law in this Province." [29]

The Proprietor gave further instructions for granting land and regulation of the early settlers in a letter to his land commissioners, William Crispin, John Bezar and Nathaniel Allen. Penn was anxious that his town be laid out on the finest site in the colony, even if previous colonists were already established on the desired land. He urged his commissioners to persuade the old settlers to move by giving them "a new graunt at their old rent, nay halfe their quitrent abated, yea, make them as free as Purchasers, rather than disappoint my mind in this Township: though herein, be as sparing as ever you can, and

urge the weak bottome of their Graunts, the D. of Yorke haveing never had a graunt from the King, etc." [30] He gave the
commissioners permission to grant less land in the town to the
purchasers than he had promised in the "Concessions," if they
found it necessary to do so. The difference was to be made up
by granting the balance in the "liberty" lands on the edge of
the town. The variance between these two statements caused
untold trouble in the years which followed. In addition, Penn
urged the men to begin the organization of the town with store
houses, markets, and a building for the government. He asked
that 300 acres in the town be set aside for himself, in order
that he would have half again as much land as anyone else,
even those who purchased 10,000 acres.

William Penn joined in the establishment of a joint stock
enterprise called the Free Society of Traders. It was formed
early in 1682 by 200 persons who pledged £10,000 to the enterprise. The proprietor contributed to the capital being raised,
granted the company 20,000 acres for a nominal quitrent, and
allowed the company manorial rights on its land. James Claypoole, the treasurer of the company, described the plans and
accomplishments of the body that summer. He said that 100
servants were being sent over immediately to build houses,
plant crops, and improve the land. He added that the company
planned to make glass for the entire continent and the islands
of the Caribbean. Other commodities to be produced were
wine, oil, linen, iron and lead. Two thousand pounds had been
set aside to develop the fur trade, and 400 acres had been
granted in the capital town for offices, houses, warehouses and
other buildings. He stated that Penn was most cooperative,
and promised a charter "wth as many priviledges as wee could
desire." Claypoole added, "through ye blessing of god wee may
hope for a great increase And it may come to be a famous
Compy." [31]

Nicholas More was the first president of the Society. The
company began its existence in a pretentious manner, but
never proved profitable. The promised capital was never provided by the members, and the company slowly dwindled.

Both the company and its officers soon became involved in lawsuits. Finally, in 1721, the Assembly passed a bill which called for the dissolution of the Free Society of Traders and the distribution of the assets of the company. Lieutenant governor Sir William Keith approved the act in 1723, and set the machinery in motion to end the company.[32]

William Penn granted extensive powers to other organizations, of which the most familiar was the Frankfurt Company, a German group which held 15,000 acres, and later held 25,000. It was represented in Pennsylvania by Francis Daniel Pastorius.[33] This company developed an elaborate organization but did not find families to settle the grant, and Penn regained control of the land in 1700. In the meantime, Pastorius had joined the Dutch Quakers at Germantown under the leadership of Benjamin Furly, to purchase 18,000 acres. These purchasers had no formal agreement to bind them together, and Furly did not come with them to the New World. Nevertheless, they succeeded in establishing a community.

Two Welsh companies were formed, Charles Lloyd and Company, with 10,000 acres, and Edward Jones and Company, with 5,000 acres. Dublin merchants founded John Gee and Company which purchased 5,000 acres, and there were several other land companies, including the London Company which purchased 60,000 acres in 1699.[34]

The Governor reserved several large manors for himself and for his children when the grants were made to the purchasers. The most familiar of these commodious estates was Pennsbury, on which was built the famous manor house of the same name.

The land which had been deeded to William Penn by Charles II was largely in the possession of the Indians. Penn followed the example of many of his English predecessors in the New World, dating back to Roger Williams, in purchasing land from the aborigines as it was needed. The most famous of his treaties with the Indians was the one which was presumably signed at Shackamaxon, at the home of Thomas and Elizabeth Fairman, under the Treaty Elm. According to tradition this was a great occasion, with solemn councils on the one hand

and games and contests on the other. While documentary evidence is lacking to substantiate the traditional tales, passed on from one generation to another, and immortalized by Benjamin West and Voltaire, there is no doubt that Penn did purchase land from the Indians. He wrote to the Privy Council in 1683, "I have followed the Bishop of London's counsel, by buying, and not taking away, the natives' land." [35] More land was purchased as needed throughout the twenty years covered by this study, and generally amicable relations were maintained, although in several instances Indians molested whites, and vice versa, and there was a considerable fear of the Indians during King William's War.[36]

There should be some mention of the proprietor's policy in regard to Delaware. The grant of the Lower Counties to William Penn was similar to that of Pennsylvania. James granted what was called New Castle County to Penn for ten shillings and an annual payment of five shillings.[37] He granted the area south of New Castle to the Whorekills to Penn for an additional ten shillings and an annual payment of one rose, plus one-half of all the quitrents and other profits made from the same.[38] Thus, Penn also planned to collect quitrents from the settlers in the Territories. Those who owed payments to James were now to pay Penn. As new lands were granted, the terms fixed upon by Penn were to be in operation.

How does Penn's land policy fit into the "holy experiment"? On the surface, it is not related at all. It was a financial arrangement between the proprietor and his tenants. Where Penn made concessions to prospective purchasers in grants of land and in establishing quitrents, it can be successfully demonstrated that these concessions were bestowed to attract more colonists. The founding of Pennsylvania was a spectacular and successful business venture for everyone except Penn. Brochures were distributed, agents traveled, and companies were formed to guarantee the colonizing of the province. William Penn believed that he had at least £16,000 coming to him from the colony, the payment owed to the estate of Admiral Penn by the crown, and he sank additional thousands of pounds in

Pennsylvania in the early years. He hoped to regain this sizable fortune both by the sale of land and the collection of quitrents.

Further, Penn looked to the quitrents to provide an income for his declining years and a suitable inheritance for his children. It seems apparent that Penn was engaged in dual enterprises. He wished to establish the "holy experiment," and at the same time he looked to the colony for a substantial monetary return in future years. This does not mean that in William Penn's mind there was any separation between the "holy experiment" and his financial activities. In fact, the following quotation from a letter to Robert Turner in 1681 indicates the opposite. "I have been these thirteen years the servant of truth and Friends, and for my testimony sake lost much, not only by the greatness and preferments of this world, but £16,000 of my estate, that had I not been what I am, I had long agoe obtained; but I murmur not; the Lord is good to me, and the interest his truth has given me with his people may more than repaire it: For many are drawn forth to be concerned with me and perhaps this way of satisfaction has more of the hand of God in it than a downright payment." [39]

If Penn really believed that the "holy experiment" was established in part to give God an opportunity to reward him for his faithfulness in the past, is it to be wondered that he was bitter against the colonists when they failed to fulfill their financial obligations to the proprietary? We must conclude that to William Penn the "holy experiment" and his land policy were closely related. No one will ever know how successful the "holy experiment" might have been if it could have been separated from the wranglings over money matters in the decades which followed.

MARYLAND-DELAWARE BOUNDARY DISPUTE

In 1684 William Penn was faced with a serious boundary dispute with Lord Baltimore of Maryland which threatened his hold on Delaware, and in August of that year he hurried home to England aboard the *Endeavour* to defend his rights to the Lower Counties. The story of the boundary dispute between Pennsylvania and Maryland is a familiar one, and the Mason-Dixon Line which finally settled the differences has a prominent place in American history. Less well known is the boundary dispute between Maryland and Delaware which plagued Penn in 1684.

Lord Baltimore claimed all of Delaware. He stated that the charter given to his family in 1632 had granted all of the land not held by Christians on the west bank of the Delaware, and that the Dutch and Swedes had usurped his rights. He added that as long as the land was in the hands of the Duke of York he had made no claim, but if it was to pass into the private possession of William Penn he had more right to the region than anyone else.[40]

Most students of this matter agree that Penn's claim to Delaware was defective from the beginning. The grant to the Duke of York from Charles II, of the land formerly in the possession of the Dutch, extended only to the east bank of the Delaware River. James had presumed that since the Dutch ruled the western shores of that river and of the Delaware Bay, that he might rule also. However, when James granted the Lower Counties to William Penn his title was either non-existent or of doubtful legality, although he was in actual possession of the lands. The Duke recognized this fact, and the deeds of feoffment included the previously quoted provision that Penn, at his own expense, would obtain a better title to the land for James from the Crown. James would presumably give the title to Penn. These facts strengthened the case which Lord Baltimore was making, but also caused dissension between Penn and the political leaders of Delaware in the years which followed.[41]

William Penn ignored the claims of Maryland, and in 1681 wrote a letter to James Frisby and others who lived in the disputed area in which he said, "I hope to take this opportunity to begin our acquaintance, and by you, with the rest of the people on your side, of the country; and I do assure you and them that I will be so far from taking any advantage to draw great profits to myself that you will find me and my government easy, free and just." [42]

Despite these conciliatory words, when Penn arrived he had some trouble with the settlers in the western part of Delaware, and ordered John Simcock, William Welsh, James Harrison, and John Cann to put down those who were cooperating with Baltimore. He told them to seize one man at a time quietly, to prevent others from learning what was happening. He asked his representatives to attempt to obtain a jury verdict against them, for "be assured that one judgement of ye jury of that county were worth two of any jury of this Province." [43] "Endeavor all you can to know ye motives inducing to disaffections, and in your conversations refute them as dangerous, foolish and ungrateful on their side." He suggested further that when they had finished their temporal business, "I should be glad you had a good meeting or two amongst them," and deliver "serious rebukes with truth mixt with sorrow." If this referred to meetings for worship it provides an example of the "holy experiment" in action when devout Friends combine meeting for worship with jailing recalcitrants.

William Markham and Lord Baltimore made an attempt to settle the differences before Penn arrived, although Markham seemed to be sick most of the year and missed some conferences, while at other times Baltimore did not appear. Penn and Baltimore met to reach a compromise, but it became evident that the dispute could only be settled by the Lords of Trade back in England. After William Penn learned that Baltimore had sailed for England to present his side of the story, he followed. Penn thought that he had taken with him several important papers, especially true copies of documents from New York which proved the early possession of Delaware by the Dutch. However, upon arrival at Worminghurst, Penn wrote back to James Harrison, "Phil Lemain [Lehnmann] has most carelessly left behind the York papers yt T. Lloyd brought & should have come as the ground & very strength of my coming, so yt I am now here wth my finger in my mouth." [44]

In March, 1685, Penn wrote to Thomas Lloyd and the Council, "he [James] under whom we claym, is King, power is now added to Right, & I have his positive word since as well as before he was king, So I must be easy." [45] The records of the Lords of Trade indicated, however, that there was a great deal of delay before a decision was reached. Other business intervened; an important counsel for one side was out of town on circuit; Penn was gone at one time, and Baltimore obstructed the settlement at another point in the negotiations. On November 7, 1685, a decision was handed down which divided the peninsula between the Delaware and the Chesapeake Bay, from Cape Henlopen to the fortieth parallel, giving one-half to Baltimore and the other half to James II, or now to Penn. [46]

Difficulties continued to crop up in the years which followed. Smuggling was carried on between the two colonies and each blamed the other. At one time Maryland passed a law to place a special tax on goods imported from Pennsylvania, and another time men invaded New Castle, in search of runaway seamen. The division of the peninsula was illogical in some ways. However, it did provide Penn with a protected outlet to the ocean, and made possible the formation of the state which was first to ratify the Constitution of the United States.

Penn had every reason to look on his colony with pride at the end of its first two years. There was no reason to suspect that the "holy experiment" was not launched successfully. Penn had only to remember that there were *eight hundred persons in attendance on First and week days, at Friends Meeting in Philadelphia,"* to drive out any doubts about his colony. [47]

If Penn entertained uncertainty about the future of Pennsylvania, it was not evidenced in the benedictions he bestowed upon her, which Robert Proud reproduced for posterity: [48]

My love and my life is to you, and with you; and no water can quench it, nor distance wear it out, or, bring it to an end:—I have been with you, cared over you, and served you with unfeigned love; and you are beloved of me, and near to me, beyond utterance. I bless you, in the name and power of the Lord . . . Oh, now you are come to a quiet land, provoke not the Lord to trouble it: And now liberty and authority are with you, and in your hands, let the government be upon his shoulders, in all your spirits; that you may rule for him, under whom the princes of this world will, one day, esteem it their honor to govern and serve, in their places . . . And, thou, *Philadelphia,* the virgin settlement of this province, named before thou wert born, what love, what care, what service, and what travail has there been, to bring thee forth . . . My soul prays to God for thee, that thou mayst stand in the day of tryal, that thy children may be blessed of the Lord, and thy people saved by his power;— my love to thee has been great, and the remembrance of thee affects mine heart and mine eye!—the God of eternal strength keep and preserve thee, to his glory and thy peace.

CHAPTER FIVE

ECONOMIC CONDITIONS OF PENN

AND THE COLONY

ALTHOUGH WILLIAM PENN was considered a wealthy man when he founded Pennsylvania, his financial situation steadily worsened during the last two decades of the seventeenth century. The conditions which led to his imprisonment for debts in 1708 already existed at the turn of the century. The colonists, after suffering considerable hardship and deprivation during the early years of Pennsylvania, became more prosperous, especially with the beginning of King William's War in 1689.

The people of Pennsylvania continued to think of Penn as a wealthy man after his fortune changed, and used every means possible to escape paying their quitrents and to prevent being taxed. They rejected Penn's requests for loans, and only began to give him a modest return on his investment after his return to the colony in 1699.

Penn's father, the famous admiral Sir William Penn, had been richly rewarded for his services during the upheavals in the middle of the seventeenth century, and his estates in Ireland and in England were inherited by his Quaker son. Because of his excellent education, his grand tour of the continent, and his close contact with the Restoration Court, the younger William Penn had acquired elegant manners and expensive tastes. Though he joined the hated sect called Quakers, Penn never entirely forsook his earlier way of life. Like many of his contemporaries, Penn frequently found himself expending more money than he received. He was engaged in various enterprises, and Pennsylvania was the largest of these. He did not know how to be economical, he was of a generous nature, and he lived in a fine style. For example, he spent more than £2,000, Pennsylvania currency, during the two years he resided in the colony between 1699 and 1701, although he allowed his deputy governor a salary of only £200 annually.[1]

Pennsylvania brought in a large amount of money initially from the sale of land. But comparatively little land was sold after 1682, and the quitrents which he had expected to pour in beginning in 1685, did not materialize. He established impost duties on goods entering Pennsylvania, but allowed the law to be suspended in exchange for a promise of gifts from some of the substantial settlers.[2] It was not re-enacted until after his return in 1699.

His expenses continued unabated. He paid the salaries of the deputy governors some of the time, and paid some of the other officials, such as the attorney general. It cost him money to appear in the English court, and to obtain action from officials who expected what amounted to bribes. Penn began the development of his personal estates in Pennsylvania expecting that income from quitrents could carry them, only to have more bills sent from the colony.

He kept up a steady correspondence calling upon his friends to help him. On July 11, 1685, he wrote to James Harrison expressing sorrow that the public was so unmindful of him and his expenses that it was unwilling to undertake what was owed to him. He added that he was ashamed to admit how much he had spent on Pennsylvania. He also had financial difficulties at home, "My business has been thrown off with other Peoples. first, by ye late K[ing]'s Death, then the Coronation, next the Parl[iament,] now this [Monmouth's] Insurrection."[3] In a postscript nineteen days later, he added, "send no more bills, for I have enough to do to Keep all even here."

Penn was beginning to think that gentle requests for the money which was owed to him were not enough. He decided to deal with the colony more firmly. For example, hearing that his monopoly on the sale of the lime used in construction was being threatened by other people, Penn asked Harrison to prevent others from opening more lime quarries. He demanded that Thomas Lloyd force Thomas Holme, the surveyor general, to finish making a map which would describe the colony more fully; " 'tis of mighty moment . . . all cry out, where is your map, what no map of your Settlements!" [4]

By the end of 1686 the truth about the payment of quitrents was apparent to William Penn. He had agreed out of consideration for the colonists in the first years that no quitrent would be due until 1685. He might have meant that he should have been paid in 1685 for 1684, but generously agreed that at the beginning of 1686 they would owe for 1685. However, the settlers then tried to push payment forward one more year, and claimed that they began to owe quitrents in 1686, which were due to the Proprietor in 1687. Penn was upset by the news of this attitude and wrote to Thomas Lloyd asking him to threaten the people with legal proceedings if they did not pay their quitrents, which he calculated were worth £500 annually. Penn wrote about this time, "I can spare little, & would have the People Know it. I have spent 3,000 £ since I see London, besides Bills I pay yt became due since I arrived, tho drawn before I left America." [5]

Penn was deeply grieved by the failure of the Quakers in Pennsylvania to fulfill their financial obligations to him and he was taken aback by their attitude. Members of the Society of Friends had always been scrupulous about paying what they owed, and he failed to understand how they could rationalize the refusal to pay him. In addition, it was difficult to accept the fact that his trusted agents in the colony were seemingly unable to press the freemen for payment. He decided, "The Great fault is, that thos who are there, loose their authority, one way or other in the Spirits of the people and then they can do little with their outward powrs." [6]

In January, 1687, Penn stated that he would sell the shirt off his back before he would ask the people for money again, and threatened to stay away from Pennsylvania indefinitely. "This is no Anger, tho I am grieved, but a cool & resolved thought." [7] Apparently he disposed of his shirt, for he never ceased to demand that money should be sent to him.

Penn gave other indications of inconsistency. In a letter to his land commissioners, William Markham, Thomas Ellis, and John Goodson, he called on them to speed the collection of the quitrents, and urged that money be collected instead of produce. He then promised to give each of the men ten bushels of English wheat for their services to him.[8] Yet Penn was able to point out a contradiction between the protestations of love for him which constantly flowed from Pennsylvania, and the failure of the people to pay their quitrents. The freemen implored him to return to Pennsylvania, and of these requests he wrote: "methinks the country yt desires me so much should have some care to get my own easily, if I must spend it on ym wthout supply." [9] By supply, Penn meant government duties, which if collected, would have paid the officials of the colony.

In March, 1688, Penn again complained that bills were sent to him to be paid when the colony should have taken care of them. He said, "I say, this looks hard towards me, & not Inviting . . . have some care of my small Revenue or Rents, yt they be not devoured In fetchings." [10]

John Blackwell was named governor in 1688 largely because Penn believed he could collect the quitrents. He wrote to friends in Pennsylvania, "you must know that I have a rough people to deal wth about my quitrents, yt yet can't pay a ten pound Bill, but draw, draw, draw still upon me." [11] Although Blackwell failed in many ways, he was diligent about the money owed Penn. In April, 1689, he wrote, "I have severall times proposed to assist it [collection], but when I presse it, I finde more than usuall dis-composure etc." [12] Thomas Lloyd, who was not an admirer of Blackwell, wrote, he "is very active in his receivership . . . A Rent roll he is composing[,] the same may be serviceable tho his chief end may be the getting in of his Salary . . . he is hitherto somewt peevish in the manner of the receipt of the pay[,] weighty money (current I suppose in Boston) is much insisted upon." [13] Penn was encouraged for a few months, and especially when Blackwell stayed on as receiver general after resigning his position as governor, but the old Cromwellian left in the spring of 1690.

By that time, Penn's financial position had grown worse,

for his great friend, James II, was overthrown by the Glorious Revolution in 1688. Penn lost the income from his Irish estates, and was in hiding or imprisoned for several years. The government of Pennsylvania and the Territories was taken from him, and a Royal Governor, Benjamin Fletcher, from New York, took control.

Not long after the government had been restored into Penn's hands in 1694, he was again writing about his quitrents. He asked that the money which was collected should be kept, or remitted to him, and not spent. He added, Pennsylvania "is the foundation of my present incumbrance." [14] In 1696 he wrote to Robert Turner, "I have not seen Six pence these twice six years, my Plantation expensive & yet ruinous, a lovely place & good beginning, but Every one minding their own things, But my eye is to the Lord." [15] Turner replied, "I as a friend Advise thee, & that thou send some honest man & family if one can be [found,] to look after thy Quit Rents & Affairs here." [16]

Many of Penn's offices were filled by needy relatives, and the colony sometimes felt burdened with useless officials sent over by Penn to be supported by the inhabitants. The Governor wrote to Samuel Carpenter in 1698, expressing great resentment because the colonial government had refused to pay a bill for him amounting to £315, "wch has done me, ye greatest Injury in my Credit, I ever sustained." He added that he was sending over another relative, a half-brother of his first wife, Gulielma, to be Surveyor General, "being Mathematticall, more than tradeing, so gave it over, haveing also great losses."[17] Penn went on to complain that the colony had never paid the cost of defending Delaware against the claims of Lord Baltimore, and had defaulted on thousands of pounds of quitrents. "This makes my heart heavy . . . after all my expences, sufferings & losses, [that] I am no more vallued or regarded. D[ea]r Fr[ien]d In a strange place I should not meet with so mean a treatmt."

The colony owed Penn approximately £5,000 in quitrents by the time he returned late in 1699. A portion of that sum had been collected, although it is impossible to determine how much of it. Undoubtedly most of that which was collected went to pay for various fees and salaries in the colony, and Penn always claimed that he had received not a single farthing by the time he returned.

One of the prime reasons for Penn's financial difficulties was the fraudulent action of Philip Ford, his steward in Ireland. Penn had been lulled into trusting this man by his scrupulous action at the beginning of their relationship, and because he was a fellow Quaker. As late as 1696 Penn had complete confidence in the man, for he later wrote of a transaction in that year, "I then not so much as suspected the baseness and extortion of the account." [18]

William R. Shepherd went over the entire matter carefully, and a few salient facts from his study may be gathered together here.[19] Ford's actions began at the moment when Penn was ready to sail for Pennsylvania in 1682. He appeared with an account, which stated that Penn owed Ford £2,851, for money advanced and for the expenses of collection in Ireland. Penn signed the document, and when Ford presented another one which he said was to secure the payment of the money, he signed it as well. However, the second paper provided that if Penn did not pay Ford £3,000 in two days, he should grant Ford 300,000 acres of land in Pennsylvania, at an annual quitrent of four beaver skins. Ford also obtained Penn's signature to a bond for £6,000 to pay the 3,000 pounds.

By compounding the interest every six months, charging fees, and practicing chicanery, Ford convinced Penn that he owed him £5,000 in 1685, due in 1687. Shepherd wrote that before the due date Penn agreed to an enlargement of the amount, and to cover what he owed, executed a deed, "by which he mortgaged the province and territories to Ford for 5,000 years at the quitrent of a peppercorn, unless at the end of a year he paid £6,000."

In 1693, Penn tried to borrow £10,000 from the colonists, and attributed his financial situation to the wretched condition of his affairs in Ireland. It is apparent from what was later written, that he covered up the story of his indebtedness to

Ford to avoid discouraging prospective purchasers of lands, and settlers who might not wish to enter into agreements with a man involved so deeply. Eventually, Ford was leasing Pennsylvania back to Penn, and at the same time demanding new assurances for payment of what was owed. Just as Penn was to set sail in 1699, Ford and his wife, by threatening to prevent the voyage and to expose all, obtained Penn's signature to a statement that he had examined all of the accounts, found them all correct, and released Ford from suspicion of fraud.

From a legal standpoint, Penn had lost the proprietary rights to Pennsylvania, although he still maintained control over the government. Philip Ford, Jr., was in the colony during Penn's stay, apparently looking the place over and keeping watch on the Proprietor. The elder Ford asked Isaac Norris to spy on Penn for him, and with great misgivings Norris sent occasional letters to the extortionist. In one letter the colonial merchant wrote, "I believe he has Real Desires to Extricate himself from his trobles and Incumbrances And is full of thought About it but the Cercomstances of ye country does not Admit such a Dispatch as could be wisht by Those who Desires his Comfort & quiett in his last days and the Countrys Prosperity." [20]

Eventually the sordid situation was exposed to the public; there was a legal battle, Penn was imprisoned for failure to pay, and he was released after his friends raised the money to rescue him. They settled the entire claim for £7,600. It would appear to be unbelievable that a man of William Penn's stature and ability could have allowed himself to become enmeshed in a financial morass of this kind, but the facts cannot be contradicted. Much of Penn's anxiety for money and for the welfare of the colony becomes understandable, considering that this financial weight constantly threatened to drag him into disgrace. Because his proprietary rights were severely clouded by the agreements with Ford, Penn was anxious to maintain his right to rule Pennsylvania. Therein may lie the key to the compromises which the Proprietor made with the Crown in 1694, to regain the government. Certainly the inordinate desire for appropriations from the colony, when he arrived in 1699, can be explained by remembering his financial incumbrances.

The Scriptures say, "the love of money is the root of all evil." The "holy experiment" was besmirched by unseemly striving over worldly treasure. Penn did nothing immoral, he only asked for the payment of honest debts. But for a person living in frontier circumstances, the discharge of one's obligations is sometimes impossible, and always distasteful.

CONDITIONS IN PENNSYLVANIA TO 1690

The history of the establishment of English colonies in North America is full of tales of the conflict between businessmen in London waiting to share dividends from the new colony, and settlers eating berries, or hunting and fishing to keep from starving. The hardships of the Pilgrim Fathers and the demands made on them by their financial backers in England are described eloquently by Bradford. The stories which came out of Jamestown in the early years of the bitter experiences, the misfortunes, and the incredible living conditions did not prevent the Virginia Company from desiring and expecting profits.

The story of Pennsylvania is similar, although the hardships of the settlers were never as severe, and the demands of William Penn and other investors were never as cold-blooded as those of some financial backers. Since there were other settlers in the neighboring provinces, and because there were English, Dutch, and Swedish people living in Pennsylvania and Delaware, the idea has developed that Pennsylvania was practically a mature colony from the day Penn landed in 1682. That belief was strengthened by the stories of the phenomenal growth of Philadelphia, which became the second most populous town in English North America by 1690, outnumbered only by Boston.[21]

There is little evidence available on the actual conditions of the first decade. A few useful bits of information can be gleaned from the minutes of the Council and Assembly and from the laws enacted during the period. If any day to day journals were kept by the colonists, they have been lost. It is necessary to depend on references to economic matters in the letters of the day. Most of the letters from Pennsylvania to friends and business associates in England have been lost.

However, a painstaking search does reveal a number of illuminating references to personal hardships such as sickness or living in caves, the shortage of money both in the colony and for exchange, the fear of Indian attacks on property, and the pressure exerted by absentee landlords.

To be sure, there were wealthy persons among the first colonists who never suffered hardships. They sent over servants to build houses for the masters to live in upon arrival, clear the land, plant crops, and prepare the way. James Claypoole, in a letter to his brother written in December, 1683, described the house which his servants had prepared. It was forty by twenty feet, with a cellar.[22] Penn, in writing about Pennsylvania to his friends and in describing the province in his brochures, encouraged other settlers to join the exodus. He did not stress the hardships, and painted as favorable picture of conditions as possible, in good conscience.

However, there is another side of the picture. The people landed on a river bank covered with dense forest, and what land was not forested was not worth farming. They settled in a climate which was new to them, and sometimes suffered severely. Many had put down all their money to pay passage, buy land, and accumulate necessities and were short of money from the very beginning. It is a hard life cutting down trees, plowing ground full of stumps and roots with primitive plows, and trying to find enough food to maintain a bare existence.

One colonist, Richard Townsend, told the story of a deer appearing in a providential manner when his family needed food. The deer stayed near him while he was mowing grass in a meadow, and when Townsend went towards him, the deer ran into a tree and knocked itself unconscious. The man then carried the deer home, where a neighbor killed it for him, "the carcase proved very serviceable to my family." [23] Unfortunately, the hand of God intervened only on rare occasions, and many families were unable to obtain fresh meat in such an easy fashion.

Thomas Langhorne wrote a letter to Francis Dove and others in February, 1687, which described the situation of the man whose property he had just purchased. He promised to pay the man, a Robert ......, £180 Pennsylvania value, which was less than £150 sterling, for 860 acres of land, a mare, eleven swine, and some corn which had been already harvested. Ten acres had been cleared and fenced, and there was a dwelling on the land so poor that Langhorne would have to build himself another house. He wrote, "the toyle & Charge is great to gett things into any like order hear," but since he believed that "the Lords love & good hand" were with him, he expected to meet the challenge. The family of the man from whom he purchased had been sick most of the time since they had come to Pennsylvania, and had been of no help to the farmer. He had been sick for a period, and had to leave the land. He had been forced to sell the city lots which he received with the land for a barrel of pork, to have enough to feed the family, and he had gotten into debt. Langhorne commented, "soe yt for my part I admire yt things is noe worse then they are for I doe understand yt many more capable then he & better assisted & suplyed every way has made worse then he has done." [24]

The colonists not only faced difficulties with the land and the climate, but the aborigines were also frequently troublesome. It is generally accepted that the Quakers and the Indians had little trouble in Pennsylvania, and by and large that is true. Nevertheless, there were difficulties. In February, 1685, Thomas Holme the surveyor, wrote to James Harrison that the Indian chief, Taminiy or Tammany appeared in lower Bucks County and told the whites that he had not sold the land after all, and demanded that they get off. Further, he threatened to burn down houses they occupied if they resisted. Some became so frightened that they left the colony and went over the river into New Jersey. [25] In November, 1685, the Council was told of action by the Indians against the people of Concord and Hert-

ford, in which the aborigines were guilty of "Rapine and De-
structions of their hoggs." [26] In May, 1686, the Council was
notified that swine had been killed by Indians in Southampton
Township.[27] There was considerable fear of the Indians at the
outbreak of hostilities with the French in Canada, in King
William's War.

Living conditions were often very primitive in the early days,
and many of the first settlers lived in caves cut into the banks of
the Delaware or other streams. It has become almost fashion-
able in Pennsylvania to have had an ancestor who once lived in
the caves, but such life was anything but favorable or desirable
in the 1680s.

Penn wrote to the Council in July, 1685, to report that John
Songhurst and Benjamin Chambers, who had been employed
to settle estates and build up lands for absentee landholders in
England, had produced practically nothing, which "opens their
mouths" against Pennsylvania. He asked Thomas Lloyd to investigate the matter.[28] Penn knew that he was unable to make a
profit from his manors, and should have realized that Songhurst
and Chambers were unable to produce dividends for their em-
ployers. In other letters, Penn told the Council or Thomas
Lloyd personally that letters which came back from Pennsylvania were discouraging some from coming over. He asked Lloyd
to do something to help Richard Whitpain and Company, "it
make a fear ful! cry here, & whereas Gil. Mace would have gone
over & many wth him & J. Marlow . . . would have sent over his
relations & some famelys, all is flatt, Some hardined agst us, to
break covenants, instead of soliciting ye persons concerned to
mitigate ye matter." [29] The Whitpains continued to make a
loud noise to the disgust of the other Quakers.

As late as 1686 the colony was not self-sufficient, and did not
produce enough for the needs of the inhabitants. In that year
Penn shipped over twenty-five barrels of beef and 100 pounds
of butter and candles from Ireland for the use of his family,
whom he expected to bring over the same year.[30] However,
Pennsylvania was already shipping some grain to New England
and Barbados by that year and the slow trickle of trade grew

steadily.[31] The following year saw seven ships enter Philadelphia from Boston, which brought in lumber, West Indies goods, wine, fish, iron, and European goods, and carried away grain, flour, deerskins, tobacco, whalebone and pork. However, these exports did not pay for the goods imported, and gold had to be provided to make up the balance.[32]

The settlers were very optimistic about their future, despite the hardships they faced. Langhorne wrote that wherever he went in his search for a place to settle, before he decided upon the farm on the Neshaminy, people encouraged him to throw in his lot with their community.[33] Thomas Ellis, back in Dublin, wrote of the advantages to be gained in Pennsylvania. Some were opposing the migration to the New World because they had "estates of their own & leave fullness to their posterity." Ellis hoped that such persons would "not be offended at the Lords opening a door of mercy to thousands in England Especially in Wales & other nations who had no Estates either for themselves or children, And that all their industry could not afford them the meanest food & Raymt that might properly be sayd to belong even to slaves or servants." [34] Claypoole stated, "I do believe it will prove a verry healthy Country & that great improvements may be made in a few years by Industry & skill." [35]

Stray references are found concerning the development of pursuits other than agricultural during these early years. In 1686 Penn wrote to his Land Commissioners requesting that they investigate the mine which had been started in the colony. He wrote that the owners included one man who was a "Papist," and that he believed that they had the land under an irregular survey. He wanted the commissioners to stop the mining operations for some unknown mineral and to send him specimens from the mine. In the same letter mention was made of a windmill, which was in operation in competition with the water driven mills.[36] In the early years the Free Society of Traders outfitted ships to search for whales, and they caught twelve in a single season in the Delaware Bay.[37]

There is little doubt about the industry of the colonists during the early years, but it is equally true that there was little return for their efforts at first, and there were many hardships to be faced. It should be added that while the settlers were working hard to establish themselves they sometimes seemed to remember the "holy experiment." On one occasion Claypoole wrote, "I am not for striving or making hast to be rich, but my Intent and desire is to goe on quietly and moderately, and to have a regard to the Lord in all my wayes, and . . . to seek the Kingdome of God and the righteousness thereof, that his plantaton work may goe on as well as ours, that righteousness may run down like a stream, and peace & truth may kiss each other." [38]

Penn did not feel that the "holy experiment" was always in their minds, and he sometimes doubted that it was in the minds of the colonists at all. He protested that the province failed to grow and prosper because the people were so unstable and quarrelsome, especially in the government. He wrote to Thomas Lloyd, "I am extreamly sorry to hear that Pennsylvania is so litegious & brutish." He added that it was common talk in England that 15,000 people had decided to go to Carolina instead of Pennsylvania in the single year of 1686, because of the ill reports which came out of it. He had been so shaken by the news that he promised to give £100 to any person who could "bring a savour of rightenousness over that ill savour," and said that "it almost tempts me to deliver up to ye K[ing] & lett a mercenary goverr have the tameing of them." [39]

As has been indicated, one of the problems facing the proprietor and the colony in the early years was the failure to pay quitrents owed to Penn, or to supply money to support the government. In 1685 Penn wrote, "Prepare them to think of some way to support me yt I may not consume my own to serve the publick." [40] In 1687, he stated that if the rents were not paid, "I will have the damage to extremity or reenter *my land with an high hand,* and that the best Lawyers here assure me I may do." [41]

In addition to the hardships the colonists met in building and developing the province during the first decade, they suffered from a shortage of specie which could be used to make purchases or pay quitrents. That there was not even money to serve as a medium of exchange within the colony is indicated by the passage in 1683 of laws which placed a premium of twenty-five percent on specie, and which provided that "Wheat, Rye, Indian-corn, Barley, Oats, Pork, Beef, & Tobacco, shall be accoumpted Current pay at the Market price." [42] These conditions existed in other colonies as well as Pennsylvania.

Samuel Carpenter, who undertook to collect the subscription which was pledged to William Penn in 1684 in exchange for allowing the imposts to drop, exerted a great deal of time and effort with little result. People did not have cash, and although it was agreed that the pledges could be paid in produce, in the early years there was little or no spare produce.[43] In 1686, John Kinsey, a carpenter, complained to James Harrison that he had finished building a mill ten weeks earlier, and still had not been paid, though he was willing to be paid in goods instead of in money.[44]

In 1688 the commissioners of state and the Council attempted to gain the approval of the Assembly for a supply bill for the government, but failed. The men wrote:

The Freeman in Assembly mett having A high Regard and deep sense of the Governts onasions [occasions] and their owne duty towards the Supply thereof doe declare they are willing to grant any Reasonable aid proportionable to their ability, Provided it may be fixed on such things as tend not directly to ye manifest impoverishment and discouragemt of the Governt of thy Province and Territorys wch they Conceive the Imposition of a duty on skins and Peltry will doe by driving the Comorce to our neighbour Provinces and soe do faile the end of the sd intended aid, and that the excise of beer will be so grievous to ye people, so inconsiderable, and the Charges of collecting so great that it will not in any degree answer the end intended, But desire a duty may bee laid on fforeigne Comodities wch are of noe great use as Rumm and wine[,] Sugar etc and especiall on the sd Comodities Imported in vessels not belonging to ye Governmt wch they would have ffree from any impossition, And all other dutys on Rumm & wholly taken off.[45]

It would appear from this quotation from the letter to Penn that the Assembly was motivated as much by desire not to pay as by inability to pay. One wonders how the excise on beer could be at one and the same time "so grievous to ye people," and "so inconsiderable" that it would bring in little money.

But there is no reason to doubt the truth of what Andrew Robeson wrote to Charles Jones & Co. about his work as the representative of their business interests in Pennsylvania. He included a long list of persons who owed money or had large mortgages which he was trying to collect. He added that collecting was very hard, "much charge, travell and trouble has been and it troubles me that it should be so; for my former exercises in England of this nature were not accompanyed with such vexatious circumstances; but this is a new Country and things May mend." He suggested that they send a man to spend full time "to pursue your concerns." [46] He also described the sending of money from Pennsylvania to England. He was dispatching fifty pounds to the company by Thomas Holme, which had been "lying in my hands[,] being I can get no returnes that I dare trust especially to pay out your ready money upon uncertain bills: this is a ticklish Country in reference to those matters."

A letter written by Governor Blackwell to Penn in 1689, indicated that there was enough money in circulation in the colony to push prices high, although he strongly disapproved of artificially placing the value of money above its face value. In relation to the high prices, he wrote of "the Extensive Extortion (I can call it no otherwise) wherewith the poorer sort of people are oppressed by the wealthyer traders." He wrote that goods worth £100 were priced at £200 because of the inflation, a fifty per cent freight rate was added and when the retailer added another £100 the price reached £400. He admitted, however, that wages were higher. For example, sawyers were receiving as much as three times the wages paid in New England.

Blackwell also made a direct hit on Penn with his statement that with inflation as it was, the quitrents were worth only one-half their face value when translated into English money. He prophesied that if inflation continued, the whole province will "not be worth a groat, pardon the Expression." Blackwell closed his summary of the monetary conditions of the colony with the puritanical statement that he remembered the day when a businessman took but one penny profit in each shilling.[47]

The following year, 1690, may be thought of as the turning point in the economic life of the colony. William Rodeney wrote to Penn in that year, "We supply *New England* with abundance *Wheat, Bread, Flower, Beef, Pork and strong Beer,*" and that they sold to Maryland and Virginia.[48] Richard Morris wrote, "The Country-men finding the profit now coming in, do clear away the Woods, Plow and improve their Lands in *Corn, Hemp* and *Flax,* and enlarge themselves in great stocks of *Horses, Oxen, Cows, Hoggs, and some Sheep,* so that they *can, and do now spare great quantities* of *Corn* to our Neighbor Provinces, which formerly we were forc'd to be beholding to." [49]

The outbreak of war between England and France was a boon to the colony, as it could sell what it produced at a good profit with little likelihood of overproduction. With increased demand and the sinking of merchant shipping, there was a ready market for everything. Penn had written to Robert Turner that prices had trebled because of the war, and added, "our calamitys here are your market & gain. wherefore lett ye Province be industrious while they have ye advantage. god has given us a good corn land." [50]

The beginning of the war coincided with the retirement of Penn from public life for several years, including two years when Pennsylvania was ruled by a royal governor. When Penn regained the colony in 1695, the settlers were accustomed to caring for themselves, were less willing than ever to pay quitrents, and were not open to suggestions that they owed Penn anything.

While the facts presented are scattered, they strongly suggest that during the first decade the colonists lacked the ability to pay William Penn his quitrents or a tax for the government. The settlers were having a difficult time planting a new colony on the frontier. They suffered from a shortage of ready money and of the commerce which might have provided them with bills of exchange. William Penn is to be censured at least slightly for his unwillingness to make allowance for this condition.

There is a hint in these pages of a reluctance to meet the obligations of the colony to William Penn. The "holy experiment' could have weathered the economic crisis which was reaching its conclusion in 1690, but more damaging to the utopian spirit of the colony was the unwillingness of the colonists to meet William Penn half way.

A MAP OF
THE IMPROVED PART
OF THE PROVINCE OF
PENNSILVANIA
IN AMERICA

By Thomas Holme
(1687).
One section of the
original map printed
in six sections.
Reproduced through
the courtesy of the
Historical Society of
Pennsylvania.

CHAPTER SIX

POLITICAL DIFFICULTIES

1684 TO 1688

DESPITE THE EXCELLENT foundations established during its first two years, Pennsylvania failed to live up to the expectations of the Founder and his friends who had hoped that the plantation would be an "example to the Nations."

Instead of remaining in England a few months and then quickly returning to his "holy experiment," William Penn waited fifteen years before seeing Pennsylvania again in December, 1699. During those years the early idealism was slowly forgotten. Pennsylvania eventually became a prosperous colony populated by men and women who enjoyed a goodly share of freedom and who were more enlightened than some of their neighbors. However the creative spark, the spirit of dedication, and the sense of purpose envisioned in the "holy experiment" were gone.

The change which slowly engulfed the colony was the result of a combination of forces. The constant wrangling over finances between Penn and his people boded no good for the utopian dreams. The government, which had been left in the hands of the freemen, proved unsuccessful in many respects, and a grave disappointment to the Founder. In desperation, Penn tried a Puritan soldier as Governor. The wrangling grew so intense that Delaware seceded from Pennsylvania. The Quakers fell to quarreling, and were split in two by the Keithian Schism. With the government unstable, the empire at war, and Penn in hiding because of accusations that he was a Jacobite, the Crown decided in 1692 to take over the government of

Pennsylvania. After the political authority was restored to Penn the colonists rewrote their constitution without his consent. In the meantime, antagonistic groups had begun to chant that Pennsylvania favored illicit traders and pirates and was a den of immorality. With the Crown once more threatening to seize the colony, the Governor was forced to return to Pennsylvania in haste, late in 1699. By that time, the "holy experiment" was a near-forgotten dream.

In politics the "holy experiment" was fully tested in the four years which followed William Penn's return to England in 1684. The absentee Governor retained the right to confirm the actions of the government, but this proved to be a weak method of control. He also exerted influence through frequent letters of instruction and counsel. Neither of these methods for regulating the colony were very potent, and the people were virtually left to govern themselves. For more than three years the freemen enjoyed self-government through their elected representatives in the Council and Assembly, with the Council assuming the executive responsibilities in addition to its other broad powers. During the last months of the period, William Penn appointed five men to serve collectively as his deputy governors, but he named men who were in the colony and who had been elected to the General Assembly in the past.

In 1684 Penn felt confident that the Council was filled with men of integrity and intelligence, and he entrusted it with the executive power of government when he returned to England. He did not expect to remain in England for more than a few months, nor did he feel that governing Pennsylvania would be difficult, because firm foundations had been established. The eighteen members of the Council virtually controlled the province and territories. To be sure, these men were elected by the freemen, and were checked by the consultative power of the Assembly as well as by the authority of the courts, but the Council dominated the government despite these restrictions.

Penn was fortunate in his choice of the president of the Council. Thomas Lloyd, a physician from Dolobran in Wales, had arrived in Pennsylvania in 1683. He was a minister among the Quakers who was intelligent and businesslike, and he provided enlightened leadership. Unfortunately he traveled frequently to New York. Equally unfortunate, he had little power as President. Lloyd was a fine man of the type Penn expected to arise and carry the burden of his government. This is indicated by a letter which Lloyd wrote in 1684, shortly after Penn sailed for England. "We are glad to See the faces of servicable Friends here, who Come in God's freedom, who are persons of a Good Understanding & Conversation: & Will Discharge Their Stations Religiously; Such will be a Blessing to The Province. The favorable Revolution of Providence hath founded the Government so, here, That a Man is at Liberty to Serve his Maker Without Contempt, Discouragement, or Restraint; Truth indeed Makes Men Honourable, not only here, but in most Places at last; But here Truth Receives Good Entertainment at first." [1] This man was the most important person in the colony until his death in 1694. It is regrettable that so little is known about Thomas Lloyd.

The Council proved unsatisfactory as the executive branch of government in several respects, but the important weakness of the arrangement was that it met infrequently. When the Council was not in session there was no visible government. The individual members, even the President, had no power to issue orders or make decisions. The chamber had a secretary, but he had no authority to act except under express order of the Council. When the Council met each week it was able to observe what was happening in the colony and the freemen could appeal to it for advice or assistance. However, it sometimes met only one or two times a month, and often met less frequently. There were no meetings of the Council from the end of October, 1684, until March 30, 1685; and from November, 1686, to March 1687. In the ten months from the adjournment of the General Assembly in May, 1687, until the following March, only seven sessions were convened, although some of them lasted two days. In 1688, there was one meeting between May and December 18, the day Governor Blackwell arrived.

The Council met infrequently because there was little business to be handled. Few matters of importance came before the body except in the weeks before calling the General Assembly, when proposed legislation was drawn up, and when the General Assembly was in session. Other meetings were cluttered with minor matters. In one period of several months, the following items claimed the attention of the Council. A sheriff died, and a replacement was needed. Someone died unnaturally, the coroner was ill, and a substitute had to be found to examine the body. A man was accused of fornication, and the case came to the central government. There was a dispute over boundaries which the Council was asked to arbitrate. The assistant surveyor general of Chester County was accused of prejudice, and had to be suspended. A widow protested that her deceased husband's estate had not been settled properly. Pig-stealing, servant-beating, tale-bearing, and other picayune matters which local magistrates should have settled were all carried to the highest authority of the colony.[2]

Another reason for the infrequency of Council meetings is seen by examining the responsibilities of the members. The men were busy attempting to establish themselves in the New World, and did not have as many servants as William Penn. If they were farmers, they were overwhelmed with the task of clearing away the forest to have fields to cultivate. At periods of the year, when plowing, planting, or harvesting had to be completed, it was impossible to lay aside all work and travel to Philadelphia to participate in the government. The members from the towns were building up their places of business, and had to devote hours to such tasks as their particular occupations entailed.

Travel was arduous and time-consuming in a period when there were few roads. Even travel by water could be dangerous and wearisome. Men resented laying aside their work, traveling for an entire day to reach Philadelphia, and after spending one or two days on government business, wasting another day to reach home again. This was especially true because there were no salaries for the councillors. Provision was made in the laws for a small payment but apparently it was seldom collected. The resentment caused the Council to say when it had been gathered together to hear a letter from William Penn, "What were we sent for so far[,] for so little." [3] While such an attitude can be understood, still it meant a severe blow to the "holy experiment." Penn had expected men to give willingly of their time and energy to make the government work, and now the members of the Council either refused to attend the sessions or grumbled and protested when they did come.

The irregular meetings of the Council meant that too frequently there was no visible evidence of the government in Pennsylvania. The courts met for only a few days a year, and the county officials devoted a minimum of time to their responsibilities as the upholders of the law. Only the executive branch of the provincial government was likely to be active continuously. If the Council failed to convene at regular intervals, there was no source of government which could be seen and respected by the colonists. When he established the commissioners of state, Penn stated in a letter to Phineas Pemberton: "I hereby provide against absence, for before, there was no visible deputy when the P. Council sat not, they being my deputy, now there shall be one, Sitt they or sitt they not." [4]

Penn stated in the preface of the First Frame that there were two divine reasons for having governments, "first to terrify evil-doers; secondly, to cherish those that do well." The failure of the Council to provide a government which was apparent at all times, resulted in a spirit of anarchy in the colony. Penn recognized the spirit but he could not explain it. The commonwealth had been created with the assurance that the people were followers of Christ, that they had an inner discipline, and that they could govern themselves personally or through the Friends business meeting. It was a disappointment to learn that outward evidence of government was necessary to force obedience to the laws.

The minutes of the meetings of the Council during these years are sketchy. It is difficult to determine why action was taken, how decisions were reached, or even the tenor of the meetings. However, many of the colonists wrote long letters to the Governor describing conditions in Pennsylvania and criticizing the government. Those letters have been lost, but fortunately, William Penn frequently made comments to the Council about them.

These letters generally indicated that the Council sessions were tempestuous affairs and a credit to no one. Quotations from one letter indicate the criticism Penn leveled at the Council:

> The noise of some Differences that have been in the Province, have reached these parts, with no advantage to the reputations of the Country
>
> Not entering into the Merits of the Matter; Quietness is that which in so troubled an Age of the World, has great Invitation in it—If any thing be amiss lett it be by more hidden and gentle ways remedied[.] An Infancy of Government can hardly bear the Shakes a riper Age may and sometimes as a last Remedy must endure.
>
> Heat is no where commendable, but in Government dangerous—So Emulation, and too much Positiveness, or an Overweeningness in Opinion[.] Next to Religious Duty, Selfe deniall in the Administration of a Government is both Requisit and laudable I recommend it to you in prudence and Conscience.
>
> If faults are committed, lett them be mended without noize and animosity. The Pomp and Clatter of Complaint is oftentimes a greater Grievance to the Publick than the thing complained of.

He gave them orders to first, punish vice, "Let it not escape your righteous Rod." Penn admitted that he had beeen too merciful, "In that follow not my Example." "The Repentance of the Person is not enough for the Publick allways," he added, and urged corporal punishment. Secondly, he called them to settle their disputes quietly; and thirdly, to be kind to strangers. He urged them to do what was right that God might have his glory, the King his honor, "and you your Comfort and just Interest and Advantage." [5]

In fairness to the Council the words of one of its members, Phineas Pemberton, must be studied. He believed that the Council had been a credit to Penn and Pennsylvania, despite criticism expressed by others in the colony. "The Council Ever Since thou went has been very agreeing and unanimous wch has been a great Stay to us and I hop the lord will preserve and raise the heads of them who are true harted to him and the govermt[,] above the surging waves of ye pestiferous apostates & runagadors that would flow over them." [6] The very words used by Pemberton to describe those in opposition to the Council were a fair indication of the hard feelings which were seething through the "holy experiment."

The greatest single source of conflict in Pennsylvania during the first twenty years was the struggle between the Council and the Assembly. These years were no exception. The differences became so pronounced that for two years no agreement could be reached on the bills proposed by the Council and no laws were enacted.

William Penn considered the Council to be the legislature of the colony, and thought of the Assembly as a representative gathering of the freemen to express approval or disapproval of proposed legislation. Of the struggle by the Assembly to achieve equal status with the Council, Penn wrote in 1688:

the Assembly, as they call themselves, is not so, without Gov'r & P[rovincial] Councel, & that noe speaker, clark or [minute] book belong to ym[;] that the people have their representatives in ye Pro. councell to prepare & the Assembly as it is called, has only the power of I or no, yea or nay. If they turn debator, or judges, or complainers you overthrow yr Charter . . . here would be two assemblys, & two representatives, whereas they are but one, so two works, one prepares and promotes, the other assents or Denys—the Negative voyce . . . is not a debating, amending, altering, but an accepting or rejecting pow'r[,] minde I entreat you, that all fall not to pieces.

The Assembly never accepted this definition of its position and authority in Pennsylvania. Instead, it considered itself equal with the Council in a two house legislature. It thought of itself as the House of Commons in the colony, and constantly struggled to enlarge its share in the government.

Only in 1685 were laws enacted by the General Assembly. The following year a quarrel developed over the right of the Assembly to amend the bills proposed by the Council. Laws were enacted for one year at a time, and the first bill proposed to each General Assembly called for the extension of former laws for another year. In 1686 the Assembly attempted to amend this vital proposal by demanding the repeal of two former laws. The Council refused to accept this innovation and stated that if the first bill was not enacted none would be law. The passing of a few bills without the continuance of the old laws would leave the colony with those few laws alone. Yet if no laws were enacted, the pretence could be preserved that the General Assembly had not met, and the old laws would remain in operation.[8] In 1687 no laws were promulgated by the Council, and so none were enacted by the General Assembly when it met. It should be added in defense of the General Assembly, that each spring when it met it expected William Penn to arrive during the summer. When the two houses could reach no ready agreement concerning the laws, the members eased their minds with the belief that Penn would call an extra session of his legislature when he returned, and that suitable laws could be enacted then.

The session of 1685 gave other evidence of peace and concord in addition to the fact that agreement was reached on eleven laws.[9] The Assembly had difficulty in obtaining a copy of the Charter of Liberties from the Council, it protested that the bills had not been promulgated in a proper manner, and Nicholas More, a Provincial Judge, was impeached. Otherwise a good spirit prevailed. The Assembly reported to Penn, "there was a right and good Understanding betwixt the President, Council and Assembly, and a happy and friendly Farewell . . . The Honour of God, and Love of your Person, and Preservation of the Peace, and Welfare of the Government, were, we hope, the only Center to which all our Actions did tend . . . to you, dear Sir, and to the happy Success of your Affairs, our Hearts are open, and our Heads ready at all Times to Subscribe ourselves, in the Name of ourselves, and all the Freemen we do represent." [10]

The records indicate that the Assembly convened in 1686 at the Bank Meetinghouse, on Front Street above Mulberry, or Arch.[11] The first joint meeting saw the privileges of the Assembly recognized by the Council, namely: "Free Access to the

Governor and Council: Freedom of Speech and Debate; and Liberty of their Persons." But thereafter differences arose. The Assembly asked why nothing had been done about the impeachment of More, and received an evasive answer. When the lower house met alone, it voted unanimously that it had the power to impeach criminals at any time during its sessions. The two bodies differed about the holding of joint sessions of the legislature, and the final break came over the enactment of laws.

Because there were no bills to discuss at the 1687 meeting of the General Assembly, it convened for only three days.[12] During that time the Assembly presented a number of grievances to the Council, and the upper chamber promised action on some of them. Two examples indicate the nature of the queries. The Assembly complained that when a member of the Council was suspended, no new member was chosen in his place. The upper house promised to remedy that condition. The Assembly protested that there were no provincial judges appointed from Delaware, and the Council agreed to remember the Lower Counties when naming judges in the future. In addition, the Assembly wrote to the provincial court to protest the calling of an Assemblyman before it while the lower house was in session. In the resolution supporting a man named Henry Bowman, the body wrote of the highest court in the colony as "any inferior Court of this Government."

All these things grieved William Penn, and he wrote several times about the wrangling in the government. He not only regretted such a spirit because it was harmful to the "holy experiment," but believed that the reports of quareling were a hindrance to the successful colonizing of Pennsylvania. In 1685 he wrote to James Harrison, "the Reproaches yt I hear dayly of ye conduct of things, bears hard upon my Spirit too. the Lord order things for his glory." [13] At the same time, Penn attempted to understand why these differences arose. Writing about the quarrel between the Council and Assembly in 1686, he said he was not worried, "for I Hear how things stand. I regard it not; I have faith to beleive much of that will vanish when I come, that rise since I was there. In new & mixt Colonys, disorders will be, tho at all times they are wounding." [14] Penn was correct in stating that affairs ran more smoothly when he was in the colony. Many protested his absence during these years, and on one occasion in 1686 he replied that if he had not been in England to represent them, "Some busybodys would have had their mouths stopped for good and all." [15] In another letter that same year, after telling the Council of the protection he had given the colony by his presence in the court of King James and also of the persons he had persuaded to go to Pennsylvania he wrote, "this I beseech thee to read from house to house to the Sober and discreet, friend or other [non-Friend]." [16]

Another troublesome problem during these four years was caused by the reports sent back to England about justice in Pennsylvania. Some of these stories were based on fact, but others were the result of jealousy and disappointment. In 1685 the Assembly brought charges against More as a provincial judge, and called for his impeachment. He was accused of issuing unlawful writs for sessions of the court on such short notice that justice could not be done. He was accused of issuing threats to a jury which brought in a verdict that met with his disapproval.[17] He was impeached for overawing witnesses, changing the sense of their testimony, and then convicting them of perjury. He was accused of overruling the justices of the county court at Chester, in "a most Ambitious, Insulting, & Arbitrary way, . . . thereby drawing the Magistrates into the Contempt of ye people." He had reputedly declared that neither he nor his actions were accountable to the president and Provincial Council, "by Despiseing and Conteining their Orders & precepts, and Questioning and Denying their Authority." [18] These and other accusations were laid before the President and Council for a decision.

John Briggs, or Bridges, of Kent County, told the Assembly that when he was at the Governor's house More had asked him what the Assembly was doing, and when told replied, *"either I myself, or some of you will be hanged"* and urged Briggs to oppose the impeachment. Patrick Robinson, clerk of the Provincial Court, was called upon to produce the court records; when he demurred, he was put into the custody of the sheriff, who left him at liberty. Robinson accosted Speaker John White, on the street and said, *"Well, John, have a Care what you do, I'll have at you, when you are out of the Chair."* The fact that neither of these men was a Quaker did not change the fact that their words and practices damaged the reputation of the colony.

William Penn wrote to the Council in the summer of 1685 about the actions of Nicholas More, and mentioned that there had been many serious complaints against the courts. He added, "Great good will is towards it [Pennsylvania] in many brave minded people, yt are wealthy, to carry on ye Improvemts, . . . pray Retrieve ye Credit of ye Province in doing Justice in ye business, & reporting a true account to me." [19]

In 1686 a special provincial court of three men was established by Thomas Lloyd, President of the Council.[20] The court heard a case involving the Free Society of Traders. Patrick Robinson, appearing for Nicholas More who had been president of that body, attempted to disqualify Harrison as a judge on the grounds that he worked for Penn, a stockholder of the Free Society. Harrison refused to step down. If he had the court would have fallen, for when the court met in Philadelphia, three judges were needed on the bench.

The judges sent Penn a description of the session, and said of Robinson, he then "denied ye Jurisdition of ye Court & sd yt all yt wee had done in either Law or Equity was biast, & much more to ye same effect, & insensed ye people in Court agt us." He was ordered to leave, but recalled the following day. Again Robinson behaved in an insolent manner, and maintained that he had come of his own accord, and not because of the order of the court. "We told him he had denied ye Kings Authority by which wee satt there, & thee in whose nam we Sat which we were resolved to defend to our power, & desired all Magistrates to take notice of any yt spoak sleightingly of yt power or yt disturbed or broak ye pease, Lett them be punished according to Law." [21] Robinson was fined £100 and put in custody until he paid the fine, and he threatened to appeal "beyond ye watter."

In 1687, Penn wrote to the commissioners of state, asking them to draw up a remonstrance or declamation, "to give the lye to thos vile & repeated slanders cast on ye Province, or you rather & the rest of ye Magistracy, whom they represent, 1st as ambitious, Seeking preheminence, 2ly, as partial, to offenders, yt process truth [Quakers], not ye same punishmts as to others, witness J. Moon's case, . . . 5ly an unwarranted prerogative to pardon where example requires execution for the sake of others 6. quarrels among the Magistrates whereby the[y] make them selves cheap to the people they should be awful to. . . . I say, these & ye like things ought to be most solemnly considered by you & answered as afore said." [22]

While there was good reason for complaining that justice was not always meted out in an unbiased fashion, much of what was reported in England was in itself greatly prejudiced, at least in the opinion of the governor.

In the last years of the century Pennsylvania was under heavy fire from the English government because of flagrant disregard of the laws and regulations governing foreign trade. Little was said during the early years about infractions of the laws, but Penn issued several warnings to remind the colonists of their duties. The first warning was contained in a letter to the Council written in July, 1685.[23] In the meantime, the first surveyor general of the king's customs, William Dyer, had arrived.[24] In the fall of the same year, Penn wrote to Pemberton urging strict obedience and cooperation with Dyer. He mentioned that there had been trouble between the latter and Governor Gawen Lawrie in East Jersey, which had drawn a *quowarranto,* and that there had been difficulties in Maryland. He added, "Wherefore, be wise, few and safe in words and in behaviour civil and oblidgeing to yt officer or any else of ye Kings. This I write to thee because I vallue thy prudence and fidelity above thy degree, and to ye wiser sort thou mayst communicate my caution." [25] In one letter of instructions to the commissioners of state, Penn called on them to make sure that the king's customs were collected.[26]

Another matter related to the responsibility of the colony to the king came up in 1686. In September Penn wrote to Thomas Lloyd about the laws of Pennsylvania, and reminded him that they would be called before the Lords of Trade as provided for in the Charter from Charles II. Penn's proposal for meeting this situation fitted nicely into what was happening in the colony, although the morality of the suggestion could be questioned. He wrote:

because I know the franchises & constitution of them, Exceed what is elsewhere, and intended to be elsewhere; to the end we may use the advantages the Pening of my charter gave us (& by Sr. Wm Jones, was intended to me & the Colony) with what Success we are able, Know, that if once in five years, ours are presented to the said Committee, or the King rather, it is as much as we are obliged to. my Councell therefore advises, that the very next Session after the receipt of this, a Bill be prepared to vacat all the Laws as they now stand, and prepare another with such abrogations, alterations and additions of laws as shall palliate the thing.

. . . it is done for their Sakes not mine, for the less free they are, the more free I am; but as I ever desired the best of laws for them, so I would advise the ways, most easely in a disorder'd time, to preserve them to them and theirs. This must be insinuated to the wiser only, and to thos that are exceptions, deal with them apart in my name; lett them see their interest and my good intention . . . lett them know how much they are in my power not I in theirs; and the less, for being here, in such a raign, where powr is more then a little preferr'd.[27]

This was not the type of situation that William Penn, the spiritual leader of the "holy experiment," should have allowed himself to become involved in, and in fact to sponsor. If an ordinary colony deliberately deceived the King about its laws it would be strongly condemned. It was doubly iniquitous for a commonwealth founded on the principles of the Sermon on the Mount to practice such deceit.

For this reason, it was interesting to see what the Council would do. It did nothing! The minutes of April 2, 1687, reported the arrival of the letter, a fuller synopsis of it was recorded in the minutes than of any previous letter, and then this decision was reached: "The President & Provll Councill have at this time unanimously & with Generall Express satisfacon, Concluded & ordered yt it should be so Entred in ye Councill book that ye Law so Compacted & Continued as they now are, may Remayne and be in force without acnulling Variations, or supply of additional bill or bills at this time till wee hear further from ye Gov[erno]r." [28] The Council defiantly ignored Penn's letter, and continued the laws in effect. Does this mean that these men were too stupid or too blind to see what Penn was attempting? Does it mean that they were too honest and too forthright to stoop to such a trick? Were they suspicious of Penn's motives and afraid to repeal all their laws? No one can answer these questions from the evidence available. As it turned out Penn's fears were groundless, for James II fled late in 1688, and the new government did not question the laws of Pennsylvania until 1693.

By this time it was obvious that there were many problems in the colony. The Council was not performing as effectively as Penn had expected, and it now refused to follow Penn's advice on the submittal of Pennsylvania laws to the Crown. The Assembly was creating difficulty by its demand for additional power, and there were complaints about the work of the law courts. In addition, Penn was deeply concerned over the actions of other persons in the colony. In one letter in 1685 he complained that Thomas Holme, surveyor general, was accused of refusing to survey unless plied with wine and gifts. The informants claimed to have spent ten or twelve pounds bribing him. Penn added that he loved Holme and believed that Holme loved him, but such action damaged Penn's reputation, and must be halted even if it meant the removal of Holme from office.[29]

Early in 1687, Penn denounced James Claypoole vigorously for engaging in underhanded operations to gain favor in the colony. Penn wrote: "I am in my spirit secreetly dissatisfyed with J. Clayp. conduct, he is but low, & came far & seeks preferment[,] has writ to A[lexander] P[arker,] G[eorge] W[hitehead,] G[eorge] F[ox] to speak to me; & if he be not prefrd to all the rest, I know who will be out of all patience, . . . [He is] inclinable to be to inferiors insolent, to superiors weeping[,] his numerous family & sometimes hott house are some small Apology . . . I desire that thou [James Harrison] & J. Simcock would deal plainly with him as to his behaviour & not lett anger or designes rest in his bosom agst his neighbors." [30] Despite these remarks, less than a week later Claypoole was named one of the new commissioners of state.

Penn was urged to believe that John White, the speaker of the Assembly during these four years, was to blame for the 1686 impasse over the enactment of laws. He wrote to Thomas Lloyd asking that White be removed from office if to blame and "think not hard of it." [31] To Harrison he wrote: "I hear J. Keen is saucy & injurious to us of our side, if so, visit him in my name, with this plea in his ear, that I shall bring authority with me to Examin him & his proceedings, & that Country will be too hott to hold him if he mend not his manners." [32]

In the same letter, Penn said, "I am very much afflicted in my Spirit that no Care is taken by those that have a Concern for the Lord's Name & Truth, by Perswasion or Authority to stop these scurvy Quarrels, that break out, to the Disgrace of the Provinces[,] there is nothing but Good said of the Place, and little thats Good said of the People." This indignation was the combined result of all the difficulties, irritations, and conflicts which had come to Penn's attention in the past two years. He faced a disagreeable fact: the "holy experiment" was not succeeding. In statesmanlike fashion Penn decided in February, 1687, that a change was necessary which would give the executive more power and stability and at the same time allow the people to continue to govern themselves. Penn indicated that he still had faith in the "holy experiment" and felt certain that with this modification it could be successful.

In a document dated February 1, 1687, five men were named as commissioners of state "to act in the execution of laws, as if I myself were there present, reserving to myself the confirmation of what is done, and my peculiar royalties and advantages." [33] Penn added that the appointments were made "to the end that there may be a more constant residence of the honorary and governing part of the government, for the keeping all things in good order."

Eight instructions were enclosed with the commission. These dealt with the infrequent meetings of the Council, the conflicts between that body and the Assembly, immorality in government, and the question of the laws and their enforcement. Penn concluded the instructions with the paragraph quoted in the first chapter, calling on the commissioners to "Be most just, as in the sight of the *all-seeing, all-searching* God;" and to uphold the principles of the "holy experiment."

Penn insisted that the Council be required to attend meetings, "for I will no more endure their most slothful and dishonorable attendance, but dissolve the frame, without any more ado." In addition, he requested the Commissioners to "suffer no disorder in the Council, nor the Council and Assembly," and to prevent the freemen from encroaching on the powers which remained in the hands of the governor. He prohibited parleys or open conferences between the two houses of the legislature, and called on his new deputies to report to him concerning past infractions.

When the General Assembly next convened, the Governor required the Commissioners to "declare my abrogation of all that has been done since my absence; and so, of all the laws, but the fundamentals; and that you immediately dismiss the Assembly, and call it again; and pass such of them afresh, with such alterations, as you and they shall see meet; and this, to avoid a greater inconveniency; which I foresee, and formerly communicated to *Thomas Lloyd.*"

In the meantime, Penn asked the Commissioners to enforce the laws: "let the point of the laws be turned against impiety, and your severe brow upon all the troublesome and vexatious, ·more especially trifling appealers." He requested the men to publish a proclamation, enclosed with the commission, which Penn had issued under his ordinance-making powers.

The naming of these men Commissioners raised some questions in the province. More was in bad repute in the colony, and Penn had expressed his vexation with Claypoole. Turner and Eckley had been appointed provincial judges with More and others in 1684. Lloyd was an obvious choice. Before complaints could come back to him, Penn wrote to Phineas Pemberton defending his choice. "I chose those about the Town & that did not agree[,] to agree them by giving all of them a share." [34] He hoped to please all, Quaker and non-Quaker, by giving them representation. Penn's comment to Pemberton on his commission and instructions to the five Commissioners is illuminating: "my Letter to them is sweet yet close, and a good opening on my Spirit with authority."

In a further attempt to raise the standard of government in the province and territories, Penn compiled some of the fundamental charters of the English heritage, including Magna Charta, Confirmation of the Charter of the Liberties of England and of the Forest, *De Tallageo non Concedendo*, an abstract of Penn's Charter from Charles II, and the Charter of Liberties of 1683. He had them printed in the colony with an introduction signed "Philopolites," under the title, *The Excellent Priviledge of Liberty & Property*, ... In his introduction Penn explained that he prepared the booklet to help those "who may not have leizure from their Plantations to read large Volumns." [35] He added that he was aware that there was a scarcity of law books in the colony. Saying that the documents included in the collection were fundamental, he expressed the hope that noble resolutions would spring up in the hearts of the settlers, "not to give away any thing of *Liberty* and *Property* . . . [for] it is easie to part with or give away great Priviledges but hard to be gained, if once lost, And therefore . . . lay sure Foundations for our selves and the Posterity of our Loyns."

Penn now waited for the good news to return from the colony, but nothing happened. There was no mention of the new commission in the minutes of the Provincial Council until February 9, 1688, more than a year after Penn wrote the letter.[36] One's first reaction would be that something went amiss, a boat sank, Penn forgot to send the commission, or something else delayed it. However, on August 4, 1687, the proclamation which Penn enclosed was promulgated throughout the colony.[87] Further, in a letter written by Penn to Harrison on September 8, 1687, he answered arguments used by the latter against the new form of government. One can only conclude that those who received the commission did not approve of it or of parts of it, and deliberately withheld it for a time.

It is obvious from Penn's letter that there was strong opposition to the new plan. He wrote that he was "sorry thou shouldest show thy self so disturbed at what I have done, as to call it changeing of the Government. I say this was harsh, & unkind as well as untrue, for if such a man as thou art, an ancient friend, my Friend, the Steward of my family, can make those constructions, what will not thos do yt are none of thos relations. but was putting in dr. More, ye change it cannot be, for you [Quakers] were four to one & I resolved to Ballance factions, not to Irritate nor give Strength to them. I judged it a way to quiet things till I came, and thy placeing his death as a perticular hand of god to hinder his preferment, savours not wth me at all, I think it too partiall & harsh, he has often been a dying man, & twas a wonder he lived so long." [38]

Probably these persons not only laid aside Penn's commission, but they then wrote to him as if it were in force, or actually told him it was in force. In another part of the letter quoted above, Penn wrote, "For the Govermt[:] when I read thy lettrs—thy honest sons, A Cooks, & especially Tho Lloyds, I see all is well. Truth in authority in the Government & better then when I left the place, wch makes me glad at heart, for by this I may stay to clear my own matters here first[;] but again If I would hear & believe such as come over as well as lettrs from thence from honest Fr [ien] ds. . . . I am much wanted . . . but I believe the best, & think the best & hope the best, & ˙pray & breath to god to preserve [you] . . . for him & one another to his glory & yr comfort."

Three more letters from Penn add further confirmation that Penn had been led to believe the commissioners were in office. Two of these named new commissioners to replace those who had been in office. On September 17, 1687, Penn wrote appointing John Simcock to replace More, who had died, and Arthur Cook to replace Claypoole, if he was still too ill to serve or if he was dead.[39] On December 27 he named Samuel Carpenter to replace Thomas Lloyd, who wished to resign.[40] This last commission never went into effect, for Lloyd apparently changed his mind and continued as a member of the commissioners of state until Blackwell arrived. The third letter asked the commissioners to draw up an exact transscript of the laws as they stood, leaving the title for Penn to fill in before presenting the laws to the crown. He added that he was sorry not to be able to let them have £100 each, "yt you might follow ye publick more saveingly & cherefully." He promised them one-half of any taxes collected from the colonists, to defray their expenses, "but who shall defray myn, ye Lord only knows." [41]

A letter written December 27, 1687, indicated that Penn was becoming suspicious. He asked why the government (the commissioners) had sent no official communication to him. Private letters had come and contradicted one another, giving him no real idea of what was happening. He added that men should agree in duty even if they disliked one another personally.[42] By the time this letter arrived in Pennsylvania, the commissioners were in office.

When the Commissioners of State were placed in authority in February, 1688, presumably an additional letter of instructions dated June 6, 1687, was read. Penn called on the men to "be dilligent, faithfull, Loveing & communical with one an other in things yt concerne the publick & I noways doubt but yr breaches will heal, and yr example have yt effect, yt nothing will be left for me to do, but thank & love you & take pleasure in yt comely order & thos under you." He urged that if there were differences, "lett yt not appear to ye people, show your virtues but conceal your infirmitys[;] this will make you awfull & reverend with ye people." [43] He asked them to make sure that the king's duties were collected, called for a new customs act to support the government, and requested that "you retrive the dignity of courts, and sessions, and remove all persons unqualified, in morals or in capacity."

During the ten months in which the commissioners of state served as the deputy governor of Pennsylvania, the only important occurrence was the meeting of the General Assembly. The weeks preceding the gathering of that body were taken up with preparing bills for action by the Assembly. Seven proposed laws were presented to the lower house when it met May 10, 1688. Five of these met almost instant agreement by the Assembly, but the other two caused much difficulty. One proposed regulations on export of deerskins and the other provided for customs duties on foreign trade to gain funds for the support of the government.

The Assembly was aware of the power it had exerted in the two previous years, and it intended to enlarge its prerogatives.[44] It demanded that the commissioners of state exhibit their commission to the Assembly, since the promulgated laws had gone out in the name of the governor and provincial Council. The lower house called on the Council to name a time for a joint session of the two branches to discuss various matters, and named men to serve on a joint committee with councillors. It voted to keep the debates of the Assembly secret.

The Council, with the power vested in it by the instructions sent to the commissioners, called for a joint session to deal firmly with the Assembly. The statement read to the lower house may be summarized as follows: First, the Assembly had been in error in not presenting its speaker and itself for the approval of the governor and Council. Second, the Assembly had no power to create a committee, and the Council committee could not accept such a group. Members of the upper house did agree to accept reports from individuals and to forward such informal statements to the Council. Third, the Assembly was called to consider the promulgated bills, and it might suggest amendments. If it did not begin to debate the bills it would be dissolved. Fourth, the Council did not approve of the decision to keep the debates of the Assembly secret; that was an innovation. Some of these statements stemmed from

Penn's instructions to the commissioners, and probably the Assembly was told that these were orders from the Governor, for without a word of protest the Assembly turned to discuss the proposed legislation and bided its time.

On Tuesday, May 15, there was another joint session and the Council wrote into its minutes that the members of the Assembly had been convinced "of their Irregular proceedings in severall matters." However, when the Assembly presented a bill of grievances to the Council on Friday, the upper house acknowledged the following day that injustice had been done, and promised to "take all possible care to prevent such for ye future."

After Thomas Lloyd rejected some amendments which the Assembly proposed to add to the supply bill at a meeting on Monday, he expressed the hope that the deerskin bill could be passed, *"but should leave it to the Assembly, and that they would meet the Assembly in Conference, in order to remove all hard thoughts, &c."* Thursday saw the Assembly vote on the supply bill step by step. It was willing to accept the duties on lumber, shingles, and clapboard, strong liquors, beer and cider, but it refused to agree to a duty of eighteen pence on each barrel of molasses. The following day the Assembly attempted to gain preferential duties for goods carried on ships owned by the colonists.

When the houses met together in the meetinghouse for the last time on Saturday morning, Speaker John White told the Council that "the Assembly hath done what they have to do in relation to the Bills," but it was not enough. The five non-controversial bills were enacted into law, but the supply bill and the deerskin bill failed to win approval. When the lower house was left alone after the withdrawal of the Council, it prepared a paper to present to the Governor and Council, "as a thankfull Acknowledgement of their Kindness &c. Being put to the Vote, *resolved in the Affimative*," and the Assembly adjourned.

This was the most successful meeting of the General Assembly in three years, for it was the first time that laws had been enacted since 1685. In addition, there was more respect in this session between members of the two houses. One wonders whether the legislators did not feel twinges of conscience about their previous behavior. Perhaps Penn's earnest entreaties had found a response in their hearts, and they were making an attempt to conduct this session in a peaceful and orderly manner.

Whether this session of the General Assembly might have marked the beginning of a change of heart in Pennsylvania became unimportant because William Penn had already decided to change the form of government again, and name a single Deputy Governor.[45] It is improbable that there had been any lasting reformation in the colony, for when John Blackwell arrived in December, 1688, he had difficulty finding the officers of the government. Perhaps the commissioners had been holding sessions, but the Council met only once in the month following the adjournment of the General Assembly in May. Blackwell found the council room deserted and covered with dust and scattered papers. The wheels of government had nearly stopped turning.

CHAPTER SEVEN

PENN'S ADMISSION OF FAILURE:

GOVERNOR BLACKWELL

WILLIAM PENN frequently found the news from Pennsylvania weighing heavily on his heart, for he still expected the freemen to uphold the high ideals of the "holy experiment," despite their seeming disinterest. In the face of a flow of discouraging news from the New World, Penn continued to believe that he could, by his example and wise counsel, guide his people back onto the path of righteousness. Less than a year before Governor John Blackwell arrived in Philadelphia, Penn sent to the five commissioners these tender words of advice: "They that live near to God will live far from themselves, & from a Sense they have of his Nearness & Majesty, have a low opinion of themselves; & out of that low & humble Frame of Spirit it is that true charity grows. . . . O, that the People of my Province . . . felt this gracious Quality abounding in them, my Work would soon be done, & this Praise & my Joy unspeakably abound to us." [1]

However, like many other pleas for a spiritual renewal among the Friends, this poignant appeal seemed to fall on deaf ears. Penn was forced to admit that when he looked over the commonwealth he saw men who failed to fulfill their obligations to him. He saw a people who declined to pay what they owed him, a government which refused to operate in accordance with its constitution and his instructions, and a colony which had forgotten that it was established as a utopian community.

William Penn did not openly confess that the "holy experiment" had failed. However his decision to seek a deputy gover-

nor outside the Society of Friends was a tacit admission that in
his opinion, the Quakers in Pennsylvania were not fit to govern
themselves. The position had first been offered to Thomas
Lloyd, but his rejection of the high office was further proof that
the Quakers were unwilling to assume political responsibilities.
The Quakers seemed as religious as ever, and faithfully attended Friends meeting for worship, but the spiritual qualities
essential in a flourishing "holy experiment" were not transferred
from the purely religious side of their lives to the political.

However, the arrival in Pennsylvania of the old Puritan John
Blackwell aroused a new interest in government. Friends joined
ranks, and presented a near-unanimous opposition to this representative of their ancient foes in England, this outsider who
attempted to curtail the liberties which Penn had granted when
the government was established. Because Friends united in opposition to this foreign intruder, this did not mean that they
suddenly experienced a deep spiritual resurgence. The Quakers
fought Governor Blackwell with such vehemence and tenacity
that he sent in his resignation less than four months after he
arrived. Thomas Lloyd resorted to contemptible actions which
would have been of credit to no one, much less a Quaker minister. Blackwell in writing to Penn described Friends in these
words: "The Apostle [Epistle] to the Galathians speaks of Another Gospell than Christs etc.: and the Aples Jude & Peter
That in the last days there shall arise some sorts of men That
shall despise Dominion & speak Evill of Dignityes? I am sorry
to find so much of that among those who are called the sincere
members of your Comunion here!" [2]

The Friends may have seemed to be the embodiment of the
Antichrist to John Blackwell, but they were not so to William
Penn. During the year that the Puritan was among them the
Quakers wrote to their Governor in very affectionate terms and
gave evidence that they had regained the vision which had been
the basis for the "holy experiment." Penn was touched by their
reports and ignoring the letters from Blackwell and his supporters, determined to attempt the restoration of the old order
with the people once again in control of their own government.

A study of the year Blackwell spent among the Quakers clearly indicates that the colonists felt sorry for themselves under the domination of the old Puritan, but daily exhibited the spirit which had forced Penn to send him to Pennsylvania.

The announcement that Blackwell had been named deputy governor was contained in a letter dated September 18, 1688, directed to the commissioners of state by William Penn. The tone was conciliatory, for Penn wanted to prepare a smooth path for his new deputy by creating a receptive mood in the persons in the old government. He stated that Blackwell is to "confer in private with you, & square himself by your advice, but bear down with visible authority, vice and faction." He added, "If he does not please you, he shall be layed aside for it is not that I am displeased with your care, or service, quite the contrary, If in anything you have differed from my sense, It is I believe, because you thought it best for the gen[eral] Service. I desire you to receive this person with Kindness & lett him see it. & use his not being a Friend to Friends advantage. But you must know I have a rough people to deal with about my quitrents that can't yet pay a ten pound Bill, but draw, draw, draw still upon me . . . he has a mighty repute of all sorts of honest people where he has inhabited." [3]

The tone intimated that Blackwell was to be subservient to the Quakers in the Council, and that the primary innovation contemplated under his administration would be the establishment of an efficient system for collecting the quitrents. However, the instructions which Penn sent to Blackwell at the same time indicated that there were many other things, in addition to quitrents which bothered him. He asked that the laws be gathered together and sent to him immediately. He instructed Blackwell to make certain that justice prevailed in the colony, and to end the quarreling and feuding. He invited his deputy to criticize anything in the colony, and to make suggestions for improvement. He closed with the words, "Rule the meek meekly; and those that will not be ruled, rule with authority; and God Almighty prosper all honest and prudent endeavours." [4]

These instructions to Blackwell asked him to do nothing

underhanded, and with one exception, nothing which Penn had not asked the Council or the commissioners of state to do in the past.[5] He was to enforce the Charter and laws strictly, maintain peace and justice, see that the quitrents were collected, and do other things necessary to the well being and prosperity of the colony and of the proprietor.

The only difference was that Penn felt confident that his deputy would carry out the instructions, while he had never been certain that the Quakers would do as he ordered. Obviously, if the deputy governor did what the colonists had consistently failed to do and if he made reforms which they had refused to attempt then he would be unpopular with the people of Pennsylvania. Any person who is placed in authority over people who have been self-governing cannot help being strongly disliked. Penn certainly realized that the colonists would deeply resent an old Puritan soldier coming in to reform them. Yet, he made the promise, "If he does not please you, he shall be layed aside." This was William Penn in one of his worst moments. He condemned Blackwell to failure before Blackwell set foot in the colony.

Blackwell's mission was further complicated by a situation for which neither he nor Penn was to blame. Thomas Lloyd had been offered the position of deputy governor and had refused it. When he also asked to be replaced as one of the commissioners of state, Penn sent a new commission for Samuel Carpenter. However Lloyd evidently changed his mind for he continued as a commissioner until Blackwell arrived, and was antagonistic to the new deputy. Both Blackwell and his friends on the Council believed that Lloyd had wanted to be deputy governor himself. The kindest thing which can be said about Lloyd's actions during the months ahead is that he was bitterly disappointed when he learned that a Puritan had been named to the position.

Perhaps Lloyd sent a letter to Penn in which he changed his mind and accepted the former offer, and Penn never received the letter. Perhaps Lloyd refused out of a sense of false modesty, hoping to be persuaded to change his mind. Lloyd's actions, statements, and attitude in the year that Blackwell was in the colony, were childish, picayune and illegal. They were entirely beneath the man who before James Logan was the leading Quaker statesman in Pennsylvania. Even when the prejudice of Blackwell is discounted, the cold record of Lloyd's actions condemn him. Lloyd proved an able opponent, and with the support of the Council and Assembly he overwhelmed Blackwell and made him wish he had never heard of Pennsylvania.

The new Deputy Governor had been an officer in Oliver Cromwell's army, and later served as Treasurer at War and as one of the Receivers General for Assessments. He left England at the time of the Restoration and lived in Dublin, where he had extensive landholdings. In 1671 as a widower with seven children, he married the daughter of General John Lambert, one of Cromwell's chief lieutenants. Since 1684 he had lived in New England where he was acceptable to the leaders of the Puritan Commonwealth. He was engaged in several land ventures and did some writing about the formation of a "Bank of Credit" in Boston. However, in 1688 conditions had changed for the worse and when Penn offered the position of lieutenant governor to Blackwell he accepted.[6] The new deputy was a religious man, a person of modesty, and a gentleman. He wrote to Penn of a "very deep sense of my owne both unfitnesse and unworthiness to manage so great trust and power over a people of so different persuasions, and in some things principles from me." Writing to Thomas Lloyd on November 11, 1688, while still in Boston, he expressed the hope that he would be able to continue the good government which had been in operation, and asked for advice and assistance.[7]

The first inkling of what was in store for Blackwell in Pennsylvania came before he arrived in the colony. He sent word ahead that he would arrive in New York on a certain date and asked that someone be sent there to escort him to Philadelphia. After waiting in vain for three days in New York he crossed New Jersey alone, going to Pennsbury. From there he sent word to the Council that he would be in Philadelphia to meet the members at 3 p.m., the following afternoon, December 17. Charles Pickering, who carried the message, promised to gather together some of his friends and ride out on the road going north from town to form a suitable escort to usher the new lieutenant governor into his capital. However, when Pickering met him the following day, he rode on without speaking. Blackwell later learned that Thomas Lloyd would not "countenance any others shewing me the least respect of that Kinde." [8]

When Blackwell entered the town and rode to Penn's house where William Markham, the secretary of the Council lived, and where the Council met, no one was there. Blackwell, his servants and horses were left in the street while boys began to gather around and jeer. By this time the new deputy was very upset. He later wrote, "I was resolved I would publish my Commission there before I removed, & that if no others came I would call in the boys to be witnesses of it."

Markham put in a belated appearance, apologized, and went in search of the Council. Eventually several members, including Thomas Lloyd, arrived. Blackwell then addressed the Council, told them who he was, and expressed his dismay at the lack of a suitable reception for him. When the new lieutenant governor produced his commission from William Penn, Lloyd told him "he did not look upon that as a sufficient authority till it were under the Great Seale." [9] Blackwell expressed his indignation at such presumption, and said "that if he thought not fitt to attend it, I should publish it, & pursue the authority placed in me thereby." Lloyd asked him not to do that and requested time to consider the matter in the Council. Blackwell acquiesced and went into another part of the house. After discussing the matter for an hour, the Council announced that it had agreed to accept him but wished him to wait until the following morning to take control. After Blackwell agreed to this request, Lloyd, in Blackwell's words, "tould me I might have sent my horses to an Inn and payd my respect to those that were in authority by givving them a friendly visit before I had surprised them in this publique & unusuall manner."

After making this defense of the honor of the old government, Lloyd escorted Blackwell to a tavern where they spent a pleasant time together. Later Markham took him to the home of Griffith Jones, where he lived during his stay in Philadelphia. The following day, after business had been cared for, the Council adjourned to the home of Lloyd and the Governor reported, "I was very handsomly intertayned."

If Lloyd's hospitality healed the differences between the men, amity did not reign for very long. The first difference developed over the instructions which Penn had forwarded to the government in the past. Blackwell had been ordered to read these earlier directives and be ruled by them. Lloyd was reluctant to bring in copies of past letters from Penn, and Blackwell asked the Council to aid him. The Council agreed with Blackwell that all letters of instruction from William Penn were public property, and ordered Lloyd to deposit them in the hands of the Secretary of the Council. It should be said in Lloyd's defense that Penn had warned him on occasion to keep certain letters secret, and in a letter dated September, 1688, by implication gave Lloyd permission to select pertinent parts of that particular letter, as well as of other ones, to pass along to Blackwell.[10]

The next disagreement was a fundamental one, which was bitterly contested for months. The issue was this: did Thomas Lloyd, as keeper of the Great Seal, have the power to decide which documents might have the Great Seal solemnly affixed to them? Blackwell said no. The keeper was an appointee of the governor and subordinate to him and his deputy. In equally emphatic terms, Lloyd defended his right to decide what he would do with the Great Seal.

The first conflict came over affixing the seal to commissions which Blackwell had drawn up when appointing justices of the peace. The two men could not agree on the form of the commissions, and argued about this and other matters for hours. In the heat of the discussion Blackwell forgot to recover his commissions, and Lloyd came to see him later to deliver them. "After about two houers sitting with me, & familiarly discoursing other things" Lloyd placed the commissions in Blackwell's hands at parting. Blackwell recorded that the discussion had been so friendly that he let himself hope that Lloyd had undergone a change of heart and had put the seal on them after all. He could hardly wait until Lloyd was out of sight to look. Finally he opened them and they were unsealed. Blackwell placed the lesser seal on them, and they went into effect.[11]

At one point Blackwell felt certain that he was going to win. He heard that Lloyd was going to leave the colony to visit New York. On February 1, 1689, he asked the Council to concur with him in asking Lloyd to deposit the Great Seal with the Council during his absence in case it was needed while he was away. After some discussion the Council agreed to send Secretary Markham to ask Lloyd for the Great Seal. At the next session Lloyd appeared and presented a written protest. He declared that his office as keeper of the Great Seal was property (there were small fees attached to the position) and accused the Council of attempting to deprive him of his property without the right to defend himself. After a long harangue about property rights, Lloyd closed his statement with this emotion-laden appeal: "My love to ye Govr, people, and their Sincerity, hath made me Serve them Chearfully Sometime. I have Endeavoured their good, tho' I might ffayle in effecting of it. I may have witness in Some breasts, that I have more injured myselfe and ffamily then any persons just Intrest under my notice. I have been a great Drudge In my Sphere, but not so abused an one afore. Be pleased to be tender of Right, and lett not ye Royall Law be forgotten, of doing unto others as you would have (Such) others doe unto you." [12] Needless to say, Lloyd did not relinquish his hold on the Great Seal.

In February, 1689, when Blackwell appointed five judges for the provincial court, he drew up a commission which the Council approved after making slight alterations. This was sent to Lloyd for the endorsement of the Great Seal. Two days later a letter returned from Lloyd in which he said of the document, "it seems to be more moulded by ffancy, then fformed by law: . . . I Cannot without Violation of ye trust reposed in me, lett the same pass under ye seale in my Custody." [13] Blackwell then suggested that Lloyd be requested to bring the commission and his seal to the Council, and allow the Governor to place the seal on the commission. The Council agreed to censure Lloyd, but would not agree to Blackwell's proposal. Cook compared it to borrowing another's sword to kill a man, which did not please Blackwell. Griffith Jones condemned Lloyd severely, and accused him of deliberately stirring up dissention. He added, "It is the King's authority that is opposed, & looks to me as if it were a raysing a force to Rebell." [14]

On February 25, 1689, a legal case was brought before the Council which had been decided in a county court and reversed in the provincial court. Two copies of the record of the provincial court proceedings were introduced, and they differed from one another to such a marked extent that Arthur Cook suggested the original entry in the court book should be brought to the Governor and Council. David Lloyd, the clerk of the provincial court, held the records in his personal possession. Originally from Wales, like his distant kinsman Thomas Lloyd, David Lloyd had studied law with Sir George Jeffreys, later Chief Justice of England who is remembered for the Bloody Assizes during the reign of James II. David Lloyd had apparently done legal work in Penn's office in London before coming to Philadelphia in 1686 as Attorney General for the colony. He was the best trained lawyer in Pennsylvania and remained a leader in the province for three decades. On this occasion he was asked to bring all his records for the provincial court to the Council. He refused, "saying you may command the Judges, and ye Judges might Order him, & other slight and Scornfull Expressions he used." [15] For this and other "unseemly and Slighting Expressions" he was declared unfit to serve as clerk of any court in the province, and dismissed until he acknowledged his offense.

On March 5, 1689, the Council learned that Thomas Lloyd had renamed David Lloyd as clerk of the courts in Philadelphia County, by virtue of his powers as keeper of the Great Seal and master of the rolls.[16] Naturally the Governor and Council were outraged by this presumption, and Cook alone remained loyal to the Lloyds. Samuel Carpenter refused to censure Thomas Lloyd but even he admitted that this latest act was beyond his understanding.

John Blackwell was furious with the Quaker leader for refusing to perform the duties attached to his offices, and in his reports to Penn suggested that Lloyd behaved in this fashion because he was "indeavouring to keep all your affayrs in the same posture of Laxness and confusion, wherinto by his managemt of them they are reduced, to the high discontent of divers of the Provinciall Councill who really honour and Love you, but professe themselves wearyed out of their Esteeme of businesse by his dilatory harrangues & procedures." In the same letter he called on Penn to issue a statement supporting either himself or Lloyd. "For you are our Oracle upon all accounts; and by your words we stand or fall respectively. Wherefore Please to deal impartially & without respect to either of our persons; for I would not stand in the way of your reputation with your people." [17]

This struggle of two strong personalities which overshadowed all else in the colony was brought to a head when Blackwell introduced impeachment proceedings against Lloyd on April 2, 1689, charging him with eleven high misdemeanors, crimes, and offences.[18] In the meantime the Quaker had become the center of a new conflict, for he had been elected to the Council by Bucks County and Blackwell refused to seat him.

John Blackwell did not feel content with challenging the presumptions of Thomas Lloyd. His instructions ordered him to evaluate everything in the colony and to make reports to Penn. This he faithfully did. References in earlier chapters indicate that he frankly criticized the economic situation in the colony, and made biting comments about the Quaker community. Many of the difficulties with Lloyd arose over his attempts to straighten out the judiciary. He also made suggestions and observations about other matters.[19] Taking up foreign trade conditions with the Council one day in January, he said it was his opinion that the letters patent allowed trade only with England while in reality much trade was carried on with neighboring provinces and other British colonies. Another day he criticized the practice of enacting laws for only one year at a time, and expressed wonder that any thinking man would invest money in a place with such instability. He added that some laws were undoubtedly repugnant to the laws of England. He deplored the lack of public funds in the colony, which made it impossible to hire a messenger to call the Council, a door-keeper, and someone to search ships to enforce the laws of England. He believed that some means should be found to collect taxes for the operation of the government.

On one occasion Blackwell took up the matter of attendance at the Council, and suggested that all counties should be forced to maintain at least one councillor in attendance to the governor at all times. Arthur Cook responded by protesting that the people were so poverty-stricken that "they were not able to bear ye Charge of Constant attendance, as the Law and Charter Required," and asked the Lieutenant Governor to refrain from enforcing the law temporarily. Other members of the Council joined Cook in that plea.

All in all, Blackwell considered Pennsylvania to be in a most confused state, a condition he found difficult to understand in view of the fact that Penn had personally established the colony. He decided that part of the reason for the present condition lay in the fact that Penn's words of advice were not heeded because of "the whistling ayr in some mens heads [which] would not admitt a hearing." He added that the colony needed to be purged, for there were many who had eaten more of the "Honey of your concessions . . . than their stomachs can beare."

The Council met every week during the early months of 1689, and Blackwell continued to review the actions of the government in the past, the documents on which the government was based, and the general condition of the colony. His conclusions were then sent to Penn. He was performing his duty and there was nothing dishonorable in his actions. However, he was conducting this review of the past in the presence of those who were responsible for what had transpired. Every time that he criticized an occurrence, questioned a decision, or called for a reform, those who had served in former times, and almost always had served without financial remuneration, grew upset. This was a difficult position for the Council members who had emotional attachments to their past actions. A growing tension, a sense of frustration, and a deep resentment welled up in these men.

In the spring of 1689, Blackwell had been probing into the county courts and criticizing their past operation. Samuel Richardson began to denounce the Governor and denied that he was governor. He protested that Penn who was a governor, could not create a governor. After bitter argument, Blackwell ordered Richardson to leave the room while his conduct was discussed. Richardson replied: "I will not withdraw, I was not brought hether by Thee, & I will not goe out by thy order; I was sent by ye people, and thou hast no power to put me out." More discussion followed, and all but Cook disagreed with Richardson's statement that Governor Penn could not create a Governor. Even Cook made his point in a tactful manner, at the same time censuring Richardson for his unseemly outburst. The Council ordered Richardson to withdraw while his conduct was discussed and he acquiesced, declaring as he left that he cared not whether he ever sat there again.

THE IMPEACHMENT OF THOMAS LLOYD

All of these irritations and frustrations were insignificant compared with the feelings on the day that Blackwell called for the impeachment of Thomas Lloyd. The charges were made against the Quaker leader in an extended speech in which the Governor stated that his own powers were virtually unlimited, and relegated the Council to a mere advisory status.

Blackwell requested the secretary to read passages from the letters patent. The Puritan then began to discuss the powers granted to William Penn by Charles II in that charter. He especially emphasized his position as captain general, and the powers he held to create manors and courts baron and leet. "Let none then doubt to call him Lord Proprietor." He added that the charter required the officers and justices to cooperate with, and not oppose the proprietor under pain of high displeasure. "How then shall any presume on pretence of any Charter from the Proprietor, to withstand or oppose the power given to him selfe & his heirs? or challenge any of their incommunicable attributes?" [20]

He denounced the idea expressed by some, that William Penn was a joint ruler with the representatives of the people. Penn could not grant the people the right to share in government, he said, for the "Royall & Sovereign power, (such as the Proprietor holde by the Kings letters patente, as aforesayd) are not transferable." Blackwell added that as the duly appointed deputy of William Penn, an office recognized in the charter, he held all of the powers and prerogatives granted to the proprietor by the king, with the exception of the powers reserved to Penn.

He continued by saying of the representatives and councillors, "You are such worthy persons as the Proprietor is pleased to constitute, as a Politicall help unto him: & to declare, He will advise with, . . . But you, when chosen, are his, vizt the Proprietors; not theirs, vizt. the peoples, And when they fayle to choose fitt persons, or you refuse that observance and attendance . . . He may Reject your Councills, & take such others as will answer the Ends of the Kings just Expectations, . . . or act therin' without you." Blackwell urged the Council, "Be not lead asside . . . by the cunning craftinesse, specious and smooth-tongued delusions of any man or men of unstable mindes, unsteady principles in Governmt, un-experienced, proud, and ambitious spirits, assuming more than is meet to themselves." This was a direct attack on Thomas Lloyd.

In a different strain he continued: "This is the will of God that I should be thus Exorcized here too. . . . But what Evill have I done you? Testify against me. I know myself to be clothed with many fold weaknesses, infirmitys & frayltys . . . [but] I came with full purpose & resolution to do you what good I could." This mood did not last long, and shortly Blackwell turned to threats. He said, "I may not suffer such insolences as

I have met with: I may not beare the sword in vayne, It must cut off unruly tongues and members without distinction. I have already borne too too much contempt of my masters authority, . . . making use of corrosives only when I hope they'l prove healing."

Blackwell closed the long discourse by calling for the impeachment of Thomas Lloyd, and at the same time suspended Lloyd from all of his offices and duties until Penn's pleasure was known.

The Council was deeply aroused. This man was not merely attacking one member of the commonwealth, he was tearing down the very fundamentals of the government. Blackwell had denied that William Penn had the right to grant self-government, or even an equal share in the government, to the freemen. He was determined to serve as an absolute Governor, while the local political leaders resolved to defend tenaciously the power which they had formerly been granted. This did not mean that the Quakers were interested in democracy, but that they were desirous of maintaining the control of society in the hands of the merchants and substantial citizens both rural and urban. They were interested in defending the Quaker hegemony, and resented the Puritan overlord. Thomas Lloyd, who had made a determined stand against the new order, became a symbol both to the Quakers and to Blackwell. Those who had berated him for his petty, childish actions against the Governor began to feel that he had been justified after all.

The Council met several times during the week following Blackwell's speech, to decide whether action would be taken against Thomas Lloyd. It was a tumultuous period, and the Secretary recorded one day, "Many intemperate Speeches and passages happend, fitt to be had in oblivion." Later he added, "Here againe arose some warme debates, divers of the members expressing their in-ordinate affections for the sayd Tho. Lloyd; and saying they could not (& one of them he would not) believe him to be such a person, & so guilty as was mentioned in the Charge." [21]

Thomas Lloyd appeared at the Council session which met April 5. The Governor, in all innocence, asked him if he had anything to say to the Council. Lloyd, in all innocence, replied that he had been elected by Bucks County and had come to take his seat. Blackwell told him that he could not sit on the Council until he had been cleared of charges made against him. Lloyd refused to leave, and an argument followed which Blackwell was able to end only by adjourning the Council to his own rooms at the home of Griffith Jones. Even with Lloyd no longer with them, the argument continued. The followers of Lloyd objected to the wording of the minutes of the previous meeting and especially disliked the term "in-ordinate affection," but Blackwell refused to allow the record to be altered. The heated debate continued until the Governor determined to "Exercise his authority, as he was directed by the Honble Prop[riet]or & Chief Governor, for suppressing all factions, Seditions & animosityes, and so past off from that debate." [22]

April 9, 1689, was a fateful day. At its dawn there was no reason to fear for the future of the government. The Council was to gather together in a legislative session to spend the day going over past legislation, and preparing new bills to submit to the Assembly in May. When the sun set, the Council members returned to their homes, where they remained for a month. Blackwell, full of despair, sat down to tender his resignation to William Penn.

Before other business could be undertaken, Blackwell held up a pamphlet called "the fframe of the Governmt. of this Province, &c.," and announced that Markham, who had given it to him, received it from William Clark who obtained it from Joseph Growdon. When Blackwell asked Growdon where he obtained it, the councillor was noncommittal. The Governor then said that the printed copy was in error. Growdon placed the blame on the printer but claimed he didn't know who the printer was.[23] When Blackwell asked him if he had ordered the printing, Growdon replied that he did not need to incriminate himself. Then the Governor asked him to leave the room while the Council discussed the matter, and Growdon refused. When Blackwell turned to the Council for support to force Growdon to leave it was silent, and the meeting adjourned until 2 p.m.

When the afternoon session convened, Blackwell attempted to explain in a reasonable fashion why the Second Frame should not have been printed. Before this matter could be settled John Eckley put in an appearance, and attempted to take his seat as a councillor from Philadelphia County. When he was first elected there had been some doubt about the right of some fifty voters to vote in Philadelphia County. A new election had been held, at which both Eckley and Samuel Richardson were re-elected unanimously by voice vote.[24] Growdon demanded that all three disbarred members, Lloyd, Eckley, and Richardson be seated before his case was determined. Blackwell refused to accede to this request and went over his reasons for excluding these men.

William Yardley said that unless they could have their duly elected members seated they should be dismissed. John Hill agreed and asked Blackwell to name his own Council. Several others who supported the Governor called for an adjournment. The Quakers then demanded that they continue to meet, but with all the members present. Samuel Carpenter muttered: "I look upon it that we are judges of Our members, otherwise we may be Refused or turned out at pleasure. We are abused." The Governor asked him what he meant, but his answer "was as dark as his former Expression; and so was passed over."

Blackwell finally concluded the meeting with this statement: "I have a Conscience to be Exercised, & a duty incumbent in discharge of my trust, as well as any of you, and I conceive it lyes with more weight upon me if I suffer a miscarriage in these Councills. But I have sayd what was on my thought to say as there has been occasion; and since it appears to me, That we are hinderd on that pretence from proceeding any further, I think fitt (according to the advices of many of you) to adjourne this meeting of Councill on the Legislative account, till further occasion." [25]

It would seem that as soon as the session was dismissed, everyone rushed to report his side of the story to William Penn. Actually, Phineas Pemberton wrote the day before, complaining of the already described conditions in the government, and emphasizing that three members of the Council were denied their seats. He added, "hadst thou taken displaysure agt & punishe us by thy owne hand we cold have born it because we know thee & thy principle[,] the impressions of thy Seales, being mercy with Judgmt but the old hypocrites professors take vengeance like the philistines with a despitfull hart to destroy because of the old enmity." He concluded with the words, some are glad to see "poor friends run down & trampled undr foot." [26]

Seven members of the Council sent Penn a vindication of themselves. Of Blackwell they said, "for want of true love to us & our Principle he acts allmost in all things agst us in & out of Counsell (though not wth out fair coulers & pretences) and Renders us (to our faces in Councell) and the best of the People in the most odious terms as ffactious, Mutinous, Seditious, turbulent & the like ffor noe just occasion given as wee know of unlesse it be ffor our asserting in moderation & Sobernesse our Just rights & libertyes . . . and our unanimous resolvednesse as men & Christians not to Suffer an Invasion upon our Charter & laws wherin wee hope wee have discharged a good Conscience to God & to thee & to the people."

They added after reciting some of their grievances, "wee may Safely say that all honest ffriends in this Government and the Neighbouring parts that know of these proceedings of the Govr are much troubled and Concerned and it will bring a damp and dejection upon all the Sober honest people in Generall. as well as discourage any from comeing among us." They said that all of their hardships, sacrifices, and loss of estates would be for nothing if they lost their liberties and privileges. They wrote that seemingly all was lost, and those who could would leave the colony and carry a bad word against Pennsylvania, which would drive others away.

These men told the Proprietor about Blackwell's statement that Penn had no right to grant a share of the government to the freemen. They reported that such men as Griffith Jones, Patrick Robinson, and Markham were very influential. The Quakers were crushed, while "thyne & our Enemys and others yt have not well approved themselves as friends to thee & the Country are Encouraged. . . . [We] see the difference between an affectionate & tender ffather whose children wee know we are, and a Severe hardhearted father in law who hath no share nor lot nor Portion among us." [27]

Turning in his resignation, Blackwell made some well-chosen remarks about the Quakers in the government:

Tis admirable Sr, That coming from under persecution, No person though Ever so respectfull, if not under the dialect of a Friend, can have civill treatment, or justice done against so high a Criminal if a Friend. I am sorry for it, to say no more. But that such injustice & partiallity should be advanced, by Lying, & absurd conclusions: I expect will have a vindication. . . . the thing aymed at, is That the Criminall [Lloyd] may Succede me, (and if not, here will be no peace, nor then neither, for that his reputation for such a purpose is founded on the interest afore suggested, which is not compatible with that of just & prudent men of other perswasions) I shall lay myself & my Comission at your feet, praying my charges and grearters [guarantor] here may be discharged, if you shall please to approve my Removall to the place whence I came.[28]

Doubtless many other letters were sent to Penn from both sides.

After April 9, everything else during Blackwell's year in Pennsylvania was an anti-climax. The Governor went through the forms of government, he called the General Assembly, and the Council met on infrequent occasions. But he no longer had any desire to change things or to make critical suggestions. The government coasted during the next nine months. When Penn received the letters, he chose to accept the word of the Quakers and to discount the accusations by Blackwell and his friends. He was deeply touched by the letters from the Quakers describing their tribulations and protesting their love for him.

The Assembly gathered Friday, May 10, and chose Arthur Cook, who had previously been in the Council, as speaker. Since the Council had prepared no bills for consideration and was not even in session, the Assembly turned to petitions and began to collect grievances. The prime grievance was that John

White, former speaker of the Assembly, was in jail in New Castle. A committee was named to draw together and consider grievances. It was not until Tuesday, May 14, that twelve members of the Council were found to make a quorum and the two houses of the General Assembly could meet simultaneously.[29]

Governor Blackwell addressed the joint session, largely to inform the Assembly of what had happened since his arrival. He added, "it has been my great Unhappiness to meet with unexpected Opposition therein." In his own defense he said four things. That he had not sought this position as Governor but undertook it from good will towards his worthy friend, William Penn; that he would show all possible respect to the Proprietor and to the colonists; that he had attempted to fulfill his instructions, but no more; and "That in Expectation of his [Penn's] Arrival (which God grant suddenly, if it be his Will) I shall wait for my Vindication against the Malevolency of my Opposers." Blackwell made vague references to the revolutionary atmosphere which pervaded England at that time, and suggested that Penn's continued absence might be related to that situation. The entire story of the Glorious Revolution had not yet crossed the Atlantic.[30]

Blackwell then explained why there were no bills ready for the consideration of the Assembly. Because laws were passed for a single year at a time all of the laws would fall. Blackwell, not wishing that to happen, agreed to govern the colony by such laws as he considered acceptable and useful and to think of them as "so many Rules and Instructions given to me by my Master."

In closing he asked the representatives to allow reason, not passion or prejudice to influence them. "I expect the same Liberty and Exercise of my Judgement and Conscience as you do . . . for I take it for granted, this is a Fundamental Rule with every one of you, *To do others, as you would they should do to you.*" He promised to call them together again when news came from England which would allow them to enact legislation, and promised "as large Privileges and Exemptions as shall be judg'd reasonable to desire." [31]

The Council spent much time discussing a way to keep the laws in force for another year. Most of the members agreed that if the General Assembly adjourned itself, it would still technically be in session and the laws would continue. Blackwell did not concur with that opinion, and he wanted to make the laws valid by his own statement. Eventually, after the Assembly had gone home, the Council continued the laws in force by a declaration. This statement said in part. "We do hereby Declare, That all the Laws past and agreed upon by the Proprietor and Chief Governor and Freemen in Provincial Councill and Assembly, made before the Proprietor's going for England, shall be, Continue, and Remayin in the Same force as now they are, until We shall Receive Orders out of England about or Concerning that matter." The declaration amended the former laws in that it allowed the Governor to commission provincial judges under the Lesser Seal. It was prefaced with a statement of loyalty to the Charter of Liberties and the laws of the Province.[32]

Thomas Lloyd soon challenged the action of the Council in a paper entitled, "A Seasonable Advertisement to the Freemen of this Province." He analyzed the theory of making laws in Pennsylvania and pointed out that the Council had not followed the proper procedure. But he said that since the Assembly had been adjourned and not dismissed, the laws were still in existence. If they were invalid a proclamation would have done no good, and since they were valid they needed no declaration of any kind. The Council, Lloyd, and Blackwell agreed that the laws were valid, but each had followed a divergent path to arrive at the common end.[33]

The Assembly was mulling over grievances and it was worried about the incarceration of White, until White suddenly walked on the floor the morning of Friday, May 17. When it was discovered that he had broken jail to come to Philadelphia, the Assembly ordered him to withdraw. However after this brief show of indignation, the Assembly allowed him to be seated when it convened in the late afternoon. That evening, while he was preparing to go to bed in a room at Benjamin

Chambers' home, White heard a noise. The next thing he knew, his door was broken down and Sheriff John Claypoole arrested him on a warrant issued by Griffith Jones and Robert Turner, justices of the peace. At least two members of the Assembly, Samuel Levis and Daniel Brown, witnessed this seizure, and the next morning a stiff protest was lodged with the Governor and Council. Englishmen had long defended the right of legislators to freedom from arrest while travelling to or from parliament and while parliament was in session. The statement read, "Therefore this our Member being thus contemptuously used in the Assembly time, the Rights, Freedoms and Liberties of every Freeman broken down, slighted and trodden under Foot, we hope the Wisdom and Care of the Governor and Council, will, with as much Speed as Justice, Express their just Resentments against such Disorders, and Cause Justice to flow." [34]

The Assembly quietly fell apart after this effort to free White. When it convened Monday morning only twenty members were present. This remnant, indignant about being deserted by the other assemblymen, passed a resolution denying the absent ones the right to collect any pay for their services, and declaring that they should never be chosen again as delegates by the freemen of their counties. Other resolutions were passed, mostly in defense of White, but one expressed approval of the printing of the Charter of Liberties, thus supporting Growdon. After that nothing more is heard of the 1689 Assembly.

Another disorderly episode took place at the session of the Council where the resolutions prepared by the Assembly were presented to the Governor. While Blackwell was trying to decide whether to accept the resolutions from the small Assembly, paper was handed to him by Yardley. At that moment Eckley, Richardson, and Lloyd walked in. After a brief exchange, Blackwell adjourned the Council until the following week to prevent further argument. When the Governor left the room a few followed him, but more remained behind. Soon there was a great argument going on, and passersby stopped to listen. Blackwell returned to the door to order Lloyd to "forbeare such Lowd talking, telling him he must not suffer such doings, but would take a course to Supresse it, & shutt ye Doore." [35]

Little is known about what happened in Pennsylvania between the end of May and the end of December. Two sessions of the Council were held, in August and in November, while an attempt to meet in New Castle in September failed because only five members were present.[36]

In June Blackwell wrote to Penn, "I now only wayt for the hour of my deliverance, for, I see tis impossible to serve you in this place, and under your Condescentions to this people . . . It has been your great unhappinesse to be overtaken with mere glosing pretences of friendship, into an im-measurable credulity; Pardon the expression; and my playnesse of Speech, which aymes at nothing but your service." These people "have not the principles of government amongst them, nor will be informed . . . I pray God deliver you: for they threaten you." [37]

The meeting of the Council on August 28 decided nothing. A rumor that the Catholics, the French, and the Indians were preparing an attack on the colonists was discussed and dismissed as without foundation. The men also discussed the question of who was King of England. While they agreed that William and Mary were on the throne they did nothing about it for they had received no official notification.[38]

When the Council met November 1, the Governor read a letter from the Secretary of State at Whitehall, announcing that England and France were engaged in the conflict called King William's War in the colonies. The government was urged "with all possible diligence [to] take effectual care for the opposing & resisting any attempt of the ffrench upon his Ma'ties Province of Pensilvania." [39]

The Quakers refused to have anything to do with the raising of defenses in the colony. Simcock declared. "I see no danger but from the Bears & wolves. We are well, & in peace & quiet: Let us Keep ourselves so. I know not but a peaceable spirit, & that will do well. For my part I am against it clearly: and, Governor, if we refuse to do it, Thou wilt be Excused." Griffith

Jones, who had been out of sympathy with his fellow Quakers for some months in supporting Blackwell, expressed a more moderate Quaker view: "Every one that will may provide his armes. My opinion is that it be left to the discretion of the Governor to do what he shall judge necessary." Samuel Carpenter added, "The King of England Knows the judgemt of quakers in this case before Governor Penn had his patent. But if we must be forced to it, I suppose we shall rather choose to suffer than to do it, as we have done formerly."

At the meeting the following day, Blackwell urged the responsibility of the government under the letters patent to protect the king's property and the lives of the people. Simcock agreed to withdraw his extreme statement of the previous day and said, "We can neither offensively nor defensively take Armes. We would not be understood to tye others' hands." He added that if the Governor wanted to take defensive measures they could not prevent him. However, when Blackwell asked the Council to pass a resolution granting him the power to do as he saw fit, the Quakers balked. Carpenter said, "We can not vote One way or other to either of the Questions, We say nothing against it, in regard it is a matter of conscience to us. I had rather be ruined than violate my conscience in this case." Blackwell finally agreed to act as he saw fit without a vote of confidence, and to report his action to Penn and to the Secretary of State at Whitehall. Things would have been different in Pennsylvania if the Friends in the government had been as anxious to uphold all of the testimonies of Friends and all of the teachings of Christ as they were to stand upon the "peace testimony."

On January 1, 1690, Blackwell met the Council for the last time as Governor. "'Tis a good day. I have given & doe unfeignedly give God thanks for it, (wch are not vayne words,) for to say no worse I was very unequally Yoaked: and it being ye Day of my Redemption from that Groaning, (I say,) I shall not grieve any of you, Neither Shall I Deteyne you longer in this porch." [40] John Blackwell in delivering his farewell address, stated that he was resigning at his own request and that Penn

desired it be known that he had not been removed. He called
for God's blessing on the government, that the people might
enjoy a happy and prosperous future. He begged the people's
forgiveness for any wrong-doing he may have been guilty of,
and forgave them their sins against him. He thanked those who
had helped him, and promised strict obedience to the government as long as he should remain among the freemen of the
colony.

The government returned into the hands of the Council, and
Penn gave the Council a choice between two commissions. The
one accepted named the Council deputy governor as in 1684.
The other provided that the Council would nominate three
persons for the position of lieutenant governor, leaving the
choice of that single individual to William Penn.[41]

The attempt to reform Pennsylvania by sending in an outsider had failed. It had really failed in April, but was not officially recognized as a failure until Blackwell was replaced. Now
William Penn, heartened by the letters from his fellow Quakers, was going to give the "holy experiment" another try. He
acknowledged that the appointment of the Puritan Governor
had been a mistake, and hoped that the colonists, with the
memory of such a stern ruler fresh in their minds, would now
reform themselves.

Blackwell remained in the colony several months trying to
collect Penn's quitrents. He brooded over the letters from Penn
which had relieved him of his duties, and finally wrote an answer defending what he had done. "And if you had pleased to
have favoured me with some of the Grayns of allowance, many
ounces whereof you have cast in to their End of the ballance,
by saying, they act as men; I should have been incouraged to
plead on my own behalf, that I can do no otherwise." [42] He
added, defending his firmness, "Sr what could I conclude hence
(Especially when I was so assured by others) but that your
friends had made your constitution uneasy to you? and that
you would be glad to have a remedy? and it seems very rationall
you should desire to be eased here in. And is it now meet I
should be reproached as acting otherwise than as a Christian?"

. . . . "I am represented a skornfull & severe enemy to your profession [Quakers], I can have no more charity towards such
satanicall spirits." Blackwell was bitter, and with reason. He
had been thwarted by the Quakers in what he considered to be
his duty, and he was condemned for carrying out the instructions of his superior by Penn himself. About the same time,
Blackwell received a letter which said, "if you get their good
opinion, your ability will make you not only necessary to them,
but also chief amongst them." [43] What bitter laughter must
have greeted that phrase.

The Quakers had decisively defeated an attempt to bring
about their reform. They were unwilling that anyone exercise
control over their actions in the government, and they resented
any attempt to collect what they owed the Proprietor. At the
same time, surprisingly enough, they had enlisted the sympathy
of William Penn, and obtained from him the privilege of ruling
themselves once again. The year provided ample evidence that
the colonists knew how to secure what they desired. Neither
Blackwell nor Penn was any match for these amateur politicians
of Pennsylvania.

CHAPTER EIGHT

CONFLICT AND CHAOS

1690 TO 1693

FOR NEARLY three and one-half years, from the day Blackwell resigned until April, 1693, when Benjamin Fletcher arrived as royal governor, the people of Pennsylvania and Delaware ruled themselves. Penn could exert little control over the colonists, for he had been a friend and supporter of the recently deposed James II, and he was either in jail or in hiding from the crown during much of this time. The form of government changed several times, Delaware separated herself from Pennsylvania, and affairs were so chaotic that there are almost no public records for the period. While it is apparent that the colony was at a low ebb politically, Governor Fletcher's descriptions of Pennsylvania in 1693 indicate that there had been no gross disrespect for law and order. In addition, the Quaker community was embroiled in a religious controversy called the Keithian Schism.

Unaware of what the future held and swayed by tender letters from the Quakers which accompanied the one from Blackwell admitting failure, Penn sent word in the summer of 1689 that the government was to be placed again in the hands of the freemen of the colony. He wrote to the leading Quaker politicians: "I have thought fitt, upon my further Stop in these parts, to throw all into yr hands, that you may all see the confidence I have in you, & the desire I have to give you all possible contentment. I do earnestly press your constant attendance on the government & the dilligent persuit of peace and virtue, & god almighty Strengthen your hands in so good a work." He

asked them to make provision for his veto in all laws passed by
the General Assembly. He urged them to "avoide factions and
parties, whisperings & reportings, & all animosities." [1]

Penn was filled with a desire to see the spirit of the "holy
experiment" restored in the colony. He wished to regain the
close relationship between himself and the colonists which had
existed when he had been in Pennsylvania with them. He admitted that the appointment of Blackwell had been a mistake,
and he urged the colonial leaders to understand why he was
named, "Since no friend would undertake ye Gov'rs place, I
took one yt was not a stranger, yt he might be impartiall & more
reverenced, he is in England & Ireland of great repute, for
ability and integrity & virtue. I thought I did well, it was for
good, the Lord knows it, & no end of me my own." [2] Surely
Penn could not expect his colonists to accept the last phrase
unquestioningly.

Unable to come to the colony because he was under suspicion
in England, Penn attempted to inspire the political leaders with
high idealism. He admitted his own errors, pointed to the ones
which had been made by the colonists in the past, and called
on God for guidance for himself and for them. "The Lord
Keep us all in ye gentle minde, . . . it is a precious frame, a
noble frame, a conquering frame." [3]

Two observers believed that all the kindly and loving letters
in the world would not heal the breach between Penn and the
colonial leaders. One of these, Blackwell, frequently warned
the Proprietor that the people of Pennsylvania were self-cen-
tered and completely out of sympathy with him. He once wrote,
"I pray God deliver you: for they threaten you." The other
skeptic was Edward Blackfan, a friend of Penn who had settled
in the colony. He wrote to Phineas Pemberton, "I am sorry to
say that the Governor is not well pleased with Tho. Loyd &
others; yet hee will not have him trod under neither. . . . one
thing take for grant if the Governor Never Come to you (I
mean of his Communion) hee will never more bee well Assented with you (great men are not all ways wise) hee is so

poysoned with Markham and others writings: nothing but a verbal discourse Can mend the matter [.] I doupt thats too Late too doe it too." [4]

Blackfan very likely was right, especially about Penn's attitude towards Lloyd. The Proprietor had every reason to be critical of the colonial leader. He deliberately refused to accept Penn's choice of Blackwell as governor, and his actions were frequently arbitrary and sometimes childish. Penn's coolness to Lloyd is evident in his criticism of the decision to name Lloyd deputy governor in 1691, and his condemnation of Lloyd for allowing Royal Governor Fletcher to take over the colony in 1693, though Lloyd had no alternative.

There was also considerable reason for distrust between Penn and the colonists. Financial and political misunderstandings on both sides have been discussed. In addition, the colonists had two more reasons for becoming irritated with Penn. He constantly nagged them about inconsequential matters such as people living in caves along the banks of the Delaware River, as well as about more important things like his quitrents. He interlarded his querulous passages with spiritual admonitions and laments that the colonists were not living in the Truth. To a modern reader these portions sound pontifical and patronizing at times, and they may have sounded the same way to some of the colonial politicians. His absence placed him in the position of inquisitor, and that could not help but damage the spirit of close fellowship which was greatly desired.

In addition, the colonists still resented Penn's absence. When he was in the colony during the first two years he ran the government smoothly, he settled disputes over land, and he brought a spiritual quality to life which was appreciated by the people. The longer he was gone, the more the citizens deplored his absence and resented it. The fact that Penn promised each winter to come to them the following spring and then failed to keep his promise, did not help matters. Penn protested that he was doing a great deal of good in England, but the Pennsylvanians believed that he should abandon old responsibilities in England and come to live among them. This does not mean that William Penn was not a great man in many respects. However as an absentee proprietor and governor he left much to be desired. The breach between Penn and his people widened in the ten years following the resignation of Blackwell, for he did not return to Pennsylvania until December, 1699.

The first fifteen months of this period of self-rule were tranquil except for an episode in November, 1690. The Council under Thomas Lloyd served as the deputy governor of the colony, in addition to its usual duties. It met infrequently and Penn complained that it told him nothing, but there was little to tell. The General Assembly met and a number of laws were enacted.

The Council held several sessions in the first week of January, to familiarize itself with the responsibilities it was assuming. Most of one day was taken up with listening to letters from Penn to the Council, to Blackwell, and to Markham. The former Governor brought in all his correspondence from Penn, thinking that the instructions would prove helpful to the Council. One of the letters included an urgent request to settle estates for the widows Jeffs and Whitpain, in order to protect the reputation of the colony in the eyes of English businessmen. In the same letter Penn admonished Blackwell to end his dispute with Lloyd. "I intirely Know ye person both in his Weakness and Accomplishment, and would thee End ye Dispute between you two, upon my Single Request & Command, and that fformer inconveniences be Rather mended then punished." To Markham, the Proprietor had written a protest against those who would try to exclude all persons who held offices or performed services for William Penn from thy Council and Assembly. He resented the implication that his interest was opposed to the welfare of the country as a whole.[5] After these first meetings were held, this council did not meet again.

The newly elected Provincial Council met Monday, March 31, 1690, in legislative session with seventeen members present by the second day.[6] Thomas Lloyd was renamed president, a declaration of allegiance to the King and Queen and a statement promising fidelity and obedience to William Penn were drawn up and signed. Most of the time was taken up with reviewing past legislation and preparing new bills. A total of seventeen new bills were approved and promulgated for the inspection of the freemen and Assembly. Notice went out that the General Assembly would meet in New Castle, in response to a request from the councillors from the lower counties.

Secretary Markham presented a memorial on behalf of the Proprietor, asking that financial help be given William Penn. He asked that the £600 owed the Governor be spent to build him a house or to equip three manors for his children. Markham further expressed himself in favor of duties to collect money for the Governor's use. This petition was completely ignored and the Council went on to other matters. Markham was not in very good repute for he had supported Blackwell during his administration.

A letter from Jacob Leisler, head of the revolutionary government in New York, was read April 11. It requested the appointment of a delegate to join a discussion of ways to protect the colonies from the French in King William's War, which was beginning, but no action was taken on this matter. Several other minor issues were disposed of without much difficulty.

When the Council met April 24 in a non-legislative session, it spent considerable time discussing a petition from five freemen headed by Markham and Lacy Cock, requesting that the province and territories be organized to defend the people against possible attack by the French and the Indians. A lengthy answer was prepared by four members of the Council.[7] It made no mention of planning government defense of the colony, but did extend as a special privilege, to those who were interested, the right to provide for defense at their own expense and under rigorous requirements. For example, the Council required any militia which was established to yield full obedience to civil authority, and ordered "that all Cursing, Swearing, drunkness, debauchery, & pillaging (the Crying evills of Camps, Such Societies) be severely forbidden, & discountenanced, by you, as the bane & shame of a Christian Profession." When this answer was received the petitioners dropped the matter. However, when the Council was informed that Lacy Cock planned a journey up the Schuylkill River to find out how much ammunition the French families in that area had and to talk to the Indians, the body decided to send along Markham and Robert Turner. It also agreed to collect suitable gifts to give the Indians at a proposed council in the near future.[8] These incidents provide another example of the Quaker attitude toward the use of force.

When the Assembly convened in New Castle on Saturday, May 10, 1690, it chose Joseph Growdon as speaker.[9] The session, which ended the following Friday, was not only quiet and orderly but successful, for thirteen laws were enacted. The first one provided for the continuation of some laws for two years, and of the remainder for a single year. Another established a simple method for collecting debts under forty shillings. One law prohibited "hoggs, sows, shoats, piggs, or goats" from wandering in the streets of New Castle and Philadelphia.[10] The Assembly passed a resolution declaring that it was illegal for any person to prevent a member of the Assembly from attending the sessions unless he were accused of treason, murder, or some heinous or enormous crime. This action vindicated John White, who had been arrested during the previous session.

Only six members were present at a meeting of the Council held November 21, 1690, and William Clark presided instead of Thomas Lloyd.[11] All the business related to Delaware directly or indirectly. For example, it was decided that there should be two fairs held annually in New Castle and that no officer in any of the lower counties could be appointed without the consent of two of the three councillors from that county. However the main order of business was an expression of dissatisfaction with the provincial court, and a new panel of judges was appointed. The judges were commissioned on two separate documents. The same names were on each paper, but John Simcock of Pennsylvania appeared at the head of one list, while Clark from Sussex County was named first on the other. Two

men were sent to Lloyd to obtain the endorsement of the Great
Seal, but the keeper refused to seal the documents, and the
commissions were passed under the Lesser Seal.

If Lloyd was in town, why was he not at the meeting? The
answer came several days later when the Council met with
Lloyd in the chair, and a protest was drawn up against a
"rump" session of the Council on November 21. The actions of
that session were declared null and void. The appointment of
provincial judges came under special reproof, for some of
those named "under their present Circumstances are unqualli-
fyed for that Station." [12] Two men who had been present at the
earlier meeting, Griffith Jones and Clark, the presiding officer,
sat through this disavowal of their acts. This was the first round
of a struggle between Delaware and Pennsylvania which finally
ended with the separation of the lower counties from the upper
counties after Penn returned to England in 1701.

The second round of this contest began with the convening
of the newly elected Council in March, 1691, and ended with
Delaware temporarily separated from Pennsylvania. When communications from William Penn were opened, one contained
two commissions for deputy governor. Penn reported that he
had heard that the freemen wanted either a single person as
deputy governor again, or five commissioners of state. He announced his willingness to accept either change, though he expressed preference for the second type of executive.[13] When the
matter was discussed in the Council on March 30 and 31, it was
discovered that all the Quakers from Pennsylvania, plus John
Curtis and William Stockdale from Delaware, supported a single executive. The remaining men from Delaware preferred
commissioners of state. When the minority discovered that it
was going to be defeated it stopped attending the meetings and
refused to return.[14] On April 1 these men drew up a remonstrance against the majority decision. They resented the idea
of a single man making all appointments. They had already
discovered that the members of the Council from the province
imposed officers upon their counties against their will. They
disliked the idea of raising money to support a governor. Fur-

ther, they refused to allow the matter to be put to a vote, for they claimed that the Quaker members never allowed a vote unless they could win. The Delaware men said that they would withdraw and govern themselves rather than submit to a deputy governor.[15]

When the Council convened on the following day, Secretary Markham, who supported the people of Delaware, withdrew and took the minutes of the Council with him. Undeterred by this action, the Council then filled in the commission for a single deputy governor. Penn had asked for three nominations for the single position, and the Council named Thomas Lloyd, John Goodson, and Arthur Cook, but left no doubt about their preference for Lloyd. The bell of the town of Philadelphia was rung, and a proclamation was read "before a considerable appearance of friends & others to their Generall Satisfaction." [16] Thomas Lloyd was deputy governor of Pennsylvania, but apparently not of Delaware.

John Delavall and John Bristow were sent by the Council on April 3 to request the members from the Lower Counties to rejoin the body in order that bills could be promulgated and judges commissioned. When they refused, Lloyd named the judges himself, for it was nearly time for the courts to meet.[17]

Thomas Lloyd wrote a letter to the absent councillors on April 4, calling on them to reconsider. His first paragraph did nothing to heal the wound. "I am sorry for this breach, which you have made . . . you have withdrawn your attendance, without any just cause; lay aside obstinacy, wilful neglect and self interest, I cannot conceive what can support you, at last, but the absurd lenity of the Government. . . . Consider well the confusion, to which this your rashness may expose you, and many innocent inhabitants of the lower counties; and return unto your duty, and representative service here." At that point Lloyd softened, and wrote that the Council would "lovingly" receive them back. Further, he promised that the people of the lower counties would never be forced to pay any of his salary, unless they willingly offered to share that expense. He also assured the absent councillors that he would not disturb their local government. He added, "if you desire to be *apart*, let it be done with the same solemnity, whereby you were united to us." [18] The members of the Council from the counties in Delaware answered this appeal with a reiteration of their dissatisfaction with the new type of government and with their inferior position in the old one.[19]

With the division of the colony irretrievable for the time being, the Council decided to report to William Penn on the events of the past two weeks. In the letter written in November Penn had expressed fear of new troubles in the colony and had urged the Council to deal with "factious profane men of turbulent furtive spirite . . . O my ffriends put an end to these jarrs and heats, and let humility and wisdom over rule all passions and Interests." The Council had failed to heed those words of admonition. However, the letter had closed with the complaint that no one ever told him what was happening in the colony, and the Council now proceeded to answer that complaint. In this the members were not entirely motivated by a love for Penn, for they wished to describe what had happened before the other side had the opportunity to do so.

The Council explained that it had chosen to accept the commission for a single Deputy Governor, and had chosen Thomas Lloyd. The members assured Penn that this decision was not meant to show disrespect for the Proprietor, who had expressed a preference for the commissioners of state, but the step was taken because they believed that a single executive would be more successful in supressing "vice & disorders in publick houses." [20] The commissioners nominated must have included Markham, Robert Turner, and John Cann, for the Quaker councillors took great pains to point out the evils of these three men. "Captain Markham (wee on the spot doe see) is a chief upholder of those Clubbs wch are so much countenanced by his presence, even at unseasonable houres; & John Cann keeps a publick house in New Castle." They added that Cann had been accused of selling liquor without a license, and had been in trouble with the Lords of Trade. They said that Turner would have voted with the men from the lower counties and put such men in office, if the commissioners were in control. The fact that seven of the nine councillors from Delaware had withdrawn from their body was reported in an off-hand manner, either to deprecate the importance of the move, or because they believed it was a temporary situation. The Council then replied to attacks made by Penn on the Assembly in his November letter. The members expressed displeasure at the way Penn accepted rumors and lying words against the government, and spoke of "those Methods wch thou of late has been misled into."

When the General Assembly convened on Monday, May 11, 1691, no laws had been promulgated and there was not a legal quorum in either house. Since it could do nothing else, it decided to send a letter to Penn. The men protested that they were peace-loving people who "abominated and obhorred" what was happening in the colony. They made a point of denouncing the attempt to raise a militia in Delaware, and said that if such projects were started in Pennsylvania they would cause the Quakers to "Leave our half made plantations our unfinished houses and Return poor and with Griefe to our Native Country."

The letter insinuated that Penn was attempting to limit their rights as Englishmen. It said, "Certainly the King our Sovereigne Intends not that a Subject shall Exercise Greater power over his people in a foraign plantation than he Doth himself at home in Parliaments." This was nonsense, for the people of Pennsylvania had more freedom than colonists anywhere. Penn sometimes wrote sternly and threatened to use power against them, but he always gave them what they wanted. This letter closed by entreating Penn "to receive noe Misrepresentations of thy best & truest friends & the peoples Representatives," nor expose them to the scorn of "Such as never Contributed to the Improvement of the Province Either by their Industry or Manrs." [21] This letter is another example of the way the colonists played on the sympathies of Penn while complaining that he did not treat them with enough consideration.

Robert Turner, who was having trouble with the council

about his position as deputy register general, was an old friend of William Penn's, and wrote a letter which expressed some of the views of the party out of power.[22] Of Thomas Lloyd he wrote, "This new Governor by all meanes is labouring to Ingraishait him selfe unto ye people, by offeringe great ffavours naturalising, & grantting Corporations & markitts in land yt it might Redound ye honour to to [sic] him & slightinge to yee." He added that there were many who loved and admired Penn, but would not oppose those in power for fear of reprisals. Thus he insinuated that the followers of Lloyd did not love Penn. But he was honest enough to admit that few in the Lower Counties were interested in helping the Proprietor, for they were motivated by self-interest. Turner urged Penn to remove David Lloyd as attorney general, a position he had held since 1686, and name Patrick Robinson instead. Of Lloyd he said, he may "be turned as a nose of wax, but not towards yee." [23] Turner was not only a leader in the political group which opposed the Quaker leaders, but was active in the support of George Keith, who was interested in challenging the beliefs and leadership of the "weighty" Friends in the Yearly Meeting.

In answer to these various communications, Penn wrote calling on the Council to forget past differences and to join the people of Pennsylvania and the Territories together again. He asked them to "fforgive, and pass by your respective heats & objections & studdy peace & love." [24] Penn needed assistance in settling this serious cleavage in the colony. He called on George Whitehead to write to the Quakers, and this worthy stalwart of the Society wrote to Thomas Lloyd and Arthur Cook a few days later. He urged a just settlement, and said that news of the dispute "cause Truth to Suffer and bring You under a Contempt and will look ill here, and as if ye Lord in Displeasure did withhold Counsell from you." He warned that the separation endangered Penn's precarious hold on the three lower counties.[25]

The General Assembly met again September 10, determined to do something about the laws of the colony. A long bill was drawn up which reviewed the history of annexing the lower counties to Pennsylvania, and stated that the freemen "now sitting, in this present General Assembly, are the Provincial Council and Assembly of this province of *Pennsylvania*." By virtue of this fact, the legislators declared that the laws enacted at New Castle in 1690 were to continue in force until new ones were published.[26]

Some time during the winter of 1691–92, a truce was established between the two parties. Penn agreed to allow Lloyd to continue as Deputy Governor of Pennsylvania, and Markham was to assume the same office in the Lower Counties.[27] With separate executives who would have control over appointment of officials and other local matters, the two areas were satisfied, and agreed to elect councillors and assemblymen to serve in a common Council and General Assembly.

The joint Council met in legislative session April 4, 1692, to propose new legislation. The members agreed to one bill to re-enact old legislation, and passed three new bills. One of these was designed to regulate the provincial courts, another to regulate trade with the Indians, and the third to provide for the collection of taxes to support the government.[28] On April 6 a letter was written to Penn, describing the way in which the compromise was being worked out. This was signed by Lloyd, Markham, and all of the councillors.[29]

The Assembly convened on Tuesday, May 10, in Philadelphia. As a gesture to the representatives from Delaware, William Clark, long a councillor from Sussex County, was elected Speaker.[30] During the discussion of proposed legislation, petitions were received from freemen in Philadelphia and Chester against the proposed tax. This tax was one penny per pound of property, or less than one-half of one per cent, with a minimum of two shillings. The representatives were asked to keep "their Country free from Bondage and Slavery, and avoiding such Ill Methods, as may render Themselves and Posterity liable thereto." The session continued until May 18, but presumably no laws were enacted.

Turner saw some sign of progress in this session, and wrote Penn: "hapy was it for us in ye Province ye Lower Counties were Joyned in Som measure unto us, but better were it if wee were under one Government by 5 persons or by Presedent & Councill wch Last is taken for ye best & most Agreeinge way & I doe Advise yee to it." [31] No other reports at the time supported Turner in this estimate of public opinion. His long letter contained much gossip about persons he did not like. Turner complimented Penn for naming Robinson attorney general in the place of David Lloyd, and he added, "Thy bisonace in courts hath now some face wth it and hee proves true [.] before thou was a man troden down and art still too much."

Early in February, 1693, Penn, in great need for funds, wrote a pathetic letter to Friends in the colony asking that one hundred men be found who could each lend him one hundred pounds. He desired them to forego interest for four years, but to receive the usual interest thereafter. Penn promised to sail for America within three months after the £10,000 arrived for him, and assured the Pennsylvanians that thousands of persons would follow him to their shores and be of immeasurable benefit to the colony.[32] Governor Fletcher, who was soon after given control of the government, wrote that Friends did not respond. "Some meetings have been about it and It is reported that how much soever they appear his friends they stagger when he comes near their purses [.] those that are able want better security and those that are not (to excuse themselves) saying they would if they could." [33] Nothing affirmative was ever done about this request. There was little incentive to aid in bringing Penn to the colony as long as the government was in the hands of the crown. Money which could be transferred to England was exceedingly scarce, as is indicated in the two chapters on the economy of Pennsylvania. There were wealthy men in the colony, but they lacked ready money. Isaac Norris responded at the turn of the century that there were times when the colony was virtually bare of all gold and silver. In addition, the merchants of Philadelphia found it difficult to accumulate credit in London.

The scarcity of money and the fact that few taxes were collected by the government, were used twice during this period as excuses for rejecting demands for funds to aid in the defense of the English colonies against the French and Indians. On August 10, 1691, the Council received a request for money from Major Ingoldsby, of New York. Lloyd replied that there was no public treasury, "our Infancy hitherto not being trusted therewth." [34] In March, 1693, Lloyd replied to a similar request with the same answer. He added, "I might comically represent unto thee my personall difficulties & . . . request thy candid consideration & kindness toward me, w[ho]m a governmnt hath burthened but not relieved." [35]

It was only a matter of weeks before Governor Fletcher arrived to relieve Lloyd and to attempt to raise money in the colony for the defense of New York, for William Penn had lost the right to govern his colony and Pennsylvania reverted to the Crown.

A SCHISM IN THE SOCIETY OF FRIENDS

Pennsylvania not only suffered from political agitation in the years between the retirement of Blackwell and the arrival of Fletcher, it was also rocked by the Keithian Schism. This religious quarrel was another indication that the colony was deficient in the spiritual qualities necessary to make the "holy experiment" successful.

Religious controversy was not entirely new in the Society of Friends. When a religious group is founded on the principle of direct revelation of the will of God to each member, it is to be expected that men will occasionally have differences of opinion about the divine will. In the early years of the movement James Naylor and a few other persons temporarily wandered away from the main stream of the Society. Later, John Perrot was at the head of a small faction which differed with George Fox and the other leaders of the group. The Wilkinson-Story separation in the 1670s was a more serious threat to the existence of the Society, for it involved more persons and continued for a number of years. In the eyes of the world, however, these controversies within a small sect were of no importance.

But when the Keithian Schism broke open in Pennsylvania, the entire Quaker colony, including the lower counties, was immediately involved.[36] The "holy experiment," supposedly peopled with peace-loving Quakers, was exposed to the scorn of the world as a colony full of quarrelsome religious fanatics. The cleavage took on added significance because it soon became apparent that there were political implications in the struggle. The Christian Quakers, as the followers of George Keith called themselves, joined the faction in opposition to the Quaker politicians who dominated the colony. Thus, this breach in the Quaker Community produced serious consequences in Pennsylvania.

George Keith was a well-educated Scottish Quaker who first came to America as a surveyor in the Jerseys. He moved to Philadelphia in 1689, where he became master of the school which Friends were establishing. Instead of devoting all of his time to the development of the new school, he spent considerable time visiting meetings, preaching, and writing books and tracts.[37]

Friends were subjected to severe criticism in the American colonies and especially in New England, because they had no specific creed which could be examined by outsiders. They were accused of many heretical beliefs, of the denial of the divinity of Christ for example, and found these charges difficult to answer. In 1690 Keith drew up a paper which called for a creed and some rules and regulations for the Society, and presented it to the Yearly Meeting. The suggestion was flatly rejected with the statement that such a creed was most unQuakerly. The following year Keith produced a similar paper, but again met with no success. The Scotsman resented this refusal to adopt his proposals, and perhaps even suspected that some Friends did not subscribe to the fundamental tenets of Christianity which he had included in his document.

At the same time, Keith began to question the propriety of

Quakers holding office in the government. He decided that a true Friend who professed belief in non-resistance should not serve as a magistrate. This was the period of the separation of Delaware from Pennsylvania, and Keith deplored the fact that men who were the spiritual leaders of the Quakers were in the midst of the wrangling in the government.

Friends were sorely tried at this time, when a person named Babbitt and a crew of men stole a ship from the wharf at Philadelphia and then ravaged the shore. The Quakers were faced with a dilemma: if they used force to capture and punish this man they would violate their pacifist principles; if they left him alone, he would damage their property indefinitely. It was finally decided to commission an armed force to proceed against the pirates. However before the armed party could attack the sloop, a man named Peter Boss boarded the vessel, "without either Gun, Sword or Spear," and the men fled the ship. The armed company chased the offending men into the woods and wounded some, although no one was killed. Keith roundly condemned the officials for raising armed men, and a group gathered to support him in his steadfast attachment to Quaker principles.

At the time of Yearly Meeting in Philadelphia in September, 1691, George Keith was placed on the defensive, when William Stockdale accused him of preaching two Christs. Stockdale was a revered old Quaker minister and a member of the Council from New Castle County, which meant that his charge could not be lightly dismissed. Keith had frequently distinguished between the human Christ who lived on earth, and the divine Christ, a member of the Trinity, but he denied that he had preached two Christs. He demanded that the Yearly Meeting decide whether it was he or Stockdale who was guilty or heresy. Six sessions were held by the ministers of the Yearly Meeting to listen to statements from Keith and his witnesses, but no decision was reached about the orthodoxy of the beliefs of either man.

In January, 1692, at a session of Philadelphia Monthly Meeting, Thomas Fitzwater accused Keith of "Denying the Sufficiency of the Light within," which the latter vehemently denied. This quarrel continued through the winter. In the spring of 1692, Friends who had been meeting all winter in the Bank meetinghouse near the river, agreed that as usual with the arrival of better weather they would hold First Day meetings for worship at the Center meetinghouse, on what is now City Hall Square. Keith and his followers refused to go with the others to the meetinghouse in the country, and continued to meet near the river. The doors of the Bank meetinghouse were locked against them. The so-called Christian Quakers seldom met with the main body after this time.

Thomas Wilson and James Dickenson arrived in the colony near the end of April, 1692. They were public Friends from England who were visiting among the Quakers in the New World, and they tried to bring about a peaceful reconciliation. But they failed completely, and perhaps even widened the breach.

Throughout the summer months the speakers for the two factions visited Friends meetings and called for support of one side or the other. When the Yearly Meeting met in Burlington in September, 1692, Keith held his own session in the courthouse. There was some communication between the two groups, and Keith was disowned by the old organization. Approximately seventy persons, or one-fourth of those in attendance at the meetings, joined Keith in the new organization.

In the meantime, the Christian Quakers had drawn up twelve questions which they planned to present to the main body of Friends. The first eight of them dealt with doctrinal matters, but the last four implied criticism of the Quakers who participated in the government. Some questioned the share Friends had taken in the Babbitt affair, and the last question asked, "Whether there is any Example and Precedent for it in the Scripture, or in all Christendom, that Ministers should Enforce the Worldly Government as they do here?"

William Bradford, the lone printer in the colony and a supporter of Keith, printed this document without the consent of the government, and John McComb, a tailor and victualer, distributed the copies. The Quaker magistrates responded to this attack on their authority by arresting Bradford and McComb on the charge of printing unlicensed books without the name of the place or the printer provided thereon. Bradford saw his press and type confiscated by the magistrates, and McComb lost his license to operate a shop. Keith protested the decision in the trials of his two supporters, and deplored the cruel treatment meted out to Bradford and McComb. What had started as a difference of opinion about a printed declaration of faith had grown into conflicting charges of theological soundness and heretical beliefs, and had eventually developed into a full-scale political quarrel. By the time the twelve questions were prepared, it was suspected by the political leaders that theological terminology was being used to camouflage an attack on the government of the colony.

George Keith, however, wanted to continue the fiction that this was only a religious quarrel, and carefully stated, "We did not, nor do not intend anything against the present Government, or Magistracy, but own them in Commission to be Magistrates, and account it our Duty to obey them, either actively or passively." Taking refuge in his protestation that nothing he said was intended to attack the government, Keith reviled Thomas Lloyd, the Deputy Governor, "calling him Impudent Man, telling him he was not fit to be a Governor, and that his Name would stink." Furthermore, he called members of the Council "Impudent Rascals," and made slighting remarks about the magistrates.

The Quaker political leaders, enraged by this disrespect for authority, issued a proclamation against the schismatic leader on August 25, 1692. This document denied some of the charges made by Keith and demanded that he cease to issue pamphlets and make speeches "that have a tendancy to Sedition, and Disturbance of the Peace, as also to the Subversion of the Present Government." The magistrates were careful to point out that this proclamation was aimed at the suppression of Keith's civil transgressions, and had nothing to do with religious differences between themselves and the Scotsman.[38]

The Keithians failed to subside into complete silence, and on October 5, 1692, indictments were handed down by the Grand Jury against several of the leaders. Peter Boss was indicted for making scandalous, reproachful, and malicious expressions against Samuel Jennings. Keith and Thomas Budd were indicted as the authors of a book which contained accusations against Jennings, who was a justice of the peace. Keith was also indicted for "Defaming Samll Richardson he being a magistrate of this County, in Bidding him go home to his Whores And calling him heinious old man said he took up maids Petticoats [,] Exposing his reputation before some hundreds of People Contrary to that Law in that Case made & Provided." [39]

The charges and countercharges were apparently allowed to get out of hand, and the trials were a credit to no one. The three men were found guilty. Boss was fined six pounds, and the other two were fined five pounds each. These fines were never paid. Requests by Keith and Budd for an appeal to the provincial court or to the Council were denied.

After all this Keith occasionally attended the regular Friends meeting for worship at the Bank meetinghouse, but was made unwelcome in the gallery assigned to the Friends in the Ministry. Whereupon his followers built another gallery at the opposite end of the meetinghouse. With speakers addressing the assemblage from both galleries simultaneously, the situation became intolerable. When some men destroyed the new gallery with axes, Keithians demolished the old one as well.

The following year, when Penn lost his province to the Crown and Fletcher arrived as royal governor, two members of the new Council appointed by Fletcher, Robert Turner, a Keithian, and Patrick Robinson, obtained a reversal of the old charges against Bradford, Keith, Budd, and the rest. Keith determined however, to go to England to defend himself, and he left Philadelphia late in 1693. He was unsuccessful there, and later became an Anglican. He returned to America as a representative of the Society for the Propagation of the Gospel. His Christian Quakers did not last very many years without him. Many confessed their errors and returned to the main body of Friends, while others joined the Baptists or the Anglicans who were beginning to organize at the time.

Daniel Leeds, who edited an almanac, was a follower of Keith and continued a running attack on the Friends of Philadelphia. Bradford, who fled to New York after his troubles in the Quaker city, was his printer. A new edition of the almanac appeared in 1700 while Penn was in the colony and the Governor wrote to Lord Bellomont, Governor of New York, to remonstrate against it. "I hear ye printer has printed an Almanack for one Danll Leeds a Quondam Quaker with Reflections upon both o[u]r Governmt & p[er]swasion & am sure Ld Bellumont will not Indure Such Ill Manners & Unneighbourlyness to Pass upon pswasions & Governmt undr his [government]." [40] The attacks of the Christian Quakers on their old comrades reached the depths in 1701, when Leeds published a tract entitled, *News of a Strumpet Co-habiting in the Wilderness or, A brief Abstract of the Spiritual & Carnal Whoredoms & Adulteries of the Quakers in America.*[41] In this scurrilous document Leeds accused most of the religious and political leaders of crimes and misdemeanors, with great emphasis on sex offenses. As has been suggested, by this date the Christian Quaker movement was nearly dead. The end of the religious separation did not erase the scars which had been left upon the "holy experiment" by this religious conflict.

CHAPTER NINE

ROYAL INTERLUDE

1693 TO 1695

LATE IN 1688, James II was threatened by William of Orange and his Protestant subjects and was forced to flee to France. Most of those who had surrounded him were naturally considered his partisans. To escape disgrace or death some bowed before the new monarchs, William and Mary, and maintained their positions, but more of them fled the country with James. William Penn continued to go to Whitehall daily as if nothing had happened.[1] His was not a comfortable situation, but he saw it through to a successful conclusion.

Penn had been very close to the exiled King, and had exerted considerable influence over him for good. A nobleman reported in 1687. "Quaker Penn attends the King very close and preached at the Bath in the Tennis Court but the report of his being made one of the King's Privy Council is false, though the King consults him in all matters of moment."[2] Penn himself wrote, "The Lord has given me a good Entrance and Interest with the King, tho not so much as is said."[3] He was seized by the government December 10, 1688. After he issued a statement professing loyalty to the Protestant faith and the new government, although freely admitting his admiration for James II, he was released on bail. Penn was taken twice more in the two years which followed, and acquitted on each occasion.

In February, 1691, fresh accusations were made against Penn and despairing of ever freeing himself from suspicion despite his three acquittals, he went into hiding. He remained in England, perhaps under the surveillance of the government, and did a great deal of writing. By the time he reappeared in public in November, 1693, Pennsylvania had been seized by the crown. The crown's prime reason for entering William Penn's colony in 1693 was to incorporate Pennsylvania into the defense installations of the English government. William III was engaged in war with France, and believed that it was dangerous to leave an unprotected colony in the middle of the Atlantic seaboard where the French could easily gain a base for operations in both directions. Because of Penn's friendship for James II, who was allied with Louis XIV, there were rumors that Pennsylvania held treasonable allegiance to the deposed ruler, and was pro-French.

While William III expressed admiration for William Penn, he had no sympathy for the Quaker belief in pacifism. He called it a "doctrine without sanction of any law in statute or in morals, human or divine. Those who professed it pretended to teach more that God had taught in His own Word. . . . They pretended to exceed Christ in holiness." [4]

The return of the government to the Quakers in 1690, after Blackwell, roughly coincided with the beginning of Penn's precarious situation in England. While he was unable to exercise proper control over the colony political chaos and internal disorders arose. These were magnified by unfriendly spectators who reported the conditions to the Lords of Trade. Thus it is seen that the English government had three reasons for seizing Pennsylvania: the lack of preparations for defense against the French, internal disorders in Pennsylvania, and Penn's inability to cope with either of these problems because he was hiding from the Crown. During 1692 there had been considerable talk about entering the Quaker province. On October 21, 1692, Benjamin Fletcher, who had recently gone to New York as the new royal governor, was also made royal governor of Pennsylvania and the Lower Counties.

William Penn faced an impossible task in attempting to prevent the government from seizing his colony, but he made a valiant effort. Rather than attack the Crown directly, he determined to thwart the intent of the government by persuading

Fletcher to refuse to assume executive authority in Pennsylvania. He also wrote to his colonists, urging them to resist the invasion of royal officials and to lodge protests in London against the procedure. He tried to both intimidate Governor Fletcher and to flatter him. "I give thee this caution—that I am an Englishman, and that country and the Government of it inseparably my property," was his first approach, as he warned him to stay out of Pennsylvania and avoid possible legal action. He added, "Thou has formerly discoursed largely in favour of free and property principles; I expect proof of it in my own case." [5]

Penn did not incriminate himself by writing letters to his subordinates in Pennsylvania advocating revolt. Instead, he wrote to individuals who were expected to carry the message to Thomas Lloyd. One letter was addressed to Turner and warned: "A Day of Temptation is coming over you, as a just Exercise from the Lord for your Animositys & divisions, in which blessed are they that are clear & innocent." [6] Penn called on the colonists to stand firm in defense of the patent, and if they were unable to prevent Fletcher from entering the government, they were to draw up a petition to present to the Lords of Trade. He promised that Friends in England would appear to support the petition. He added, "if that doesn't do—Westminster Hall—And if that fail—The House of Lords will do us right."

In another letter he gave explicit directions for a campaign against the royal commission. To answer the charges that a defenseless Pennsylvania left neighboring provinces open to attack, he urged them to "Set forth the falsehood of it by your singular situation by land and sea, your hazards, charges, labours—that the Government was your motive more than land, and that you were a people who could have lived at home, and went there not upon motives of guilt or poverty." [7] Unfortunately, the inhabitants paid little attention to Penn's suggestions. They accepted Fletcher's entrance in a docile manner, and only began to express concern when he attempted to disallow all the laws and the guarantees of the Charter of Liberties.

Governor Benjamin Fletcher wrote to Thomas Lloyd on April 19, 1693, to inform him that he had received a commission from the King and Queen for the government of Pennsylvania and the Territories. He announced that he would leave New York Monday, April 24, and hoped to meet the Council and principal freeholders on arrival.[8] He arrived in a festive Philadelphia, just before noon, April 26, was met by Sheriff John White, and escorted to the market place where their Majesties Letters Patent were publicly read.[9]

The arrival of a royal governor did not change the government of Pennsylvania as much as one might think. The most important innovation was that the Council was appointed by Fletcher instead of elected by the people. This loss of privilege was somewhat balanced by the fact that the Assembly obtained the long sought right to initiate legislation. The laws were to be transmitted to England within three months after passage, where they could be declared null and void. All who held positions in the government were to take an oath of allegiance to the Crown. In other respects, the government remained much as it had been in former times.

Fletcher's first public act was to choose councillors who would be loyal and of assistance to him. He had been ordered to name no more than twelve persons to his advisory body, and three would be a quorum. He offered the first place in the Council to Thomas Lloyd, "knowing that he would not accept it." [10] The Governor then named nine other men, and during the last months he was in control of the colony added three more.[11] All these men had been active in previous years. Four were Quakers, although at least some of these were Keithians and opposed to Thomas Lloyd and the main body of Friends. Markham was named lieutenant governor on Tuesday, April 27. Since Fletcher remained in Pennsylvania only a few weeks during the twenty-three months that he was governor, Markham and the remaining eight original councillors were responsible for the operation of the government during this period. Although Markham was related to William Penn and had served him in a number of ways, Fletcher did not feel that these connections disqualified him for office. He had served in the Royal Navy and had held positions of responsibility before Penn sent him to the new colony in 1681. He continued to enjoy the trust of the Proprietor, who named him as his deputy in 1695 when the crown returned the colony to Penn.

Fletcher had been directed to re-establish law and order in Pennsylvania, and to force the colony to share in the common defense effort. Aside from reorganizing the colonial government at the top level little was done internally to make Pennsylvania a royal colony. There is no evidence that Fletcher found any great disorder among the people in the commonwealth. The Keithian members of his Council persuaded him to reverse the judgements against Keith, Budd, and Bradford, but that can scarcely be used as evidence of "great Neglects and miscarriages . . . Disorder & confusion," as Fletcher's commission described the situation.[12] The Governor appointed a number of justices of the peace and left the responsibility for maintaining law and order in their hands.

There is no indication that Fletcher had any success in raising a militia in Pennsylvania, although there was apparently some military activity in Delaware. He held a conference with the Indians to make certain that the Pennsylvania frontier would be free from attack. During the meetings one Indian spokesman said, "Wee are now glad to know our Governor: when the Quakers governed sometimes one man & sometimes another pretended to be Governor," and added that the Quakers refused to help the Indians against the French and their Indian allies. Fletcher promised more assistance in the future.[13]

It soon became apparent that Fletcher had come to Pennsylvania to obtain funds for the defense of New York and was not particularly interested in anything else. Once he had obtained money in 1693, he returned to the northern province. He appeared in Pennsylvania only once more, when he came to ask for more financial assistance the following year.

The only way to secure funds was by legislative appropriation, and Fletcher called for the election of an Assembly, to meet May 15. He ordered the freemen in both Philadelphia and New Castle counties to choose four representatives, while the citizens of each of the other four counties were to have three Assemblymen represent them, making a total of twenty. Ten days before the Assembly was to convene, a letter to Governor Fletcher from the members of the old Council of Pennsylvania was read in the Council. It protested the actions of Fletcher and requested "that no other measures be taken, for electing, or convening, our legislative power, than our recited laws and constitutions of this government prescribe." [14] The Council advised Fletcher to ignore the communication, especially since the men who wrote it failed to recognize him as Governor of Pennsylvania.

Friends held a testimony against taking oaths, which according to Fletcher's instructions would have excluded them from the government. However the Governor allowed them to subscribe to a declaration of fidelity, "Provided this be entered in the Journalls of your house as an act of grace from their majesties, and not taken as a president." [15] Fourteen members of the Assembly subscribed and the other six took the oath. When Fletcher appointed justices of the peace he found that most of the important men in the colony refused the positions because they would be forced to administer oaths as a part of their duties.[16]

Joseph Growdon was chosen speaker and presented to Governor Fletcher, where he protested his unworthiness according to custom, and the Governor graciously replied, "if I had been to choose a Speaker from amongst ye representatives returned for this occasion, I had pitched upon you as best quallified." [17] Fletcher added that he wanted the Assembly to appoint a clerk to keep the minutes of their sessions and to bring them to the Governor for his perusal at the end of each day.

He then launched forth on the subject which interested him most. He told the General Assembly it had been called to lay a tax on the people and to aid New York financially in defending the colonies against the French and the Indians, as requested in a letter from Queen Mary. Knowing that many of the men had religious scruples against giving money to conduct a war, he promised that the money they appropriated would be converted to nonbelligerant uses, "& shall not be dipt in blood." To further weaken their resolves he reminded them that they built walls around their property, and used locks, "Mastiff doggs" and other protections against thieves and robbers. He said that the government used "forts, garrisons & Souldiers," in exactly the same way to protect crown property, and that this protection was extended to Quaker pacifists as well as to "the rest of their subjects."

Fletcher added that the legislators would be permitted to propose the confirmation of former laws or to write new ones conformable to the laws of England.

The Assembly spent the next several days trying to decide whether Fletcher as a royal governor had the same powers as an executive serving under William Penn's Charter of Liberties. The members didn't know whether his powers should be recognized by the Assembly if they were different. Fletcher's answer to these two questions was precise: "The Constitution of their Majesties Government, and that of Mr. *Penn's,* are in direct Opposition one to the other: If you will be tenacious in sticking for this, it is a plain Demonstration, use what Words you please, that indeed you decline the other." The Assembly, with some hesitation, agreed, "that wee may saflie act in Legislaon in Conjunction with the present Gor, according to the king's Letters patents," but added a clause in which it attempted to retain some of the privileges held under the former constitution.

At the same time, the Assembly was working with the old laws, attempting to draw up a list of those which were not repugnant to the laws of England. Fletcher began to get impatient for he had originally planned to finish affairs in Pennsylvania in a few days and return to New York where there were pressing matters awaiting him, especially on the frontier. Though he received a copy of the minutes of the Assembly each evening, he still wondered what the Assembly was doing. On May 23 he called Growdon before him and demanded to be told why the Assembly had produced nothing in nine days (it was the seventh working day). The speaker replied that the Assembly was not accustomed to preparing bills for the Council had that duty formerly, but he promised to bring in something very soon.

On May 24, a bill was presented for the Governor's approval which contained the titles of more than 100 of the former laws. Fletcher, was incensed. How could he approve of laws when only the titles had been presented to him; he demanded to see the laws. Consternation struck the assemblymen. There was no copy of the laws on the master rolls, but someone said that Markham had a book of laws "which [we] have much regard to." Late in the afternoon Edward Blake, Samuel Carpenter, David Lloyd, and John White, as a committee from the Assembly brought a book to the Governor and told him it contained a true copy of the laws. Fletcher was skeptical and said, "these scripts of paper are handed about from one to another, and everie one may alter them att pleasure." A joint committee was appointed by the two houses, which decided which list of laws was true and which laws should be reenacted by the present General Assembly.

The Assembly forwarded thirteen bills to the Council on May 30, and by the end of the morning session the following day thirty-one bills were in the hands of the Council. This body approved twenty without amendment, approved five with amendment, and laid six aside. That afternoon the men who had represented the Assembly several days earlier, Blake, Carpenter, Lloyd, and White, reported that the supply bill had been read twice in the Assembly and asked about the status of the bills sent to the Council. Fletcher replied that he would not read the supply bill until it had been passed three times and signed by the speaker. White repeated the query and added that such procedure was customary in the House of Commons. Fletcher repeated his statement that he would not look at the money bill until it had been passed. David Lloyd then threw down the gauntlet: "To be plain with the Governor, here is the Monie bill, and the house will not pass it untill they know what is become of the other bills that are sent up."

Fletcher exploded at this effrontery. He said: "Gentl., You have not dealt fairlie by me; you have no candor; you have sitt these fifteen days & nothing done: . . . I came not here to make bargains nor expose the king's honour, I will never grant anie such for all the monie in your Countrie . . . in short, you must expect to be annexed to New yorke or Maryland."

When the four assemblymen took this message back to their colleagues a long debate followed, while in the Council there was serious talk of dissolving the Assembly. It was finally decided to wait until eight o'clock the next morning before taking such drastic action. Both houses were in session by 5 a.m. the next morning, and shortly after seven the Assembly sent over the supply bill. A joint session followed, during which the Assembly acquiesced to all the amendments suggested by the Council except for one which would have provided a salary for the councillors as well as for the members of the lower house. The Governor then dissolved the Assembly.

It is apparent from the *Charter and Laws of Pennsylvania* that Governor Fletcher confirmed eighty-six of the old laws and that thirty new ones were written.[18] Most of the new laws were in reality old ones reworded. Although the Assembly passed the money bill last, Fletcher placed it at the top of the list to make a better impression in England. One of the bills established a post office in Philadelphia and listed rates for mail. Fletcher had been indignant because laws in the past had not been passed under the Great Seal, but now he could not decide how to endorse these new laws. He did not want to use William Penn's seal and could not use the New York seal. He wrote to the secretary of the Lords of Trade, William Blathwayt, asking him what he should do.[19]

The money bill proved a disappointment. It provided for the collection of a one penny per pound tax on all real and personal property, and a six shilling tax on those not rated according to property. The very poor were exempted, as was William Penn and his "late deputies in government," presumably Thomas Lloyd and Markham. The tax was expected to bring in about £760, half of which was to go to Fletcher and the other half to the crown. The Governor reported to the

Council of New York that he "Could prevail little with the people and Government of Pennsylvania," and they had given him but a "trifling" amount of money, a mere "introduction of future supply." [20]

Fletcher made other comments about Pennsylvania and its people. To Blathwayt he wrote:

I have spent some weeks there but never yett found so much self conceite [;] they will rather dye than resist with Carnall weapons, nay they would perswade me their Province was in no danger of being lost from the Crown, tho they have neither Armes or Amunition, nor would they suffer those few to be traind who were free for it, their minutes of Council and Assembly which are now Transcribing for you, will appear a farce. . . . they have no regard for the Queen's Letter, so that instead of assistance it is like to prove a trouble.[21]

To the Earl of Nottingham, Fletcher wrote, "Some Quakers who have acted in the Government by Mr. Penn's commission and are very fond of lording it over their brethren are now sending their delegates to court" to get Penn restored or to be transferred to the supervision of the government in Maryland. On a more optimistic note, Fletcher concluded, "I received an address from the peaceable and loyal inhabitants of Phila. County and I hear that the like are preparing in other counties. This will show you that those who will trouble you are but a faction." [22]

The only permanent result of this General Assembly was the increase of power in the lower house. The Assembly had been vaguely flailing in the air for a decade, but there had been no permanent visible advancement of power until 1693. The lower house slowly advanced from the position it held this year until it became an important organ of government in 1701. The royal order to initiate legislation in the Assembly was largely responsible for its metamorphosis from a group which gave its assent or dissent into a powerful branch of the legislature. The growing independence of the body can be further illustrated by a protest signed by one-half of the members, which defended the right of the freemen to learn the fate of other proposed legislation before passing a money bill. The statement ended with these words: *"the Assent of such of us as were for sending*

up the Bill for the Supply this Morning, was merely in Con-
sideration of the Governor's speedy Departure; but that it should
not be drawn into Example or Precedent for the future."

In contrast, the Council was much weaker under royal rule
than it had been under Penn. The members knew that if they
disagreed with Fletcher they could be removed, which made
the body more timid and weak than before. In addition, the
Council was deprived of financial support because of the jealousy of the lower house. After the Governor returned to New
York, Markham and the Council met weekly. In these sessions
the same topics were raised which had been discussed in former
years, and as before there were weeks when too few councillors
attended and business was postponed.

William Penn, back in England, was becoming increasingly
anxious about what was happening in the colony, for apparently
no one had written to him. He was still in hiding from the
Crown, his funds were cut off, and now with his colony taken
from him it is no wonder that the letter he wrote in September,
1693, was full of complaints and reproaches. He was bitter
towards Thomas Lloyd for not resisting the coming of Fletcher.
"I perceive T.LL. took pett at my silence and so left things
drive to their present period." Penn accused Lloyd of deliberately forcing the separation of Delaware from Pennsylvania to
get the office of deputy governor, and added, "he might have
stood upon his commission, Grounded upon a Legal and Solemn Patent, He needed no other argmt" The Proprietor suggested that Lloyd's enemies were responsible for the occupa-
tion of Pennsylvania by the crown, "because I would not
remove him, & they had rather I were outed than not carry
their point agst him, & yet he, I hear, thinks I should have done
more for him." [23]

Thomas Lloyd deeply resented the accusations made against
him by Penn, and wrote a reply which must have made Penn
halt and consider. He wrote,

I loved & served thee faithfully, . . . yet thou hast endeavoured to expose
me, & [give] Friends wrong Apprehensions of me: I am not the Man thou
takest me to be; Our God doth . . . justify me, in most of the particulars

wherein thou wouldest blemish me: Thou understandest me not; for if thou didst, thou wouldest not thus treat me: Thy own Credulity to ill-effected Persons hath long misled thee; . . . their Misrepresentations to thee of thy near Friends & their Insincerity towards thee, will be apparent to thee tho late; The Lord preserve thee from thy false Friends, as well as from thy open Adversaries . . . tho thou has changed, yet I continue thy assured Well Wisher.[24]

Unknown to Lloyd, several of his friends wrote a letter to Penn in his defense while he was out of town. They protested that Lloyd "faithfully discharged his Duty to thee & the Province, to the satisfaction of Friends here," and were much disturbed that Penn should "have such hard Thoughts of him, who asserted thy Right: & yet write so favorably of them, who, thou sayest, acted contrary to thy express orders." These men denied that Lloyd forced the split between Pennsylvania and Delaware in order to be Deputy Governor, and said that he took the office, "but by the Importunity of his Friends." They added that Lloyd had wasted his estate in the service of Penn, "& has thy hard Thoughts besides." [25]

Thomas Lloyd died within the year. He was stricken with a malignant fever September 5, 1694, and died five days later. He had been an exceedingly able partisan, a dogged defender of what he thought was right, and one of the great men of colonial Pennsylvania. James Dickinson wrote of him: "His care was to keep to the experience of the power of Truth in his Gift . . . wch made him the more comely in the Eyes of all those who loved the Truth for the Truths sake." [26] Haverford Monthly Meeting prepared a memorial about him which recommended him highly as a minister in the Society of Friends. It said in part:

His sound and effectual ministry, his godly conversation, meek and lamb-like spirit, great patience, temperance, humility, and slowness to wrath; his love to the brethren, his godly care in the church of Christ, that all things might be kept sweet, savoury and in good order; his helping hand to the weak, and gentle admonitions, we are fully satisfied have a seal and witness in the hearts of all faithful friends who knew him . . . We may in truth say, he sought not himself, nor the riches of this world, but his eye was to that which is everlasting, . . . He reviled not again, nor took any advantage, but loved his enemies, and prayed for them that despitefully abused him. His love to the Lord, his truth and people was sincere to the last.[27]

Those who have followed his political career must take exception to some of the kind things said about him, but he was sorely missed in Pennsylvania in the years which followed.

Penn did not know that Lloyd was nearing his death. If he had he might have written in a more kindly manner. All Penn knew was that he had lost his colony and seemingly no one cared. He grasped at any straw which would help him understand why things did not go smoothly and profitably for him. In attempting to remain neutral in the quarrels which sometimes shook the colony, he appeared, in the eyes of each side to favor the other. The same group of men who wrote Penn in defense of Lloyd added that all of Penn's real friends in Pennsylvania wished that he would be more considerate of them, and stop turning to their enemies, "which hath been a matter of Grief, & Exercise to those that love thee well." For William Penn it was a trying time, and the "holy experiment" must have been nearly forgotten.

Late in January, 1694, Governor Fletcher wrote to Markham and the Council about holding another General Assembly in the spring, and added, "I study nothing more than your prosperity[. I] . . . depend much upon your Council and advice which shall be always very acceptable." [28] The Council set April 10 as the date, and issued writs for the election of assemblymen.

Fletcher was called to Albany at that time and the session had to be postponed. However enough men had gathered to form a quorum and the Assembly organized, with David Lloyd elected speaker by the twelve men in attendance. Markham tried to send the legislators home at once, but Lloyd was granted permission to hear some petitions. He then asked to have the session extended to a second day, and Markham reluctantly agreed to a short meeting. When the Assembly and Council met on the following day, Lloyd announced that the Assembly had something for the Council to hear. Markham answered that he had positive orders from Fletcher to adjourn the General Assembly. Lloyd demanded that they be shown the orders but Markham refused.

Lloyd then disagreed with Markham over the date of May 1 for the adjourned session, and said that the majority of the members of the Assembly would like to attend the yearly meeting of Friends at Salem, West Jersey, which began April 27. By the time that May 22 had been agreed on the clerk of the Assembly finished copying the paper which the Assembly had been preparing, and it was read. Markham refused to discuss it, and told Lloyd to take the paper back and introduce it when Governor Fletcher was present. Lloyd answered that although he had orders to bring in the paper, he had none to take it back with him. At this, Markham abruptly adjourned the session. Lloyd, determined to have the last word, replied, "Wee thank the Leiutenant Governor." [29]

The General Assembly convened on May 22, 1694. Governor Fletcher, who addressed the members the next day, spent some time describing the melancholy sight of four score deserted farms, abandoned because neighboring colonies would not help New York in the defense of her frontier. He then called on the legislators to appropriate more funds for the war. "I hope you will not refuse to feed the Hungrie and Cloath the Naked. My meaning is to supply those Indian nations which such necessaries as may influence them to a Continouance of their friendship to those provinces." [30] In addition, Fletcher promised to redress any grievances the Assembly had. Tuesday, May 29, the Governor delivered a second speech asking for money for the hungry and naked Indians.

While the Assembly was preparing grievances and discussing the possibility of raising more money, a report was brought in of the collection of the tax for the previous year. According to the assessment the six counties owed nearly £761. Slightly more than £400 of that amount had been paid. New Castle and Bucks counties had paid nothing, and Sussex county had paid slightly less than one-half. Chester had paid approximately ninety per cent, and Philadelphia and Kent counties had paid more than seventy-five per cent.

When the Assembly did agree on a supply bill the tax was set at the same rate as in 1693, but the first £400 was appropriated to Thomas Lloyd and William Markham, one-half to each, for their past services as deputy governor. The remainder was for the use of their Majesties for the Indians or for whatever was desired. The bill also provided for a new tax collector in place of the one named by Fletcher.

The Governor was greatly upset by this proposed bill, and denied that the Assembly had a right to raise money for any purpose except to give it to the Crown. The Assembly drew up a remonstrance in which it claimed the right to appropriate money as it saw fit. The following day a second communication was sent to Fletcher, in which the Assembly expressed resentment that its gift of the previous year had not been properly appreciated, and complained that the Indians had not been told that the money had come from Pennsylvania.

By this time Fletcher was furious. He told the men on June 9, "you have now satt nineteen dayes without the Least Consideraon of their Ma[jes]ties Service in the Securitie of the province; you have applied the first part of yor time in the searching for grievances, which all appear to be the effects of yor owne weaknes . . . Now Gentl. finding no prospect of yor Inclinaons for their Maties service or your own saftie, I think fitt to dissolve this present assemblie, and you are hereby dissolved." [31] On May 21, the day before the General Assembly convened, the Council had recorded that in its opinion no money would be granted during the session. It proved to be an accurate prophecy.

Despite the sharp difference of opinion in regard to the money bill, six other laws were enacted during the session. Three of them were restatements of old laws, while the remainder related to trade and commerce. In addition, Fletcher and the Council devoted some time to regulating the ferrying service across the Schuylkill. Penn had granted a monopoly of that trade to Philip England who had paid a fee, but two other men were running ferries in competition. In recognition of Penn's proprietary right to grant franchises, Governor Fletcher agreed to support Philip England in maintaining his monopoly.[32]

The dissolution of the General Assembly virtually marked the end of the royal government in Pennsylvania. Fletcher continued to serve as Governor until the end of March, 1695, but he was no longer interested in the province and little of importance took place. Markham and his Council met but accomplished very little.

Even before the General Assembly met in 1694, Penn had petitioned the Crown for the return of his government. That July the Attorney General, reported that while Penn's right to govern Pennsylvania was unquestioned he might temporarily forfeit his right to the crown in times of emergency, as for example, if he failed to provide for the defense and protection of his province in time of war and imminent danger. He added that when the emergency no longer existed, "the Right of Governmt doth belong to the Peticonr [Penn]" [33]

With this decision to support him, Penn began a campaign to regain his government. He promised to return to Pennsylvania in the near future and to transmit to the Council and Assembly all orders given to him by the crown. He promised "they will at all times dutifully Comply with and Yeild Obedience thereunto." To strengthen his assertion Penn submitted a statement drawn up by the members of the Pennsylvania Assembly the previous year, which humbly expressed their gratitude for the confirmation of their rights and liberties by the royal government, and as a "dutyfull Acknowledgemt of their Maties care and Tender regard herein have humbly presented to their Matys an Assessmt of Money upon all Estates within the sd Province and Countries for the Support of their Mats. sd Governmt." [34] Fortunately Penn had not heard the results of the General Assembly which had just been dissolved.

William Penn also promised that the colony would obey all requests for the "Supplying such Quotas of Men or the defraying of their part of such charges as their Maties shall think necessary for the Safety and Preservation of their Matys Dominions in that part of America." When he appeared July 27, he agreed to retain Markham as deputy governor, promised that none of the laws passed by Fletcher's administration would be repealed, and offered to subscribe to the declaration of fidelity to their Majesties.[35] Thus on August 9, 1694, by order of the Queen in Council, Pennsylvania was restored to the Quaker Proprietor even though King William's War had not ended.[36]

The "holy experiment" had been severely buffeted on many occasions, generally because the colonists lacked the spiritual depth necessary for its success, and Penn was deficient in those qualities of leadership which would have helped him to lift the people to utopian heights. The compromise with Fletcher, whereby funds were provided to carry on the war in violation of the spirit of the peace testimony of Friends did further damage to the "holy experiment." William Penn now went far beyond that concession in his efforts to regain the province. He promised obedience to any commands from the Crown, specifically mentioning his willingness to grant money and men to aid in the defense of the Crown's provinces in America, and by implication agreeing to raise defensive installations in Pennsylvania.

Certain that the Quakers would resist this further breach of the peace testimony, Penn wrote, "Wee must Creep when wee cannot goe and it is as Necessarie for us in the things of this life to be wise as to be Innocent[.] a word to the wise is enough." [37] Penn undoubtedly believed that nothing should be allowed to stand in the way of regaining control of the province, and he hoped that the colonists would cooperate with him to achieve that end.

CHAPTER TEN

GOVERNMENT UNDER WILLIAM

MARKHAM, 1695 TO 1699

WHILE WILLIAM PENN promised the Lords of Trade, in August, 1694, that he would go to his colony "with all Convenient speed," he did not reach Pennsylvania until December 2, 1699. He appointed William Markham, who was serving as Lieutenant Governor under Benjamin Fletcher, his deputy governor in a commission dated November 24, 1694. Markham took office under this document on March 26, 1695, and filled the position until Penn arrived nearly five years later. His was the longest rule in the two decades covered by this study. In keeping with the unsettled political history of the period, Markham ruled under two different constitutions and two separate commissions, and at one period in 1696, governed the colony without any constitution.

Two characteristics of the colonists had become apparent by 1695. The first was that the colonists were able to care for themselves and were no longer dependant upon William Penn for guidance and assistance. There had been many examples of bumptious independence and self-conscious striving to be free from the Proprietor before but now it was different. Instead of looking anxiously to see how Penn would respond to their actions and statements, the Quaker leaders did much as they pleased and silently defied Penn to stop them.

In turn, Penn wrote few long, pontifical, scolding letters to the government. He expressed opinions about many things and sometimes gave voice to his disappointments, but his patriarchal tone of the first decade had disappeared. The most striking example of this change is that he expressed neither approval nor disapproval of the so-called Markham's Frame; and left the third frame of government hanging in abeyance until he arrived. Penn had been absent from the colony for ten years when it was restored to him by the Crown in 1694, and he had been absent fifteen years by 1699. The passage of time made the colonial leaders forget William Penn the man. He became a figure in the distance who wrote letters and tried to collect quitrents. The growing spirit of independence rested in part on the prosperity of the colony. The settlers had made a successful colony out of Pennsylvania, seemingly without any help from Penn, and they no longer felt like the children of a kindly Proprietor.

The second characteristic of this period was the clear indication of two factions in Pennsylvania. Ever since Nicholas More expressed opposition to the actions of the Council in 1683 there had been a small dissident group in the colony. Blackwell had received support from several men, in opposition to the majority of his Council and the Assembly. When Delaware seceded from Pennsylvania at the nomination of Thomas Lloyd for deputy governor in 1691, a small group in the northern colony sided with Delaware. This group was related in part to the Keithian schism. The same people supported Fletcher in opposition to the Quakers in 1693 and 1694. Now, when Markham deserted the disaffected group to assume the leadership of the Quaker faction, and enacted Markham's Frame in response to loud insistent demands, again there were several men who steadfastly opposed the majority. They were joined before the end of the period by Anglican recruits, which meant that with the help of Delaware the opposition nearly equalled the Quaker majority. While this spirit of faction had no place in a "holy experiment," it was an accepted part of Anglo-Saxon government everywhere.

These two characteristics meant that the government under Markham was more conventional than it had been earlier, and that Pennsylvania looked more like neighboring colonies than it had before. Despite these appearances, there were still conditions in the province which made Pennsylvania unique.

Markham's rule can be divided into three periods. In the eighteen months before he decided in September, 1696, to call the General Assembly for a second time, nothing very important happened. During the next few months there was much activity as a new constitution was adopted, money was appropriated to the Crown, and a vigorous dispute broke out between two factions. The third period lasted from spring, 1697, until Penn set foot in Pennsylvania in December, 1699. Some comments will be made about the first period, ending in the fall of 1696, before turning to the more interesting three years which followed.

Three subjects came up for discussion in the spring of 1695 and continued to hold the spotlight. The Crown asked for money and men to aid in the defense of the New York frontier from the French and the Indians. Pennsylvania was ordered to prepare defensive measures in case of attack by a French fleet. The colonists demanded a new constitution in place of the old one written in 1683. The only move the colony made in the direction of accomplishing any of these tasks was to set up a watch at Cape Henlopen to warn the colony if a French fleet sailed up the Delaware Bay.

When Markham became deputy governor he was ordered to gain the consent of two assistants, John Goodson, and Samuel Carpenter, before taking any action. Little is known about the relationship between these men and the Governor except that Markham wrote to Fletcher at New York in May, 1696, explaining that he had been prevented by his assistants from calling together an Assembly similar to the ones in neighboring colonies.[1]

The Deputy Governor supposed that Pennsylvania and Delaware were again under the Constitution of 1683 since the colony had been restored to Penn, and he issued writs for the election of members of the Council.[2] The body convened April 20, 1695, but the entire membership did not appear until May 25, because of confusion about elections.[3] When Markham addressed the Council on May 20, he reminded the members of their obligation to reply to the Queen's letter which requested contributions for the defense of the English colonies.

In a diplomatic gesture, he commended the Council for appropriating money for the Crown's use in the past, "Tho ye principles of most of you were agt giving anything to Maintaine warr," and expressed the hope that they would respond again.[4]

It soon became apparent, that the men were more interested in drawing up a new frame of government than they were in appropriating money for defense. Markham tried again, May 29, to convince the Council of the urgency of the matter.[5] The body replied the following day that it felt incapable of doing anything in answer to the Queen's letter without the concurrence of the Assembly, and added that it would be impossible for the lower house to meet until September since the men were busy with their crops until that time.

Fearful lest this answer lead to difficulties with the Crown, Markham warned: "Gentl., You are my wittnesses that I have done my dutie: [I] Onlie wish that this your delay may not be taken for a deniall The Consequences whereof may prove verie fatall to us all." The Council promised to bear the blame if its action caused difficulty. The Deputy Governor then asked the members about the defense of the colony and reminded them that Penn had made solemn promises about undertaking the defense of the province and lower counties. The Council refused to answer the question, and Markham dissolved the legislative session of the chamber.

On September 10 the General Assembly met. Markham addressed a joint session and stressed the need for answering the urgent requests for military aid. Various letters were read, including one from the Queen and one from Fletcher.[6] The following day members of both houses were named to a grand committee which was to bring in a suitable answer to the Queen's letter and write an act of settlement or new constitution.[7] The Assembly, which was meeting in Sarah Whitpain's house, named Edward Shippen of Philadelphia County Speaker for the session.

Virtually nothing was done in the two houses while the grand committee met. On September 19 it reported that the members wished to contribute to the defense, as far as in them lay, but requested that any financial aid which Pennsylvania offered should be applied to non-military needs. It further petitioned that the colony be allowed to contribute money rather than men.

The members of the two houses announced to Markham on September 27, that they had reached agreement on a supply bill and an act of settlement, and hoped that he would approve them.[8] Markham replied that he was pleased with the first bill but did not feel free to approve of the revision of the constitution which was proposed in the second one. The General Assembly replied that he could not have one without the other. When further discussion seemed fruitless, Markham dissolved the General Assembly.

During the year which followed the dismissal of the legislature, Markham sat uneasily in the chair of the deputy governor. He had refused to agree to the Act of Settlement out of loyalty to Penn, and now he was fearful lest the failure of the government to provide money for continental defense would lead to a new seizure of the colony by the Crown. He wrote to Penn for instructions, but letters were intercepted at sea by the French. It was an anxious time.

Markham received a letter from Whitehall in the summer of 1696 directing him to build up the defenses of the colony. He could do nothing, for the Council members resolutely refused to protect their own colony.[9] Several letters came from Fletcher demanding aid, and Markham put him off as best he could. In May, 1696, the Deputy Governor wrote that the legislature would appropriate no money unless the freemen could have a new constitution. Markham defended his refusal to accede to their demands, saying,

I never was for the Proprietor's form of government and doubted if he had power to grant many things in it; but I know very well it was forced from him by friends who unless they received all that they demanded would not have settled the country. Since they refused the old charter, thereby releasing the Proprietor from his obligation to them, I had no reason to bind him again, and that faster then he bound himself before.[10]

Despite the opposition of his assistants, Markham determined to make another attempt to reach a compromise with the representatives of the freemen. He decided in September, 1696, to call together a General Assembly patterned on the ones in the neighboring colonies. This meant that he would appoint his Council and provide for a public election of members of the Assembly. This decision indicated that Markham realized he had no chance of forcing the government of Pennsylvania to accept the Second Frame of 1683 and meant that he was governing the colony without any constitution.

There were eight men in attendance at the Council which met September 25, 1696.[11] Three of these men were Quakers, Edward Shippen, Anthony Morris, and David Lloyd. Two of these Friends had been speakers of the Assembly in the past, and perhaps Markham believed that they would do less harm on the Council than in the Assembly. Markham told the councillors that they had been chosen because they were loyal to King William and to William Penn, and because "I know you are all men that are fastned to the Country by visible estates, I mean such as the Law calls Real estates, of which each of you have a plentiful portion, and thats a great securitie that you will study the interest of the Country, and will advise me in what you believe to be for the saftie and preservaon of it." Since Markham believed that the naming of this Council changed the government, he asked Patrick Robinson, secretary of the Council, to administer a new oath of allegiance to him.

When Markham told the Council of the repeated requests for action on defense and for cooperation with a new Parliament act entitled, "An Act for Preventing Frauds and Regulating Abuses in the Plantation Trade," the Council recommended that the Assembly be convened.

The Deputy Governor ordered the secretary to issue writs to the sheriffs of the counties for elections October 16. As during the Fletcher administration, Philadelphia and New Castle counties were to have four representatives each, and the other counties were to have three. John Simcock of Chester County was named Speaker of the Assembly which convened October 26, at Samuel Carpenter's house. Markham addressed the General Assembly the following day, and again stressed the responsibility of the legislators to the Crown and urged that plans be initiated for the defense of the colony. The Assembly, which just a year earlier had rejected the Charter of Liberties of 1683, now responded to this address by protesting the way the General Assembly had been chosen and said it could do nothing until the people had been restored to their "former constitutions." [12]

The Deputy Governor convened the joint bodies again on October 30 to announce that he had just received positive word that the colony was to be governed by the Second Frame. John Goodson had resigned his position as assistant to Markham and Arthur Cook had stepped up with a commission naming him as the successor. This document included instructions for Markham, and ordered him "to act according to Law & Charter." [13] Since the Deputy Governor had just laid aside the Second Frame he was embarrassed, and vainly protested, "no man ever heard mee say that the Charter was void." To complicate matters further, the legislators now decided they did not want the constitution of 1683 in effect despite their earlier remonstrance.

Apparently Markham decided that as he had already laid aside the Charter of Liberties, the General Assembly might as well prepare a new frame of government. He gave the men permission to amend the old constitution, and four days later, November 3, he submitted a new frame of government to the Assembly himself. This action was to the advantage of Markham in two other ways. When he granted the so-called Markham's Frame it made him popular with the ruling element in the colony. At the same time it was possible to answer the urgent requests for appropriations to aid New York, for on November 7 the Assembly simultaneously passed the new constitution and a money bill.

The supply bill appropriated £300 to Governor Fletcher's defense installations and provided that the money be borrowed and sent to him immediately. Markham was granted an equal sum, while Robinson, who had served without pay since 1693, was awarded seventy-two pounds. Samuel Carpenter, who had advanced sixty-three pounds to pay for the pursuit of Babbitt and his men in 1691, was promised reimbursement.[14]

Several other bills were enacted, including a fire prevention law for Philadelphia and New Castle. The law entered the province of morality by providing a fine of twelve pence for every man caught smoking tobacco on the streets of the town, either by day or night. The fines were to be used to buy "Leather Buckets & other Instruments or Engines ag[ains]t fires, for the public use of each town respectively."

Markham's Frame remained in force until Penn returned in December, 1699, although it was never recognized as valid by the Proprietor. The thirteen chapters were largely copied from the Second Frame, but there were some changes. The Council was to consist of two members from each county, and the Assembly of four. The members of each body were elected annually, and allowed a larger sum of money in payment for their services. The Assembly was granted the right to initiate legislation, and was permitted to adjourn itself temporarily, provided it had not been dismissed. Thus during the legislative sessions, the Assembly was virtually equal to the upper house. Voting qualifications were changed. The property requirement for rural voters was lowered from one hundred acres to fifty. On the other hand, the vote was no longer granted to every inhabitant of the towns who paid scot and lot, as before, but only to those who were worth fifty pounds.

The legislators were uneasy about changing the government by the enactment of law. In the second chapter they wrote:

Now for as much as the former frame of government, modelled by act of Settlement and Charter of Liberties, is not deemed in all respects sutably accomodated to our present Circumstances Therefore It is unanimously Desired, that it may be Enacted. *And Be it Enacted by the Governour aforesaid, with the advice and Consent of the Representatives of the freemen of the said Province and Territories in Assembly met, and by the Authority of the same,* that this government shall, from time to time, Consist of the Governour or his Deputy or Deputies, and the freemen of the sd. Province and Territories thereof in form of a Council and Assembly.

In addition, the final chapter stated:

It is hereby Enacted that neither this act, nor any other act or acts whatsoever shall preclude or Debar the Inhabitants of this Province & territories from Claiming having and enjoying any of the Rights, Priviledges & Immunities which the said Proprietary for himself his heirs & assigns Did formerly grant or which of right belong unto them the said Inhabitants, by virtue of any Law, Charter, or Grants whatsoever, anything herein Contained to the Contrary notwithstanding.

The change between what was customary in 1696 and what was enacted in Markham's Frame was slight. Everyone but William Penn recognized by then that the Assembly had achieved equality with the Council in lawmaking. The period under Fletcher had established that fact without question. The other modifications, except for the change in suffrage requirements, were not very important. The change in voting qualifications was apparently designed to allow more men to vote in the rural areas and fewer men to vote in the urban centers, for requirements were lowered in one case and raised in the other. Sister Joan de Lourdes Leonard believed that the new constitution was drawn up to protect the Quakers from the non-Friends, especially in the towns.[15] That theory presumes that the urban poor were mostly non-Quaker.

More than 100 persons signed a petition, dated March 12, 1697, against this change in the suffrage requirements. Aside from a dozen signatures of well-known men who were opposed to the frame on other grounds, it may be supposed that the signers had been deprived of the right to vote by the new constitution.[16] Certainly the facts do not support the statement by W. R. Shepherd that the ratification of the new frame of government "meant the complete recognition of the supremacy of the popular will." [17] It would be nearer the truth to say that the document represented a new step in the move away from proprietary control and the seizure of that control by a sturdy rural and urban middle class.

The faction which was mentioned earlier in the chapter expressed strong opposition. It had gained Arthur Cook, the new assistant to Markham, but otherwise it had the same leaders: Robert Turner, Griffith Jones, Francis Rawle, Joshua Carpenter, Thomas Fairman, and Toby Leech. The split was not necessarily one of Quakers versus non-Quakers, for some Friends in good standing and some Keithian Quakers were in opposition to the majority. Also, many of the non-Friends cooperated with the majority group around Markham, who was not a Quaker.

Several men in this faction drew up a letter to William Penn, expressing opposition to the new frame. All the innovations were deplored. Since the Assembly now shared in initiating legislation bills were no longer promulgated, and this was criticized. The change in the number of men in each house and the change in voting qualifications were opposed. It was claimed that John Goodson had not given his consent to the change before it was made.[18] The letter expressed the belief that the new constitution would not become effective until Penn ratified it and urged him to reject it. The men protested that their opposition to the new charter and the taxes assessed under it was based on principle, not on economic necessity. The letter closed with the admonition, "Do not interpret this as against your friends & ours in the Assembly & Council, called Quakers." [19]

On November 7, 1696, the day the General Assembly adjourned, the members of the Assembly wrote to Penn to explain what had been done. It was reported that the Act of Settlement had been drawn:

to putt us in a frame of Government as near to our Charter of Priviledges as we could, considering thy Absence & ye present Circumstances of Affairs, it's Submitted to thy Pleasure for Approbation or Dissent, with a Salvo notwithstanding to ye people hereafter to Claim & Enjoy all their Rights formerly granted by thee to them, and we hope thou wilt find nothing therein but what thou wilt see cause to Confirm.[20]

In addition, the Assembly reported its gift of money to the Crown and protested that the government had always been ready to answer "according to our Abilities, considering ye Religious Persuasion of the majr part of us (having therein a due Regard to thee) that thou might not Suffer for any Neglect of ours." Penn was reminded of the gifts of some £500 during the Fletcher administration.

These protestations bring up the question of whether Pennsylvania Quakers really did have religious scruples against paying money to the Crown to further the war effort. While they did, it is obvious that their religious inclinations were weakened by other considerations. They disliked paying taxes for anything, and especially disapproved of sending money out of the colony. But these were matters of economics rather than of conscience. The Quakers refused to raise money to support their own government and pleaded poverty. When a request for money came from New York they at first postponed any decision, then begged to be excused because of poverty, and as a last resort claimed to have conscientious scruples against paying money for defense.

However in 1693, they appropriated money to Governor Fletcher, in exchange for the reenactment of their laws and privileges. In 1695, the General Assembly offered a similar trade, and in 1696 offered Markham a supply bill for a new frame of government. The plea of religious scruples was further weakened by a letter from Penn which questioned the practice of Friends in Philadelphia, and stated frankly that English Friends had no scruples about paying money to the government for the war effort. Pennsylvania Quakers endeavored to prevent that letter from falling into the hands of Markham, although he heard vague references to it.[21]

The Quakers consistently opposed all attempts to place the government of Pennsylvania in a posture of defense. They were willing to grant money to the Crown if necessary, and permitted others in the colony to plan for their own defense, but they refused to share in any defensive plans themselves.

William Penn's personal feelings about Markham's Frame are unknown. He neither approved nor rejected it. Much later, on December 1, 1697, he wrote to Samuel Carpenter and others saying that the granting of a change in the government "is my own peculiar prerogative." He expressed fear that if he submitted the document to the Crown it might be invalidated, which would cause great discomfiture to Penn and to the colony. He promised, "I shall do for ye best, in short, as ye Lord shall direct me & way is made." [22]

In the meantime, Markham forwarded the £300 appropriated

for the war effort to Governor Fletcher, "for ye supply & relief of those Indians of the five Nations yt are in friendship with ye English wth Necessaries of food & raymt." Fletcher was urged to give the Pennsylvanians full credit for their donation, both among the Indians and in England.[23]

One detects a note of sarcasm in Fletcher's answer. He returned the thanks of Albany for:

ye Great Charity of yor Province In Granting this Assistance tho in obedience to the Royall Commands. Upon ye Receite of yor Minute of Councill I sent for ye Mayor and directed him to call ye Aldermen and Assistance and Comunicate this yor Kindness to Them[,] Then Enter ye Minute in their Records that yor Charity may not be Stiffled or concealed[.] By this method ye Perticular Indians who frequent this place will know it at our next meeting[.] I shall acquaint ye whole five Nations.[24]

He further promised to tell London about their magnanimity. When it is remembered that Pennsylvania's quota in men and money amounted to some £2,000 annually, and the £300 was the first appropriation in three years, Fletcher can be forgiven his feelings.

After the flurry of excitement about writing a new constitution and appropriating money for defense had subsided, the next three years were fairly quiet. There was one exception, when English officials and persons in neighboring colonies stirred up agitation against Pennsylvania with claims that the Delaware Bay area was friendly to pirates and illicit traders. The minority faction made a few attempts to challenge the changes brought about by Markham's Frame, but these were unsuccessful. Otherwise, the government functioned smoothly, passed a number of laws, and was satisfactory to the majority of the colonists. Penn wrote several letters to the government and to individuals, one of which aroused the Council to attempt to stamp out immorality in the colony.

The persons who had opposed Markham's Frame decided to hold elections in Philadelphia County for the Council and Assembly under the Charter of 1683, when election time arrived in 1697.[25] The newly chosen legislators presented themselves to Markham on the day appointed under the Second Frame for the meeting of each house and were rejected.[26] Turner then sat down and wrote a protest to Penn that the Deputy Governor was depriving the freemen of "our ancient rights libertys & ffreedom." He added that the Quakers prevented members of other religious denominations from holding office, which "gives occation of mutteringe & discontent & workes against our good." [27]

Two months later, on June 26, 1697, Turner again wrote to Penn bemoaning the evil days which had fallen upon Pennsylvania.

I wish thou had sensibly & feeling sense of it. a little time more spent without Redress or discountenance from thee will cause a loud Cry in thy Ear & draw answer from some body: God will hear the Cry of the Oppressed & punish their Oppressors as in former days. Thy Ears are open to a P[ar]ty that oppress & grind ye poor whereby they take incouragmt thy many Letters of friendship to them wch they keep hid & secret from thy old & true ffriends.

He urged Penn to get out his former writings, such as *No Cross No Crown*, or *England's Present Interest*, and remind himself of the danger of supporting one faction against another.[28]

Turner again expressed indignation at the supply bill of 1696, and asked that money seized by that "unwarantable, illegal & Arbitrary Act, be forthwith Restored." He added that some had paid the tax because of threats and that others had been tricked into paying by statements that prominent persons had paid when they had not. He reported that a piece of flannel worth five pounds had been seized by the collectors to pay his taxes which were but three pounds.

During the meeting of the General Assembly in 1698, Turner, Griffith Jones, and Joshua Carpenter complained to Markham that the Quaker leaders had broken a promise to them, and asked for an investigation. They claimed that in exchange for their promise not to contest the election of 1698 the majority group had agreed not to pass any more laws until William Penn arrived. Markham ignored this attempt to halt proceedings and there was no discussion of the petition.[29] After Penn returned to the colony, this group again challenged the majority decision.

Whatever Penn's feelings were about the new constitution, he deplored the attacks on the Quakers by this minority group. He wrote to Turner, do not "strengthen yt Sp[iri]t & Party wch runs agst ye ancient unity & fr[ien]ds, as we were a People when I was among you, I will not say they have not their weaknesses; Some may be high some selfish, Some hott, yet they are a people Called and In measure Saved by the Lord. They have known & do know & measurably enjoy the Lords love & presence." [30]

Markham knew that the minority faction was writing to Penn. He wrote a long letter on May 1, 1697, to reaffirm his loyalty and to let Penn know he had been hurt by rumors that the word of his enemies was accepted. He ended on a pathetic note: "In Short I have served you faithfully but desire not to be a burden. I have trusted providence hitherto & tho it may be hard with me being a Cripple, yet cannot begg an alms tho att the door of them I spent my strength for." [31]

When the General Assembly met on May 10, 1697, the lower house named John Blunston of Chester County as speaker. Markham addressed a joint session of the legislature and among other things said: "Gentl, & you Mr Speaker, 'You are att this time mett together, not by virtue of anie writt nor call of mine, but by virtue of a Law made by yorselves, or by yor repsentatives Last Sessions, & yrfor I have the Less to say to you. I recommend to yor Consideraon a Letter which I latelie received from his Excelly Benjn Fletcher, Gor of Newyork.' " [32]

The letter reminded the gentlemen that they were expected to furnish annually eighty men or £2,000. However Fletcher asked Pennsylvania to send him twenty-five men or £600 in lieu of the men. A joint committee was named to consider the request and it brought in a negative reply. To defend the government's refusal to cooperate with the Crown's representative, the men reported that the money borrowed the previous year to send Fletcher £300 had not yet been repaid. The New York

Governor was reminded of the "Infancie & pvertie of this governmt," and the rejection concluded with a protestation of loyalty to the Crown and an expression of readiness to observe the king's commands, "according to or religious psuasions & abilities." [33]

Sixteen bills were approved by the Assembly, but only eight were enacted by the Governor and Council. One of these laws reenacted the former laws, including Markham's Frame, and declared legal the actions taken in 1696. The mere repeating of what had been written the previous year was not very satisfactory, but it was the best that could be done since the new frame of government still lacked the confirmation of William Penn.

The last day of the session of the General Assembly, Monday, May 24, Markham introduced a document he had received from the Board of Trade. Members of the government were expected to subscribe to the document, pledging their loyalty and obedience to the King and his laws. The non-Friends signed the paper, and the Quakers affixed their signatures to a similar document. The Quakers outnumbered the others twenty-four to seven, with five of the thirty-six representatives not present. The General Assembly was thereupon dissolved.

Again some of the Friends penned a report to the Proprietor.[34] They told him that the Act of Settlement had been reenacted, "wch Gives Generall Satisfaction of wch wee desire thee to Consider of and not be hasty to Expresse thy dislike least thou should thereby Gratifye thyne & our enymies & bring us into Confusion wch some desire & use their Utmost Endeavr to Effect." They denounced the faction which held elections under the old constitution but added that those men had not been dealt with harshly, for they hoped to maintain a temporary peace in the colony until Penn arrived to establish a more permanent settlement.

In December, 1697, Penn wrote to Samuel Carpenter, "tho I pawn my very plate, I will strive to sett out by ye 10 day of ye 2 mo. [April] ye Lord permiting, & desire you to dispose all to such a reception as [will] make our meeting Comforta[ble to us] both." He wished that the General Assembly had passed all of Governor Fletcher's laws again so that they would be the enactment of the present government, and not let such "an irregular Interruption, lye a President by Consent upon Record among us, this Stumbles me much." [35]

On February 9, 1698, Markham called together as many of the Council as he could find, to listen to a letter from William Penn which could only be opened in the presence of the Governor and Council. In this communication, Penn expressed great indignation at the stories of wickedness, vice, and lawlessness which continually came out of Pennsylvania. Specifically, he said that there were reports that the government allowed both Scottish and Dutch ships to trade in the colony, and embraced pirates. According to the stories all kinds of wickedness and lewdness were countenanced in the colony, especially in the taverns. He ordered the Council to take action. "For my Sake, your own Sakes, & above all, for God's sake, lett not the Poor Province longer suffer under such grievous & offensive Imputations, and you will oblige him, yt loves you, prays for you, & prays to be with you." [36]

Samuel Carpenter, Joseph Growdon, and William Clark were named to investigate the accusations in the letter. Their report denied that there had been illicit trade with Scottish or Dutch ships, and declared further that if such had come into the bay, it was the responsibility of the men under Edward Randolph, Surveyor General of customs, to suppress the same. They denied that piracy had been encouraged, and added that when a mere copy of the Lords Justice's proclamation came into the hands of the government, those listed were seized to be held for trial when a suitable court could be found, and that when the men broke out of the jail, a posse was sent after them. The committee sadly admitted that vice and looseness had increased, and stated that there were too many ordinaries in the colony, especially in Philadelphia. It recommended that a proclamation be drawn up and sent out to the people, calling on everyone to join in preventing illicit trade, in barring pirates from the colony, and in suppressing vice and wickedness.[37]

A proclamation was written and sent to each of the six counties. The accusations contained in Penn's letter were repeated, and the first two were denied. However, the justices of the peace were called upon to investigate in their counties, especially in the taverns and ordinaries, and to suppress crime. Citizens were urged to continue to discountenance illicit traders and pirates.

The General Assembly convened on May 10, 1698.[38] Markham announced that he had received a new commission from William Penn, under which he had the title of lieutenant governor. Presumably this meant that he now ruled alone and no longer had two assistants to advise him. Markham discussed instructions which had come from the English government in regard to trade, and suggested that the General Assembly enact legislation to supplement the laws passed in the home country.

Phineas Pemberton from Bucks County, was speaker of the Assembly, during a session which was not distinguished in any way. New attempts were made to enforce the collection of the tax assessed in 1696, and previous laws were reenacted in a statute which specifically mentioned the Act of Settlement of 1696.[39] One of the laws passed by this General Assembly was entitled, "An Act for Preventing Frauds & Regulating Abuses in Trade, Within the Province of Pennsilvania & Counties Annexed." It will be discussed in the following chapter. Penn made no attempt to defend this law when it was called to his attention by the Board of Trade, and sent off two letters by different ships to veto it.[40]

Little is known about what transpired in the government until the next General Assembly met May 10, 1699. When the Council convened there were no election returns from the sheriff of New Castle County. The secretary found instead a blank sheet of paper, with a note attached dated March 13. It said, "I here enclosed send you the return of the names of the Council & Assembly men Chosen here on the 10th of this instant. To give you anie reason for such an election is beyond my power; Have had no discourse with anie of the electors about it." [41] In addition, Markham had received two letters from John Donaldson, which criticized the election in that county. When these men were called before a grand committee to explain themselves, Joseph Wood, the sheriff, claimed that he had written his letter as a joke. Donaldson protested that he considered his letters to have been private, and that he intended no reflection upon the government. After apologizing and pledging loyalty to the king, Proprietor, and government, both men were dismissed. However New Castle County had no representation during this session, and it was apparent that the differences which had led to separation at the beginning of the decade were once again arising.

Ten laws were enacted in this meeting of the legislature under John Blunston as speaker. A new tax law called for the usual levy of one penny per pound, and since there were no demands for funds from the Crown all the money collected under this supply bill could be spent in the colony. A law was passed which would lay heavy penalties on a county which failed to elect and send representatives to the General Assembly in the future. Under one of the statutes, commissioners of admiralty were to be named to aid the officers of the admiralty court established by the Crown in the Delaware Bay region. Colonel Robert Quary, judge of that court, criticized the law severely.[42]

The colonial governments were required to submit all new laws to England annually, which nullified the old five year rule. For this reason Pennsylvania stopped the pretence of enacting all of its laws for a single year at a time. The laws had been reenacted in 1698 without a time limit, and thus there was no need to pass them again in 1699.

Three months after this General Assembly ended, William Penn was on board ship for Pennsylvania, and he arrived to take control before the year was out. A period of Pennsylvania's history was coming to an end.

CHAPTER ELEVEN

PENNSYLVANIA DENOUNCED

1682 TO 1701

WHEN THE "holy experiment" was contemplated it had been hoped that Pennsylvania would live at peace with her neighbors, with the English government, and with the minority groups inside the colony. Penn was confident that if difficulties arose the power of the spirit would heal all misunderstandings. However he expected the people of the province to behave in a friendly manner towards everyone and to give no occasion for disagreement.

Unfortunately, life is more complex than utopian planners think it is. The peculiar attitude of the colony towards war, the enactment of laws consistent with the "holy experiment" but inconsistent with the practices of non-Quakers and with the English law, and the freedom of the province from royal control when the king was increasing his authority in all the colonies, were in themselves enough to challenge the control of Pennsylvania by William Penn and his Quaker political leaders. Even if the Quakers had scrupulously adhered to the principles of the "holy experiment" neighboring colonies would have been jealous of the prosperity of Pennsylvania, English officials would have been angered by her independence from the Crown, and Anglicans would have resented their minor place in the province. Cries of outrage would have been heard all the way to London and it is quite likely that the Crown would have responded by attacking the privileged position of the Pennsylvanians. With the government gone, it would not have been long before the "holy experiment" came to an end.

In other words, it seems likely that the "holy experiment" was doomed to failure by external forces. The colony was situated in the English imperial framework and was not regarded with sympathy by either royal or colonial officials. But the "holy experiment" was suffering from internal difficulties long before outsiders' cries against Pennsylvania reached a crescendo. That failure was apparent to outsiders, who took delight in describing to the Crown the quarrels, vice, and immorality which they saw. While much was made of the fundamental conflict between the principles and practices of a Quaker colony on the one hand, and the prerogatives of the Crown on the other, doubtless the decision of the English government to seize Pennsylvania was influenced by the tales of immorality in the "holy experiment."

At the same time, the criticism of the colony and the repeated attacks on the government and commercial practices of the people contributed to the breakdown of the utopian dream. Pennsylvania was continually on the defensive, and was constantly forced to remember that hostile eyes were watching everything which was done. The colony was already self-conscious because of its goals, and the knowledge that everything was closely scrutinized increased tension among the freemen, which in turn made it nearly impossible to maintain the spiritual equilibrium and serenity so necessary to the "holy experiment."

There were three principal sources of complaints against Pennsylvania. Officials in the neighboring colonies, particularly New York and Maryland, made complaints to the Crown. Royal officials in the colonies, especially those stationed in the province, raised a great outcry. The Anglicans joined the chorus late in the century.

From the very beginning Pennsylvania was unpopular with her neighbors to the north and south. Both New York and Maryland had directed their eyes to the vacant space between them. In the early part of this study some mention was make of the boundary dispute between Maryland and Delaware which forced Penn to return to England in 1684. Other disagreements about boundaries continued for many decades. In addition, many in the New World were suspicious of Quakers, and there were already a number of Quakers in the various colonies. Little was known about the pacifist views of Friends before King William's War, but it was enough for good Calvinists and Anglicans to know that they were a new, peculiar, proselytizing sect.

Pennsylvania early drew criticism because it interfered with the old monopolies of the Indian fur trade, it attracted foreign commerce from the neighboring ports, and it lured settlers from the old colonies. In 1685 Penn reported to Thomas Lloyd that a petition had arrived in London from New York which complained that trade had decayed and that it was difficult to rent houses because of activity in the Jerseys and along the Delaware.[1] In 1687 further protests were lodged with the Lords of Trade by the New York government, and it was suggested that Connecticut, the Jerseys, and Pennsylvania be attached to New York, which would be "of great profit to the Treasury." [2] In 1693, the Council and Assembly in the same province protested that people were moving into neighboring colonies to escape the high taxes which were collected for defense at that time.[3]

In 1695 Colonel Francis Nicholson, the new Governor of Maryland, issued a proclamation to discount stories of prosperity in Pennsylvania and Carolina which were enticing colonists away daily. He threatened to imprison persons found guilty of persuading settlers to migrate elsewhere as divulgers "of false News." [4] But there was virtually no difficulty with East or West Jersey.

With the Glorious Revolution and King William's War, feeling against Pennsylvania reached new heights because of the pacifism of the Quaker colony. When the news of revolutionary activity in neighboring provinces first came to Pennsylvania in 1689, Friends issued a statement on participation in the struggles. "It may be well for all Friends in all places to Keep Clear in such cases, & noway meddle or be Concerned, but always behave themselves peaceably under all revolutions." [5]

At the outset of the war against the French it was frequently stated that the Quaker adherents of William Penn were Jacobites, which explained their reluctance to join the war.[6] It has been seen in earlier chapters that Pennsylvania steadfastly refused to participate in the war in any way until Fletcher arrived in 1693. During this period an attempt was made to attach the colony to Maryland. Governor Lionel Copley wrote, "Pennsylvania is an unsettled state and should be brought under the Crown. It is so near to this Colony [Maryland] that it encourages illicit trading here. Moreover, the Jacobite party, of which Penn is known to be the head, will involve this Colony in trouble. Many think it would be well to join it to this province." [7] Certainly the letters colonial officials sent to the Crown during the early years of the war strengthened the determination of the English government to take over Penn's commonwealth.

It should be added that during the war, when New York was frequently carrying the entire load of defending the English colonies from the French, she complained against other colonies in addition to Pennsylvania. Herbert L. Osgood, in his comprehensive studies of the colonial period, suggests that only small groups of "fanatics" and "zealots" on each side really favored the colonial wars, and that everyone else hung back, waiting for someone else to do the fighting and to pay the expenses.[8]

Even before the first complaints were lodged with the Lords of Trade about Pennsylvania's refusal to join in the war effort, there were isolated examples of the charge that the colony harbored pirates and encouraged illicit trade.

Privateering and piracy were common late in the seventeenth century, and especially after King William's War broke out. Privateering was a legal action sanctioned by the government, but it tended to turn into outright piracy. Once a captain and crew began to taste the fruits of merchant shipping seized legally, their appetites were whetted, and it was easy to slip into a careless attitude and eventually into illicit actions. These men infested the Caribbean, sailed along the African coast, and preyed on the shipping of the North Atlantic. Penn wrote of them in 1697, "Truly the villany of yt people has made ye name of Eng. & Christian Stinck in all ye Eastern Coasts of ye World, & therefore encourage them not." [9]

The papers of the Board of Trade are full of references to the presence of pirates in most of the colonies, and Pennsylvania was possibly no more cursed with them than were other provinces. However, it is certain that lawless men were attracted to a colony where the use of force was frowned on in principle and seldom resorted to in practice. Lieutenant Governor Stede of Barbados, reported in the period before the Glorious Revolution that the pirates "landed at midday [at New Castle] with as much confidence and assurance as the most honest men in the world, without any molestation whatever." [10] It has been seen that Babbitt and his men seized a vessel in 1691 and began to raid the shore. The following year Colonel Nicholson complained, "I hear several of them [pirates] are in Pennsylvania, where the government, owing to the Quakers falling out among themselves, is very loose." [11]

Nicholson continued to report irregularities after he became Governor of Maryland. In 1695 he reported to the Duke of Shrewsbury that the people of Pennsylvania and Delaware were shipping tobacco illegally to Scotland, Europe, Curaçao, and Surinam. "They cunningly convey their tobacco in casks, with flour or bread at each end." [12]

Similar reports were going to the Crown from other colonies, and in 1696 a new law was enacted, entitled, "The Act for Preventing Frauds and Regulating Abuses in Plantation Trade." The act extended the provisions of the earlier navigation acts, strengthened the powers of the customs inspectors, and called for new guarantees of loyalty by the colonial officials.[13]

The passage of this law, which coincided with the creation of the Board of Trade to replace the Lords of Trade, marked the culmination of a movement which had been gathering momentum for twenty years. The English government had decided about 1675 to increase the restrictions on the colonies and to regulate the colonial possessions more closely for the benefit of the home country. One manifestation of this new policy is seen in the statement the Lords of Trade issued in the month that

William Penn set sail for Pennsylvania in 1682. "We think it not convenient to constitute any new propriety in America nor to grant any further powers that may render the plantations less dependant on the crown." [14] Penn's charter, granted in large part for personal reasons, was an exception to the direction which the English colonial policy was taking. The firm action instituted by Charles II was continued by James II " . . . with an energy and swiftness hitherto unknown." [15]

Immediately after the Glorious Revolution it became evident that the change in kings did not mean a change in colonial policy. In May, 1689, the Lords of Trade recommended to William III that something be done about the proprietary governments. "The Present circumstances & Relation they stand in to the Government of England is a matter worthy of the Consideration of the Parliament, for the Bringing those Proprieties and Dominions under a nearer Dependance on ye Crown." [16]

The creation of a new board and the enactment of the new law prepared the Crown for a struggle to establish strict control over the colonies, proprietary or not. Pennsylvania soon found herself the target of several royal officials who found much in the Quaker colony to complain about.

The surveyor general for the colonies, Edward Randolph, did not believe that the new law would be useful in Pennsylvania or in any other colony unless courts of admiralty were established to hear the cases prosecuted under the law. He was convinced that it would be impossible to gain convictions in local courts with friendly juries.[17] The admiralty court however, could come into the colony with its own judge, register, marshal, and attorney general. It could use civil law instead of the common law and operate without a jury, thus protecting the Crown's interest. In 1697 the privy council decided to establish admiralty courts in the various colonies.[18]

For the next several years Randolph and Quary flooded the Board of Trade with tales of piracy and illicit trade in Pennsylvania, and with accusations that Markham and other officials in the colony were friendly with the criminals involved. In September, 1698, Quary reported that a pirate ship had come into the bay and plundered Lewis town, or Lewes, during the last week of August, and had remained in the bay for several days. After much delay, Markham ordered the drums to beat to call for volunteers. The volunteers refused to serve because he had no money to pay them, and he would not allow the men to keep what they seized from the pirates. Quary commented that there were men willing to defend the colony, if competent persons were given the power to "command and Exercise them." [19]

In June of the following year, Quary wrote to the Board of Trade that Captain Kidd had been sighted off the capes. When he landed, Quary had seized some of his men and 2,000 pieces of eight. He added that if Markham had helped him, he could have captured the ship itself.[20]

In August, 1698, Anthony Morris, a justice of the peace in Philadelphia County, issued a writ of replevin against Webb, the marshal attached to Quary's court, to force the return of goods taken from a man accused of engaging in illicit trade. Quary was furious, and wrote, "I hope yor Lordship will now bee sattisfied that neither Comissions nor acts of Parliamt are of any force in this Govermt for they will obey none." [21] A week later in a letter to the Board of Trade he reported that Pennsylvania feared he would ruin "theire beloved profittable Darling, Illegall Trade," and think they can do as they please because of Penn's influence at Court. "I very well knewe them to bee a perverse, obstenant and turbulent People, that will not submitt to any power or Lawes but their owne, . . . they have so Long encouredged and carryed on a most pernitious Illegal trade . . . contrary to Law, wch un Lawful Trade hath beene so advantadgous to them, that no ordinary meanes can make them part with it." [22]

The Philadelphia court then added insult to injury by calling Webb before it to answer by what authority he had held the goods in question. The marshal produced the King's commission to which was attached the great seal of the high court of the admiralty with the King's picture stamped on it. David Lloyd was prosecuting for the state that day, and in Quary's words, Lloyd held up the seal, "& shews itt to all the People in a Scornefull sliteing manner useing these words, here is a fine baby, a pritty baby but wee are not to be frightned with babys. the Courte in Steed of reproveing his Impudence ware very much pleased with the witt of this man." Quary's report added that when Lloyd was reproved by the Council later he replied, "all those that did any waies encouredge or promote the Setting up the Courte of Admiralty in this Province ware greater Enemies to the rights and Liberties of the people than those that promoted ship money in King Charles the first time wch hee would make appeare and prove to them, at theire next setting." [23] Much of what Quary wrote was true, although some of it was exaggerated. The quantity of correspondence which he sent to England must have impressed the Board of Trade and Quary once admitted, "I am very Sinceable [sensible] that I have Tyred yor Lordships with my numerous Letters." [24]

Randolph visited in several colonies and only a fraction of his correspondence related to Pennsylvania. He seemed to specialize in crossing swords with Markham. During the summer of 1698 he quarreled with the Lieutenant Governor and later accused Markham of imprisoning him, which the latter denied. Randolph demanded that the Crown "put the governmt into the hands of Persons of Abilities & Loyall Principles & true to the Interest of the Crown." [25]

Other men also reported on the immorality in the colony. Robert Snead, a justice of the peace, jailed three men accused of piracy after he had seen a copy of a proclamation from England against them. Shortly after the official proclamation reached Markham's hand the men escaped from the jail, and although Markham issued a hue and cry against them, it was to no avail. Snead complained that when he first talked to Markham about the pirates Markham's wife and daughter had warned the men of his plans and they called him "informer" as he went along the street. [26] It was widely believed that Markham's son-in-law, James Brown, was a pirate, but Brown stoutly denied it.

In confirmation of all of this, Turner wrote to Penn of the "Murtherings bloody Crew of Privateers whom we were become ye greatest harbourers of . . . It's better ye Governmt were out of or hands & in ye hands of others that they might bear their own shame & Reproach which we must expect to bear while we called Quakers bear ye name of Government." [27]

The General Assembly of Pennsylvania aroused the ire of Randolph and Quary in 1698 when it passed the law entitled, "An Act for Preventing Frauds & Regulating Abuses in Trade, Within the Province of Pennsylvania & Counties Annexed." This new bill included the provision that owners of ships should be allowed to affirm, instead of taking an oath as the new English law of 1696 required, in cases where the owners had conscientious scruples against taking oaths. Randolph threatened to dismiss John Bewley, his assistant in the Delaware Bay, if he allowed another Quaker to register his ship with an affirmation, "wth out laying his hand upon ye Bible & Kiss the Bible." [28]

The new law also required that legal action taken against those accused of any "breach or Non-observance of anie of the Acts of trade or Navigation . . . shall be according to the course of the Comon Law," and the defendant shall have the right of trial by jury.[29] Quary lodged protests with the Board of Trade, and Penn was called on to explain the action of his colony. When Penn appeared before the board in December, 1698, he announced that his negative of the law had already gone to Pennsylvania. He failed to understand why the Quakers could not affirm instead of taking oaths, else "we shut out our own folks, & confirme yt grievance upon our selves." Further, he protested that the Act of 1696 was "so darkly, & if I may say so, inconsistently worded" that one would naturally think trial by jury was expected under it.[30] It should be pointed out in defense of Penn's criticism that those who were interpreting the law in England could reach no agreement on several points. The following month Penn wrote to Robert Harley about the Act of 1696, saying, "Let us be treated like Englishmen, and not loose our domestick advantages for cultivating of wildernesses, so much to the honnour and wealth of the crown." [31]

In March, 1699, Quary reported to the Board of Trade that

he was forced to hold his admiralty court sessions forty miles from Philadelphia for the safety of the court. He added that no one paid any attention to his court, its orders, or its decrees. The government is "Concerned in Exposeing & possessing ye people that all ye Acting & proceeding of ye Admiralty is Arbitrary & Illegal." [32]

Quary condemned the law enacted by the General Assembly in 1699 against pirates. He said the law provided that persons could only be prosecuted for entertaining pirates after the said buccaneer had been found guilty in the courts. The Jamaica act, on which the law was patterned, called for the raising of armed men, but that of Pennsylvania called only for men, presumably unarmed. "If the Quaker justice Sheriffe & Constable wth those of their freinds whom they shall call to their assistance can preach the pyrats into a Submission to the Kings Authority itt is well [,] if not they may goe about their business." [33]

The complaints and denunciatory letters mentioned in these last few pages are but a fraction of all the reports sent to various boards in the English government during these years. The colonists denied many of the charges and protested that other accusations were based on half-truths. They pledged their loyalty to the king and his laws, and on occasion struck back at their accusers. It did little good, for the refutation of a charge seldom catches up with the original condemnatory statement. Furthermore, the colonists were not as innocent as they claimed to be, just as they were not as guilty as royal officials painted them.

The members of the Council and Assembly drew up an address to the King in 1698, asking him to vindicate them from the accusation of being tender towards pirates and illicit traders. They issued a general denial that Scottish, Dutch, or other illegal trading had been countenanced. They protested that pirates had never been knowingly entertained in the colony, except the ones that Edward Randolph had urged to settle in Pennsylvania. The document concluded, "If in any thing We have made wrong Stepps in Government, We shall Submit and cast our selves upon the King's Clemency." [34]

The same body drew up a protest against Quary in May, 1699, which criticized his arbitrary actions and protested that a man who was engaged in considerable merchant activity himself should not preside over the admiralty bench. The General Assembly added that the colony had nothing against the Court of Admiralty, "wch was Soe much wanted and desired here," and that it was willing to aid and assist it, if kept within the "bounds & limits of the Laws of England." [35]

Markham occasionally struck back at his accusers. He not only denied the charges made by Randolph, but stated that this royal official accepted bribes. He pointed out that the Surveyor General was a coward. "I wish any that had been acquainted with Randolphs huffing and bouncing had but seen him w[he]n I Called him to an account for his Affronts here, they would have seen him truckle & as humble as any Spaniell Dogg, but no sooner gott out of the town but fell to abusing & reviling me after his base manner." [36]

The denials and countercharges sent by the government of Pennsylvania to the Crown carried little weight, and in 1699 the Board of Trade decided to stop the open disobedience of English laws by the inhabitants of the Quaker province. William Penn was called before the Board and he agreed to sail immediately to Philadelphia. He promised to remove Markham as lieutenant governor, to enforce the laws of England, especially those against piracy and illicit trade, and to establish cooperation between the government and the court of admiralty.

Penn's decision to go to Pennsylvania and direct the reform of the government halted the move to overthrow his political authority in the colony. His personal intervention however, proved only a temporary setback to those who hoped to see the province become a royal colony. Within two years a new menace developed, in the shape of a parliamentary bill calling for the seizure of the government of Pennsylvania.

In the meantime, a new group had begun a campaign of denunciation directed against the Quakers in Pennsylvania. There had always been some suspicion of the political leaders in the colony because of their religious belief, and that increased during the years of King William's War. In February, 1694, the Lords of Trade expressed concern about the number of Friends in Pennsylvania and other plantations.[37]

In 1695 a small Anglican congregation was formed in Philadelphia; this group eventually built Christ Church. The letters patent from Charles II guaranteed the Anglicans a minister and the privilege of forming a congregation to worship together when twenty adherents to the faith requested it. Governor Fletcher had encouraged the establishment of a congregation, and the English government appropriated eighty pounds annually for religious and educational work, as an aid to the project.[38] This new official organization, from which accusations against the Quakers soon began to flow to London, was composed of the same group of men who had been attacking the major sect of the colony for a number of years. The charges made by this new congregation received additional attention however, because they were based on religious grounds and they appealed to religious leaders such as the Bishop of London, under whose care the church was established.

Letters found in the archives of the Society for the Propagation of the Gospel in Foreign Parts indicate that as early as 1698 the Anglicans were complaining to the home government. One man said that he had come to Philadelphia looking for wholesome laws and quiet moderate people, and found them "in wrangles among ym selves, and imprisoning one another for Religion." He added that when the Anglicans drew up a petition to the king to ask that a minister be sent to them and to request that they be allowed to prepare some defense against the French, the Quakers objected. They said there was a law against petitions and took Griffith Jones into custody as the writer of the paper. One Quaker judge was quoted as saying that he "would sooner take a Negro yt is a heathen's Word before a Church of England man's Oath; their Malise towards us is such." Another Quaker magistrate said that French privateers had positive orders from James II not to harm Pennsylvania; "They indeed are all Jacobites." [39]

Robert Snead had written to England as a justice of the

peace to condemn the policy of Pennsylvania towards pirates.
Now he wrote to Sir John Hublon in 1698, as an Anglican, im-
ploring England to intercede to save the Anglicans from the
Quakers. "We have built a Church & here is many of ye Church
of England yt has good estates which we Cannot Call oure owne
the Quakers being so predisict [prejudiced] & inveterat against
all yt are not so, & haveing ye Governemt in their hands." [40] It
might be added that Snead fled from the colony in 1700 to escape his creditors.

In January, 1701, the vestrymen of Christ Church addressed
a petition to the Board of Trade, which stated in part, "We
have a long time Silently grown'd under the misseries and hard
ships that we have Sufferd in this Governmt & that your Ldps
may guess at our unhappy circumstances, we will presume to
give yor Ldps a few Instances." [41] They protested that although
they outnumbered the Quakers they were allowed little influence in the government, that they held few positions of importance, and that they could not obtain justice in the courts,
"for there is not one Magistrate in this Governmt of the Church
of England." They stated that the right of petition was denied
them and that a law had been enacted which declared all those
who wrote or spoke against the government would be found
guilty of sedition. The Anglicans protested that oaths were not
used in the courts, even by non-Friends. "These & the rest of
the Acts will gaul & bear upon us till his Majty thinks fitt to
Dissallow them."

They further contended that Penn had no right to rule them,
for he had not taken the oath, nor did he have the King's approbation. However they hastened to protest, "Yett we have
never fail'd of paying all due respect to them, & all Submission
& obedience to their Govern[ment]."

In October of the same year the vestrymen directed a new
letter of accusations to the Crown. Whereas the former petition was based in part on religious grievances, this one was
frankly a political document. The men reported on three legal
cases pending in the colony. They stated that a man accused
of bestiality had escaped punishment because the jury refused

to take an oath. They reported that a woman who had confessed to murdering her bastard child was at liberty and had probably been pardoned. The vestrymen wrote that a man, the "son of an eminent Quaker," committed to jail on a charge of "Notorious Rape on his Serv[ant] Mayde," was let out on bail, and freed on a technicality.[42]

All of these charges and complaints did not go unheeded by William Penn who was in the colony for two years at this time. For example, when the charges made by the vestrymen were repeated by Quary, Penn answered them in a competent manner. He stated that in the case of bestiality the only witness against the defendant had left the colony, and his reputation was none too good. In the second case, at the request of the woman's Swedish minister, he had forwarded her case to Secretary Vernon, and she was meanwhile living in the sheriff's home. Penn reported that the maid married the defendant in the rape case which made it impossible to force her to testify against him, but Penn was attempting to find some way to prosecute him nevertheless. He denied that the accused was the son of an eminent Quaker.[43]

In a long letter to Lord Sommers in October, 1700, Penn answered some of the other accusations made against Friends. He protested that Pennsylvania had not been created as a Church of England plantation, yet it welcomed all who believed in God, and allowed those who confessed Jesus Christ as the Saviour of the World to hold office, "so that Churchmen not only have their Liberty but may & actually have a share in the government." He stated that in Delaware all the officials were Anglicans except for three judges. He added that three of the judges of the provincial Court were churchmen, and in Philadelphia County the sheriff, clerk, sub-sheriff, attorney general, and two of the seven justices of the peace were not Quakers. "Yet no less than outing of us and overturning the Governmt is ye Ambition & Sedition of some violent Tempers the chief of which have neither house nor land in the Province, and eat the Bread they get in it by the Indulgence of those they would Injure and destroy." Penn hastened to add that he welcomed good, honest churchmen and their priests in the colony, but not those who were "rude factious & troublesome." [44]

To Robert Harley, Penn wrote: "We cannot yet be so self-denying as to let those that had no part of the heat of the day, not one third of the number, and not one fourth of the estate, and not one tenth of the trouble and labour should give laws to us, and make us dissenters, and worse than that in our own country." [45]

Because Penn was only human, he gained great satisfaction from reporting to the Board of Trade that the priest at Christ Church, Edward Portlock, had accepted £414, Pennsylvania value, from Captain Kidd's doctor while he was in jail. This deprived the Crown of the money which had belonged to pirates and reverted to the English government, and the clergyman had left the colony for Virginia and Maryland. Penn stated the issue clearly: while Parson Portlock "used us in ye pulpit as he pleased & among other things inveighed agst the Quakers for not fighting agst pyrates, those Common enimys of man Kinde, he was actually possest of the 624 pieces of Pyratical Gould, as I may phraise it." Penn added that an Anglican doctor named Hall had an additional 100 pieces of Bradenham's money. [46]

In the meantime some of the royal officials had joined in the campaign of denunciation. After William Penn first arrived in Pennsylvania in December, 1699, issued proclamations, enacted laws, and pledged support to Quary, it seemed that the old conflict had been settled. It was apparent that a vigorous proprietor, pledged to support the Crown, could serve as an effective governor. However in June, 1700, Penn issued commissions to the sheriffs of Philadelphia and Newcastle Counties to serve as water bailiffs; to execute writs, attachments, summons, and replevins upon persons, ships or goods on the Delaware, for the courts of record in the two counties. [47] As soon as Quary heard of this action he wrote a new series of letters condemning the Pennsylvania government. He stated that these commissions "hath broke into the Jurisdiction of the Admiralty & invaded allmost all ye powers." He said he had never labored under more difficulties in his life, and he waited for the Board of Trade to re-establish the powers of the Crown. He piously wished he could keep silent about these matters, but "I cannot wthout betraying yor Lordspps." [48]

Quary failed to report that he had been absent from the colony eight months during the past year; that the commissions had been issued after a vessel in the port fired a cannon ball into a house on the shore; that the advocate for the Court of Admiralty, John Moore, had recommended the issuance of the commissions; that the naval officer of New York, who happened to be in town, drew up the documents; or that the commissions were repealed as soon as Quary returned to Philadelphia and voiced his objections to them.[49] In other words, his complaint was a clear-cut example of half-truths twisted for his own ends.

Randolph joined the chorus of detractors in March, 1701, when he drew up a long list of old charges against Pennsylvania, and added a few new ones. He told the story of his imprisonment by Markham all over again and called Pennsylvania "ye Only receptacle for Pirates & illegall Traders." [50]

While it was true that law and order had been lax in Pennsylvania during the last years of the seventeenth century, there is virtually no evidence that such was the case while Penn was in the colony. There had been piracy, illicit trading, defiance of the Crown, and vice in the plantation during Markham's administration, and the Board of Trade was completely justified in forcing Penn to clean up the commonwealth. Now that Penn had carried out the orders of the Board of Trade he could not understand why the Crown was making an attempt to take his government from him by act of Parliament. When word of the pending bill arrived in Philadelphia in August, 1701, Penn prepared a long letter to the Board of Trade. He admitted the errors the colony had committed in the past, explained his recent actions, and defended his right to govern Pennsylvania. Becoming emotional toward the end of the letter, Penn said: "That persons gaping for Prefermt under the Specious pretence for Serveing the Kings Interest . . . should be countenanced and

encouraged, and all their Representations without further In-
quiry Credited . . . while my Endeavours equal in Sincerity and
application, I dare be bold to say, to those of any of the Kings
more immediate Governts[,] and this without one farthing allowed by the Crown, are made my Guilt and Crime, looks as
if all the old known Rules of Justice were to be read backward . . . I have been a constant Drudge to all your Direction
and a Kings Goverr in all things but a Salary." He expressed
the hope that Parliament would not "lightly suffer other mens
mistakes or ill disigns to p[re]vail with them to ruine Me and
my ffamily." [51]

Not content with writing one letter, Penn wrote to ten of
his friends in the House of Lords.[52] He wrote much the same
thing to all these men. A few examples from his letter to Lord
Romney, brother of his old friend Algernon Sydney, will indicate the kind of plea he made.

Penn stated that he had expended £20,000 on Pennsylvania
in addition to cancelling a debt of £16,000 owed to him by the
king, and asked if it was just to take his colony away from him
under such conditions. He admitted that the proposed law
would leave him proprietor of the land, but said that the property was as nothing in comparison with the right to govern. To
take away the government "is to strip us of our defence both
in our Civil & religious capacity, & to introduce that powr &
Spirit over us we came heither to a voyde." Penn admitted that
there had been mis-government before his arrival, but assured
Romney that all wrongs had been rectified, and that Pennsylvania was a well-governed province. He concluded by saying
that he was particularly grieved to think that "those who ought
[to] be our last resort for redress, should be imposed upon to
attempt It [has ruin] ." [53]

For once the detractors of Pennsylvania had met their match.
Penn finished his most pressing business in the colony and followed his letters home to England, where he was successful in
defeating this attempt to seize Pennsylvania.

CHAPTER TWELVE

PENN'S RETURN TO PENNSYLVANIA

1699

THE BRAVE DREAMS, the great expectations, and the deep faith which had motivated the founding of Pennsylvania as a "holy experiment" were largely faded in 1699 when William Penn returned to the colony. Two years earlier he had written, "The Reports are . . . that there is no place more over run with wickedness[,] sins so very scandalous, openly Committed, in defiance of law & virtue[,] facts so foul, I am forbid [by] my common modesty to relate them." [1] In these words the Proprietor described the colony which he had established as an "example to the Nations." However, the failure of the "holy experiment" did not prevent Pennsylvania from becoming one of the most successful colonizing ventures which the English attempted in the seventeenth century.

Beginning with the year 1690, it was gradually apparent that the plantation would be an economic success. Foreign trade, both the export of local commodities, and the import of goods from England and other colonial possessions, increased. By the time William Penn returned in 1699, Pennsylvania was able to provide a considerable sum of money for the support of the government, and the colony gave ample indication of prosperity in the future. The colony also proved a pecuniary success for the Penn family, although that was less apparent in 1699 than later. During Penn's final visit to the colony he successfully defended his proprietary rights and privileges from the provincial leaders who attempted to circumscribe his prerogatives.

Despite all the criticism and denunciation of Pennsylvania Penn found it comparatively simple to restore law and order in 1700, which indicated that firm foundations had been laid for a durable, responsible political existence during the first two decades. After the Governor consented to the Charter of Privileges in 1701, Pennsylvania possessed one of the finest frames of government in the New World. It provided considerable freedom for the citizens, and at the same time guaranteed the maintenance of law and order. While he was in Pennsylvania, Penn engaged in correspondence with the chief executives of the other provinces of the New World, and cooperated in a governor's conference at New York which helped to create a more favorable opinion of his plantation.

When Penn arrived in Philadelphia on December 2, 1699, "Friends love to the Governor was great and sincere. They were glad to see him again." He was "received wth much joy by ye majr and best part." [2] He had returned to rescue the good name of Pennsylvania from its detractors; fortunately he was successful.

Penn had repeatedly promised himself, the people of Pennsylvania, and the English government, that he would go to his colony in the near future. Always some pressure had prevented him from carrying out his desire. When he first returned to England in 1684 to defend his interests against the Baltimores, he found himself swept up in the whirl of court life around James II, who constantly looked to him for counsel. Following James' abdication in 1688, Penn was in prison or in hiding until 1693. Pennsylvania was in the hands of the Crown and his wife Gulielma was very ill and finally died. Taking care of his motherless children, striving to improve his financial condition, and courting his second wife, Hannah Callowhill, kept him occupied for a time. By then the urgent desire to return to Pennsylvania had abated. He had been gone a dozen years.

In the summer of 1699 things had grown desperate, with Randolph, Quary, and others complaining loudly about the attitude of Markham and his government towards pirates and illicit traders. They added the further charge that there were those in the government who were disrespectful to the officers of the Crown and to the king himself. Penn was forced to travel to Pennsylvania to re-establish law and order and to inculcate a proper respect for the Crown.

Penn gathered his family and belongings on the ship *Canterbury* late in August and left the English coast September 9. He did not touch land again until the night of November 30, when he disembarked to visit Friends at the home of Lydia Wade, near Chester. He proceeded to Philadelphia two days later, where he made a brief call on William Markham and then joined Friends in a First Day afternoon meeting for worship.

James Logan, who had accompanied Penn to the New World as his secretary, was deeply impressed by his reception by the colonists. Several months later he described the scene to Penn's eldest son: "The highest terms I could use would hardly give you an idea of the expectation and welcome that thy father received from the most of the honester party here. Friends generally concluded that, after all their troubles and disappointments, this province now scarce wanting anything more to render it completely happy." [3] Isaac Norris wrote, "all things in Church and Govermt seem to goe well since his Arrival hitherto[.] wee Belive and find him still a true man notwithstanding all the Insinuations of his Enimies Dureing his Absence." [4] In another letter he added, we "hope he will be Sp[iri]tually & Timpourally a Blessing to [us] haveing bin allready much Comforted wth him wee have reason to hope thus & bless god in ye Reception of his marceys." [5] In a third letter Norris mentioned with appreciation the sermons which Penn had delivered in meetings for worship.[6]

William Penn was not only a deeply spiritual person, but he alsq had a magnetic personality, and he captured the hearts of nearly all the Quakers in the colony. He no longer dominated the scene as he had done in the first years, but his presence brought a change to the atmosphere of the plantation. This raising of the spiritual tone made possible the innovations and reforms which Penn planned for the province. However, there were a few Quakers and many more non-Friends who were not pleased to see Penn; they quarreled with him, and caused trouble during the period. Some of these people resented his land policy, especially the requirements in regard to quitrents; others feared his wrath for their past wrongdoings; a small group wished to overthrow the Quaker rule altogether and make Pennsylvania a royal colony; and there may have been a few who engaged in quarreling for its own sake. Logan observed:

The faction that had long contended to overthrow the settled constitution of the government received an universal damp, yet endeavored what mischief they could by speaking whispers that the Proprietary could not act as governor without the king's approbation, and taking an oath, as obliged by Act of Parliament; but that in great measure soon blew over. Colonel Quary, judge and John Moor, advocate of the Admiralty, the two ringleaders, went down to the water-side among the crowd to receive the governor at his landing, who, not seeming to regard the very submissive welcome they gave him, and taking notice of an old acquaintance that stood by them [ignored them].[7]

During the early months of 1700, even some of these individuals were disarmed by Penn's personality and his obvious efforts to reform the province, and the critical reports stopped for a time.

Penn had been given definite instructions by the Crown before he left England, and these claimed his immediate attention. He was ordered to declare the "Act for preventing Frauds, etc.," null and void; he was directed to remove Markham as Lieutenant Governor and to obtain the approbation of the English government before naming a successor; he was to remove David Lloyd and Anthony Morris from all positions in the government; he was required to encourage the Admiralty Court, enforce its actions, and punish those who opposed it; he was to pass laws to regulate trade and punish piracy; he was to establish a militia for the defense of the colony; and he was instructed to report his progress in complying with these orders by writing frequently to the Board of Trade.[8]

Penn made no move to establish a militia, although he did approve maintaining a watch at the mouth of Delaware Bay.

He was reluctant to remove Lloyd from all responsibilities but he eventually did so. Relations with the Admiralty Court were sometimes strained, but they represented a vast improvement over the conditions in previous years. Aside from ignoring his orders in regard to the militia because of religious scruples and only half-heartedly complying with two other orders Penn faithfully carried out his instructions. Perhaps most important was that respect both for local statutes and the laws of England was established in a brief period of time.

William Penn removed Markham from public office immediately. Lame, unwell, and crushed in spirit, Markham was unable to leave Pennsylvania. He was forced to remain in the province where he was the butt of condemnatory remarks and unfavorable comparisons of his government with that of his successor. Markham wrote vigorous letters to the Crown in defense of his actions, but was never able to regain the respectable position he once held. His son-in-law James Brown, who had frequently been accused of piracy, was not allowed to take his place in the Assembly and was eventually shipped to Boston for trial.

Anthony Morris was dealt with in a similar fashion for his actions against the Admiralty Court, but the case of Lloyd was handled with less dispatch. It was not until the end of April, 1700, that Penn was able to report to the Board of Trade that Lloyd had been removed from his positions as Attorney General and Clerk of the courts of Philadelphia County. Two weeks later, when the deposed official was elected to the Council from Chester County, Quary appeared with sufficient evidence against him to persuade the Council to refuse him a seat. Penn did not disgrace Lloyd entirely. He was allowed to practice law, for even Colonel Quary admitted, "He was much needed and trusted in the Estates of ye People of the Province, and . . . it might be very detrimental to ye Inhabitants as well as . . . [an] Obstruction of the Course of Courts, he being the alone man versed in the Law, . . . This and the want of Instructions postponed his full disgrace." In further defense of his action, Penn added that though Lloyd denied some of the facts and all of the "Aggravation & Venom" ascribed to him, yet Penn had shown him "Resentmt, I believe, equal to your Wish, and therefore not short of my Duty." [9]

On December 23, 1699, Penn and the Council issued a proclamation against piracy and offered a reward of ten pounds for the capture of pirates.[10] A month later the General Assembly was convened to enact laws for the suppression of piracy and illicit trade. The two bills included a clause which forbade trade with Madagascar and Natoll [Natal], but it was soon discovered that none of the members of the Assembly knew where the latter forbidden place was located.[11] The members of the two houses also drew up a statement to the Crown protesting the innocence of the people of the province. They said: "We have and Always had a just abhorrence of them [pirates] and their practices & look upon them as Enemies to mankind and hope wee Shall upon all occasions Use our Utmost dilligence and endeavours to discountenance and Suppress them." They denied that Pennsylvania had been enriched by illicit trade, and said they were certain that their accusers knew it was "our Industry [and] . . . the blessing of God upon our honest Endeavours and Labours," which had made the colony prosperous. The men expressed sorrow that others were jealous who "have not Expended their substance nor Trodd the Same weary Ste [ps t] o Improve it as wee have done." [12]

Penn's response to the orders in regard to the admiralty court was less clear-cut. In the beginning he actively defended the court and urged his freemen to cooperate with Quary and his men. The judge wrote to the Board of Trade: "I must doe Governr Penn the Justice to say that he is very zealous in promoting all things that doth any ways concerne the Kings Interest." [13] He added that he hoped he would never have to complain again, which "was never easy or gratefull to me."

The members of the General Assembly stated in the address quoted above: "And as to Obstructing the Officers of the Customs and Court of Admiralty wee hope the Governmt is Cleare of it but if any particulars have been faulty In that Respect they are Answerable for the same." [14] However, William Penn soon realized that there was determined opposition to the Court of Admiralty by some of the provincials, and he began to modify his strong defense of it. He told the Board of Trade, the people "are very cool in considering of my Circumstances, thinking themselves injured in their Reputation, and unsafe in their Interests, believing the Common Law to be overruled by the Admiralty Office." [15] It was his opinion that the court overstepped its authority when it insinuated itself into such questions as "Charter-Parties, Wages, Bread, Beer, Sails, Smith Work, Carpenter's Work done at the Key or Dock," in a port approximately 150 miles inland from the sea. He added that in New York, Maryland and Boston the admiralty court had no such power. In the previous chapter mention was made of the altercation between Quary and Penn over the appointment of water bailiffs during this period.

By the fall of 1700, Penn had grown discouraged about the situation in the colony. The people of Delaware strongly disliked the law enacted to restrict illegal trade in tobacco, while the Pennsylvania Quakers resented Penn's treatment of Morris and Lloyd. To give emphasis to their feelings, the members of the General Assembly showed great reluctance about granting money to Penn.[16] The Proprietor's pessimism was premature however, for the General Assembly, which was in session at the time he wrote the letter, later provided for him generously.

Shortly afterwards, a letter arrived from the Board of Trade which complimented Penn on the improvements which "you say have been made both in the country and city, and so long as such improvements do not arise from any unlawful courses, or means that interfere with His Majesty's service and the Interest of England, nor tend to the injury of other plantations, we shall always rejoice to hear of their further encrease." [17] In a pious tone which rivaled that found in some of Penn's letters to his colonists, the communication continued: "and as we shall never be backward in giving what encouragement lies in our power to all industrious and fair improvements both there and elsewhere, so we hope you will also in your own private concerns receive more stable advantages by that conduct than by any different method."

William Penn did not meet with nearly as much adversity as some of his lieutenants had faced in previous years, but his situation resembled the circumstances which had sometimes harassed Blackwell, Markham, and others. The difference was of degree rather than kind. The two years of direct proprietary rule paralleled conditions in the early years in another fashion. Just as some of his predecessors had governed Pennsylvania under two or more types of constitutions or commissions, Penn ruled the colony under two frames and joined in writing a third, besides running the government without a constitution for more than a year.

The so-called Markham's Frame, written in 1696, had never received the approval of William Penn; nevertheless, the first General Assembly he called had been elected under that charter in the previous year. However, when the writs were sent out calling the members to meet January 25, 1700, the following statement was appended to the usual wording: "Saving to ye pr[opriet]or & Gor ye same power hee had before ye enacting of ye Late frame of governmt." [18] This body met for a few days to pass the laws which Penn had promised the Board of Trade that he would enact.[19]

In the meantime, Robert Turner, Griffith Jones, Francis Rawle, and Joseph Wilcox, who had long denied the validity of Markham's Frame, entreated Penn to set this constitution aside. Realizing that a new charter was needed, the men urged the Governor to call for the election of a General Assembly under the Charter of Liberties. They suggested that Penn, with this legally elected body of representatives of the freemen, could then revise the constitution. They stated that "such settlement will be most satisfactorie to the well effected." [20] Acting upon this advice, William Penn issued writs for an election of councillors and assemblymen on March 10, 1700, in accordance with the provisions of the Second Frame. These writs were sent out at virtually the same time the General Assembly chosen under Markham's Frame was meeting with him, which caused some confusion.

The new Council, elected under the provisions of the Charter of Liberties, began to straggle into town on March 30, 1700, and was organized the following Monday, April 1, when fifteen members had arrived. Penn opened this meeting of the legislative session by suggesting that both the laws and their execution needed to be modified. He considered some of the laws obsolete, imperfect, and harmful, and wanted them changed, but he urged the Council to move slowly. He preferred a few laws well enforced to a large number which were ignored.

Penn promised to cooperate in altering the constitution if that was the will of the representatives, but he advised them against trifling with the government. He added that it was his sincere wish that governments were not necessary, and said as he had in the past that governments were but a means to an end, and not an end in themselves.

Urging the representatives to halt political intrigue, he said, "Friends, away wt all p[ar]ties, & Look on yorselves & what is good for all, as a bodie politick, first as undr ye king & Crown of England, & next as undr me, by L[ette]res patent from yt Crown." He said that it pained him to hear that religion had been an issue in the election just held in Philadelphia. "Study peace, & be att unitie[,] ey[e] ye good of all, & I desire to see mine no otherwise than in ye publick's prosperitie." [21]

When he finished, one member of the Council moved that the people be given a new charter. Penn asked the members whether they believed the Charter of Liberties or Markham's Frame was in effect at that moment. A member replied that by reservations they had continued the best parts of the old charter while writing the new. Penn said, "The act of Settlemt served till I came; now I'm come, It Cannot bind me agt my owne act."

The Governor had called on the Council to draw up a revision of the laws to present to the Assembly for its assent or dissent. The upper house, which realized that the Assembly would no longer tolerate such an inferior share in lawmaking did virtually nothing during the two weeks that it met. The single bill it approved was written to permit the General Assembly to meet twenty days longer than provided for in the Second Frame, to allow the lower house to share in compiling new laws.

The second General Assembly during Penn's stay in the colony convened on May 10, 1700, in accordance with the provisions of the Charter of Liberties.[22] After John Blunston was introduced to the Governor and Council as the speaker of the lower house on May 13, William Penn addressed the joint session. Unfortunately there is no record of what he said. For the next month the members remained in Philadelphia discussing a number of things but they reached few conclusions.[23] Apparently many days were consumed in fruitless argument over the provisions of a new constitution, especially the question of the number of representatives from each county in the legislature. Twelve bills were under debate, but the two houses concurred on only eight of them, including a law "granting an impost upon wines, Rum, beer, ale, &c., & goods imported, retailed & sold in this province & territories." [24]

On Friday, June 7, when the General Assembly was moving toward adjournment, Penn asked the legislators about the new charter which they had been discussing. They answered that while no agreement had been reached concerning a new constitution the men were agreed that they did not wish to be governed by the charter of 1683. The Governor then asked the members of the two houses if they wished him to rule without a constitution until agreement could be reached on a new frame of government. He promised to be guided by his Letters Patent from Charles II and the Act of Union in the interim period. The men agreed to this proposal although there were a few negative votes. It was unanimously decided that the laws passed at Chester in 1682, the laws approved by Governor Fletcher in 1693, and all laws passed since that time except those repealed or altered by later laws, should remain in force until twenty days after the rising of the next General Assembly. Penn also promised that the guarantees concerning property contained in the Second Frame, of 1683, should continue.

Following these decisions Blunston and William Biles for the assemblymen and councillors from the Province, and William Rodney and John Hill for the assemblymen and councillors from Delaware and all four in behalf of all the freemen of the colony took the Charter of 1683 and delivered it back to Governor Penn. He responded:

> Friends, since you wer dissatisfied wt ye Chartr you had, & yt you could not agree among yorselves about a new one, I shall be easie in ruling you by the king's Lettrs Pats. & act of Union, & shall in the ruleing of you, Consider my grant from the king & you that I am to rule, and shall from time to time endeavor to give you satisfacon. I advice you not to be easilie displeased One with another, be slow to anger & swift to charitie, so I wish you all well to yor homes.

Until October 28, 1701, Pennsylvania had no constitution. This situation could have been dangerous with another governor or proprietor, but William Penn took no advantage of it, and in the end granted his subjects a more liberal charter than they had possessed previously.

The Governor decided that it would be desirable to gather a small group of the colonial leaders around him as a Council, even though he was no longer required to comply with any specific governmental pattern. He broke with his former practice by naming his councillors instead of calling for an election, but both Fletcher and Markham had followed the same course on occasion. Nine men were chosen during June, and the first meeting of the Council was held June 25, 1700, with six present. With the exception of Thomas Story, a prominent Friend who was in the colony temporarily to minister to the Quaker community, the men were experienced political figures in the plantation.[25] These men attended Penn from time to time during the summer.

With the approval of his Council, Penn decided on September 12 that the people should elect representatives to the lower house of the General Assembly. He hoped that the legislature could reach agreement on a new charter, revise the old laws, and pass an appropriation bill. The sheriffs were issued writs which summoned the freemen of each county to gather on October 1 to elect four persons to represent them in the Assembly which would meet in New Castle October 14, 1700. In the county elections several members of Penn's Council were selected for the Assembly and chose to serve in it rather than continue in the upper house. For example, Growdon was elected and then was named speaker of the Assembly. Penn was nettled by this attack on his appointed Council, but agreed to excuse the men from serving when they promised to return to his Council after the Assembly adjourned. In the meantime, to prevent the body from becoming too small he named three more councillors: Phineas Pemberton, William Biles, and John Blunston.[26]

One of Penn's relatives who held an office in the government, Edward Penington, expected very little from this session of the General Assembly. In a letter written October 11 to Phineas Pemberton, he expressed surprise "yt thou has flip't thy neck out of ye Collar," referring to the fact that Pemberton had not been elected to the Assembly. He added that he was "not sorry thou art for this time not one of ye Elect for I expect little good from them, & if they do no hurt it is all I can hope for all things considered." [27] The dire predictions of Penington were not fulfilled, for a good deal was accomplished during the session. One hundred and four laws were enacted, which included a complete revision of all the laws of the colony, plus three new tax bills. The legislators did not agree on a charter but many of the problems were thoroughly aired, which made it easier for the men to reconcile their differences the following year when the new frame was adopted.

Nevertheless it was a long, tempestuous session. Isaac Norris, who was in the Assembly, mentioned it in several letters. To John Askew he wrote, "I am at length come home fro[m] Newcastle wch has Jaded us all and I believe s[p]oiled many of us for Statesmen." [28] He described the session in more detail to Daniel Zachary. "I am at length got home from Wearysome

Newcastle, after near 7 weeks sessions—much tensing and some-times almost of[f] the Hinges—for they would Creek Loudly-yn wee used Oyl and Reduct or Selves to good ordr again[.] Some Turbulent Spiritts would oft indeavr to Drive it to a pitcht Battle betwixt uppr Countys and Lower[,] Quakrs & churchmen but in Short wee at lenght brot it to a pretty good Conclusion." [29] A few weeks later he was not so sure about political conditions, and wrote, "As to Publick Affairs I am Sylent for it is hard to state our case at a Distance when wee don't know it our Selves." [30]

The fourth meeting of the General Assembly since Penn's arrival took place on August 1, 1701. The men gathered once again in the following month to prepare for the Governor's departure. Penn addressed the members on August 2, and apol-ogized to the legislators for convening them during the har-vest season. He said that he had received a letter from the King which called on the colony to contribute £350 towards the ex-pense of building fortifications in New York, which letter "I now lay before you and recommend to your Serious Considera-tion, since without it, t'will be impossible to answer them." [32]

The Assembly wasted two days in the kind of parliamentary maneuvering which had been used against former executives on such occasions. The members asked to see the king's letter as well as a copy of Penn's address to them, and were not satis-fied when the Governor replied that he had spoken extempora-neously and had no copy of his speech. When the Assembly did bring in an answer it was a negative one. It protested complete "Loyalty to our Sovereign," and then proceeded to list the fa-miliar reasons for the refusal: the infancy of the colony, the taxes promised to Penn in the previous session, the arrears in quitrents, and the failure of neighboring colonies to contribute. The Assembly closed the reply with the following: "we earn-estly desire the Proprietary would candidly represent our Con-ditions to the King, and assure him of our Readiness (according to our Abilities) to acquiesce with, and answer his Commands, as far as our religious Persuasions shall permit, as becomes loyal and faithful Subjects so to do." [33]

Seven men from Delaware called on Penn to acquaint the king with the defenseless condition of the three lower counties on the coastal frontier of the colony. The legislators stated that their people had no money to buy guns or ammunition, having spent all to raise tobacco for the benefit of England. They called on the king to provide for the protection of their homes before he asked the colonists to contribute to the defense of New York. This letter must have been intended as much for Penn as for the king, and perhaps the authors wished the Board of Trade who had ordered the Governor to establish a militia in the colony, to see it. No action was taken in regard to this second address, and the General Assembly was adjourned.

In summary, it appears that one lasting contribution to the development of Pennsylvania was made during the period of the first four sessions of the General Assembly under Penn's direction. This distinctive contribution came in the third session, the one which convened in New Castle, October, 1700. The members of the two houses met to hear from Penn, who said: "I recomend to you the revisal of ye Laws; what to Continue, what to repeal, what to alter, what to explain, & what new ones is requisit to make." [34]

For nearly twenty years, ever since the passage of laws at Chester in 1682, the General Assembly had been forming a legal patchwork quilt. Statutes were added to or subtracted from the body of laws in a haphazard fashion. In 1693 Governor Fletcher had forced a revision of the laws, and a body of laws known as the Petition of Right resulted from his demands that the colonists consolidate their enactments and bring them into order. After he was replaced the legislators reverted to the casual attitude of former years.

Penn suspected that the informal way in which the General Assembly altered the laws had contributed to the moral laxness noticed in the colony before he arrived. He believed that the situation would be greatly improved if the laws were revised so that a compact, useful law code could replace the sprawling collection of statutes in force.

Some time had been spent in discussing a revision of the laws in the May session of the General Assembly, but it was not until November that the legislators reached agreement on a new compilation which would entirely replace all previous enactments. The list of 104 statutes was headed by the guarantee of liberty of conscience which Penn considered all-important, and it concluded with a law to protect Indians from unscrupulous traders. Most of the laws included in the new compilation were taken directly from the old statutes books, frequently *in toto,* although on occasion two or more old laws were combined to form a new one. The laws were passed in two parts, 1 through 90 and 92 to 104, with the ninety-first law as an introduction to the second group. No completely satisfactory reason can be offered for this separation, although most of the laws in the final group were concerned with government procedure. However there were also such laws among the first ninety.[35]

As the governor of a growing colony which was beset with many problems, and as proprietor of a feudal domain which claimed a good deal of his time, William Penn was extremely busy during the two years that he lived in Pennsylvania. Nevertheless he found time to carry on a considerable correspondence with governors in neighboring colonies, and he joined with some of them in a conference at New York in 1700. Penn's care in cultivating the friendship of the executives of the other plantations must have been motivated in part by a desire to guarantee friendly reports from them to the Board of Trade. The officials of the neighbor provinces had in the past written embarrassing observations of Pennsylvania to that body. Confident that he had been successful in this mission, in 1700 he urged officials in London to accept the impartial testimony of the Earl of Bellomont and Colonel Blackistan in support of his contention that Pennsylvania had been reformed.[36] Penn considered it his duty to correspond with the men with whom he shared the responsibility of governing the English colonies, and since he was a friendly, outgoing person, he undoubtedly enjoyed the exchange of greetings.

Although he wrote to the governors of West Jersey, Maryland, Virginia, and some of the English possessions in the West

Indies, Penn wrote to Bellomont in New York most frequently. Most of his comments to the earl had to do with colonial matters, but other subjects were also mentioned. Of Frederick, the Elector of Brandenburg, who had just taken the title of King of [in] Prussia, he wrote, "He is a good Sort of Man to all serious people that dissent from the National Worship, and instead of persecuting them, bade the others outpreach and out live them." [37] He wrote appreciatively of Bellomont's advice in legal matters, and said that he needed it "to ballance the Insolence and Ignorance too of some that pretend here to the Law, for to say that the Kings Lawyers are of another mind will be a Redoubt invincible." [38] On another occasion Penn expressed relief that the pirates were being sent home to be tried in England, "ffor tho they are some of the worst of Human Race, Life is a tender thing, and I can't forbear thinking that Am[eri]ca is not yet furnished, wth ye skill requisite in the Civil Law to be exact & safe in proceedings of So high a Nature."[39] When Governor Nicholson of Virginia was ill, Penn sent him a prescription which consisted of an infusion of wormwood, century, agrimony, and camamile flowers, to be taken hot and cold, at meals and between, "to fortify the stomack and sweeten the blood." [40]

More important was the fact that Penn joined Bellomont and Nicholson in September, 1700, at New York, to draw up suggestions for cooperation between the colonies. A list of nine recommendations was compiled and sent to the Crown. These may be summarized as follows: 1, there should be a single value set for coins in all colonies, since pieces of eight were worth from five shillings in Virginia and Carolina, to seven shillings, eight pence, in Pennsylvania; 2, a mint should be established to mint small coins, such as a silver piece worth six pence; 3, the shipping of timber to England from America should be encouraged by imposts on foreign timber, especially masts; 4, the border to the north between the English and the French should be adjusted; 5, the various colonies should make the same laws to deal with fraudulent debtors, runaways, and rovers; 6, uniform naturalization proceedings should be established; 7, appeals to England should be limited to those involving more than 300 pounds; 8, rewards paid out of the belongings of pirates should be offered to encourage the pirates' apprehension; 9, uniform control over marriage should be established to prevent bigamy and clandestine marriages.[41]

The Board of Trade should have been favorably impressed by Penn's willingness to join with royal governors in drawing up recommendations for unifying the procedures in the English colonies and strengthening the tie between the plantations and the mother country. Unfortunately, all the good work which had been accomplished by Penn inside and outside Pennsylvania counted for little in England, for a new, vigorous attempt to take Penn's charter from him had commenced in Parliament. Nevertheless, great strides had been taken in putting things to rights in Pennsylvania.

CHAPTER THIRTEEN

A FLOURISHING PLANTATION

1690 TO 1701

WILLIAM PENN must have been overwhelmed by the changes he saw when he returned to Pennsylvania late in 1699. Fifteen years earlier Philadelphia had been a small, struggling village, and a farmer who cleared ten acres of land was fortunate indeed. Even though reports were sent to Penn during his absence, they could scarcely have prepared him for the transformation he beheld.

Philadelphia had become a small city with a population of nearly 5,000 persons.[1] Forests had been removed and the land turned to farming along 170 miles of the Delaware River and Bay, and in some places the clearings extended sixteen miles inland.[2] Many of the townspeople were wearing fine clothing imported from England. Shipbuilding was in progress on the banks of the Delaware. Each year the colony sold thousands of pounds worth of goods to England, the West Indies, and neighboring colonies. When Penn finished a survey of the economic conditions of Pennsylvania he was critical of only one thing, that the people were importing more than they exported. He started several projects which he hoped would lessen the gap in the trade balance.

The story of the struggle for survival in the early years was told in a previous chapter. The year 1690 was the turning point in the economic history of the colony, for with the advent of King William's War, which provided ready markets for all Pennsylvania could raise for export, the colony began a slow, steady improvement. By 1700, Colonel Quary, who was ad-

dicted neither to passing out compliments to Pennsylvania
nor to praising her to the English government, wrote to the
Board of Trade of "ye present State of this province[,] it growes
very Populous & the People are generally very laborious & Industrious[;] they have improved tilledge to that degree that they
have made Bread[,] fflower & Beer a drugg in all the Marketts
in the West Indies." [3] But although the colony gave ample evidence of prosperity and material development, it faced many
problems during these years, such as a scarcity of specie. In
the eyes of the English government it was still one of the small-
est plantations in the New World.

References to economic life in Pennsylvania in this period
are rare and generally refer to the development of some new
type of business venture or to the commerce which flowed in
and out of Philadelphia. The great majority of the people of
the plantation were engaged in farming although there is little
information on farmers. One of the few specific references to
agriculture in documents available for these years stated that
two men with four horses could cultivate enough land to
produce 1,000 bushels of wheat. At four shillings a bushel this
meant an income of £200, "three times more than any of the
other Colonies or Islands can produce." [4] Virtually all the exports were from the farms of Pennsylvania and the Lower
Counties, although some furs, whale oil, and a few other non-
agricultural products were sold. Another observer wrote to
Penn, "Sr Your Country dayly improves wth Inhabitants & is
Cultivated wth great industry much exceeding the Neighbouring Provinces which Creats their envy and Malicious endeavors
to hindr its prosperity by having the Govrmt altered which
otherwise will if Incouraged undoubtedly in little time be the
flower of the whole Continent." [5]

There are no figures available on the population of Pennsylvania at the turn of the century, but Penn mentioned in one
letter that new settlers were coming in at the rate of 1,500 annually.[6] The Proprietor lamented that this figure was not
greater, but Jonathan Dickinson was highly gratified by the
growth and wrote, "this place is so thronged with people that

there is hardly A house Empty. & rents grow high." He was also impressed by the high quality of the colonists, saying, "they are Chiefly familys." [7]

The indentured servants coming into the colony were also above average. Isaac Norris, representative in Pennsylvania for various persons engaged in commerce, wrote to one man in England in 1699, urging him to send over young men with trades, such as carpenters, masons, shoemakers, tailors, or men trained in husbandry, who could be sold for eighteen or twenty pounds each. "Send few women Unless Youngly & fitt for huswifry Either in town or country." "Lett all be b[o]und in England[,] be Sure Give the master a charge to use them Kindly for there is Little Difference in the Charge and it gains a good Name." [8]

In addition to the immigration of colonists from the Old World, a sizable number deserted the neighboring provinces to move to the Quaker plantation. Most of those who migrated did so to better themselves financially. Some were motivated by political reasons. For example, Markham wrote to Penn that some came because in Pennsylvania, "men are protected by Laws, & not put in fear of caning or cudgelling [at the hands of Governor Nicholson in Maryland], wch has been ye occasion of severall of their inhabitants seating amongst us, and att this time more are coming of their first Rank." [9] Thus, for the third time, an observer stated that the persons who came to settle in Pennsylvania were above the average. These three statements could conceivably be the result of the kind of tactics which are the stock in trade of the modern chambers of commerce. The fact that the remarks were included in private letters would lend credence to the idea that they represented the honest opinions of the writers. Other evidence corroborates the testimony of these three men, and the statement that many of the early settlers of Pennsylvania had a great deal to contribute to the wealth of the colony cannot be easily dismissed.

During the first decade there was no attempt made to collect either import duties or levies on property.[10] The colony was striving to gain a foothold and the representatives in the Assembly strongly objected to any attempt to collect taxes. However beginning in 1693, a number of assessments were laid on the colonists. Although it was no easy task to collect the money, a considerable sum was raised during the second decade. Governor Benjamin Fletcher pushed through a tax which he expected to yield some £760. During Markham's rule two levies were made on property by the legislature. When Penn called the Council and Assembly together in 1700, duties were laid on the importation of liquor and other items, estimated to bring in a return of from £500 to £1,000 annually. Later in the year a grant of £2,000 was made to the Proprietor, to be levied on property. The success of these ventures in public finance are a clear indication that the colony was more prosperous and more responsible than it had been in the early years of its existence. The reluctance of the freemen to pay their taxes was equalled by their unwillingness to meet their obligations to the Proprietor in the form of quitrents. No longer did the colonists plead inability to pay, but they found many legalistic reasons for refusing to honor their feudal debts. The colonists made a distinction between Penn the political leader and Penn the feudal overlord.

Quakers have long had a reputation for purchasing plain, simple goods of the highest quality, and this was already in evidence in the 1690s. The epistle sent by Philadelphia Friends to London Yearly Meeting in 1698 urged the merchants to send "no flowerd Striped or Gaudy Stuffs, Fringed Curtains, Ribbon Hat Bands, Needless Furniture for Horses, as brass Bosses, or brass Nails on the Bridles, nor anything Else that may not Suit the Plainess of our Profession." [11] Norris, describing what would sell in Philadelphia, urged one correspondent to send serge, "if prettey fine plaine And Good." He added, that "Bedd ticks if fine and Large do the Better." He expressed the belief that he could sell curtains and valance if there were no printed fringes or if the fringes were small. They should be "Plaine Either white or Coullared . . . Especially the white & finest Sorts." He also thought that he would be able to sell some brown cloth.[12] The sale of such goods was a profitable venture, for he marked the price above the cost in England, "from 100 to 120 p[er] c[en]t according to ye want or Cheapness."

While nearly all the inhabitants were engaged in farming and most of the remainder were in commerce and merchandising, there were a few individuals who were active in crude manufacturing. Several water-driven grist mills, brick kilns, and mines were operated during the first years. At the beginning of the last decade of the century, William Rittenhouse, with the support of the printer William Bradford, constructed the first paper mill in the English colonies, along the Wissahickon near Germantown.[13] In 1693 a group of men headed by Richard Hayns appeared before the Lords of Trade to obtain permission to develop a trade in naval stores in Pennsylvania, which would indicate that the colony was gaining a reputation for producing such stores at a profit.[14]

The construction of ships began in the last years of the century. Norris described one partly-completed vessel as having a fifty-one-foot keel, a twenty-foot beam, and an eleven-foot hold, and he said that it would cost £325 plus iron work and rigging.[15] This figure was considerably below the cost of building a comparable ship in England, and Norris persuaded some of his English business associates to have a vessel constructed at Philadelphia. To his dismay the ship was more costly than he had been led to believe, and it took longer to complete than had been anticipated.

Unfortunately there are no overall figures on Pennsylvania's trade during this decade, but a few scattered statements and statistics indicate that commerce grew rapidly. One authority stated that by the year 1693 all the trade of West Jersey went through Philadelphia; the settlers of that province sold their raw materials and purchased what they needed in the Pennsylvania capital. He added that in the following year complaints were recorded in the Journal of the Maryland House of Delegates because trade with Pennsylvania had drawn off £1,500 sterling in two years.[16] Governor Fletcher in New York admitted in 1696 that "The town of Philadelphia in fourteen year's time is become nearly equal to the city of New York in trade and riches." [17]

The Board of Trade compiled figures on the trade between England and the various plantations for the years 1698 and 1699, which indicate that the trade of the colony was increasing. From Michaelmas, September 29, 1697, to the same date in 1698, Pennsylvania sent to England produce valued at £2,720 and purchased £10,702 worth. In the same period the following year the goods sent to England were worth £4,540, and those coming into Pennsylvania cost £17,062. These figures did not include other foreign trade. This was greater, especially the exports, with much going to the West Indies.[18]

Even though the second decade of Pennsylvania's history was a time of prosperity, several problems faced the settlers. Three of these years saw the colony hit by catastrophes beyond human control. The crops were very short in 1694, and the people lost large numbers of cattle and other livestock. The colony still felt the effects of the year in the summer of 1695.[19] In the bitter winter of 1697–1698 carts crossed the Delaware river on the ice until March and a number of Negroes died of the cold.[20] In August 1699 the dread yellow fever hit Philadelphia and took a fearful toll. Ports everywhere were closed to Pennsylvania vessels and ships did not come up the Delaware. Business came to a halt, and 220 persons died. Norris wrote, we must "Submitt to the will of our Almighty and wise God who Is now sheawing his power In order I believe to our Humilliation and To drive us near to himself—Oh yt it may have that Effect upon all." [21] Those with more scientific understanding believed the disease came from the West Indies where it had raged in former years. The following summer there was another small attack and some forty died on the two sides of the river.[22]

One problem which plagued Pennsylvania and many other colonies was the shortage of money. Specie and bills of credit for use in commerce with England and other plantations, and cash for the conduct of business within the colony were scarce. In June, 1699, Norris was willing to give a premium of sixteen pence for pieces of eight and could not find any to buy at that rate.[23] In April of the following year he wrote: "For my part I am Almost quite out of Cash and tho Several hundreds oweing to mee, yet cannot [collect] in money." [24] Norris wrote of a cargo which arrived in May: "I do think that had I offered ye whole Cargoe now come in for 30 p[er cent.] P[ennsylvania] Ready Money I should not have mett a Chap man yt would & Could buy it." [25]

Competition for business was very keen, and the first ship to arrive in the spring had a better chance of disposing of its cargo than had later ones. Norris described his activities in 1700 when the *Pennsylvania Merchant* arrived two days ahead of other vessels. "We had ye start[,] I was very quick at opening and have been Industrious in ye sale Attending it from 5 in ye Morning till Night And this to gett ym . . . [who] pick & Choose—I have disposed of about £8,001 worth of our money some at 3 mo. trust." [26]

Sometimes goods arrived in a deplorable condition, such as cheeses half spoiled, barrels of tar that had water in them, or calico which had bad water stains on it.[27] In 1700 Norris bought an expensive clock which soon would not run and did not strike. The wooden parts shrank and came unglued, the lacquer work peeled off, and the clock looked "as Scabbed as a Mangy Dog." [28] Even new settlers had trouble, for Norris wrote of a girl who had been in the colony a bit more than six months and was returning to England; "she takes to nothing here yt may be a Maintainance." Perhaps there was no longer a shortage of women, or perhaps she was not very attractive and thus no men had paid honorable court to her. She was probably a Quaker for she came under Penn's care.[29]

Although Pennsylvania gave substantial evidence of prosperity, as late as 1696 Penn stated that the settlers had not yet earned enough to repay themselves for the original investment.[30] An indication of the size of the colony in comparison with other older provinces is found in the following figures. The Board of Trade drew up quotas in October, 1700, for contributions towards a £5,000 defense fund which the colonies were expected to raise. Massachusetts was given the largest quota, nearly one-fourth of the total sum, and Virginia had the second largest quota, £828. Only two other colonies, New Hampshire and Rhode Island, had smaller allotments than the £276 expected from Pennsylvania.[31]

The weakness in the economic situation of the colony which attracted the attention of William Penn was the unfavorable trade balance between Pennsylvania and England. He wrote to the Board of Trade in 1701: "I have apointed a committee to meet weekly, of ye ablest persons in this town, for trade & estates, to consider of means of makeing beneficial returns, that we may, as little as possible lessen our commerce for the Growth of England, else they must endeavor, of meer necessity, a self-subsistance as to the things wch as yet they want from or Mother Country."[32] The colony decided to narrow the gap between imports and exports by renewing the search for whales for oil, and entering the cod-fishing trade. In addition, the plantation planned to raise more tobacco and purchase a larger amount of furs from the Indians, all for export. In the spirit of mercantilism Penn concluded, "It is trade must make America valluable to England, and if the Industry of the Inhabitants be not encouraged & well conducted, the Colonys must either Sinck, or become a great Charge to the Crown to support them."[33]

Thus it can be said that although Pennsylvania had faced hardships in the past and was still bothered by a few problems, it was a vigorous, prosperous plantation in 1701 when this study concludes. William Penn, with the single exception noted, felt it necessary to make no apologies for the economic condition of his colonizing venture, although he deplored some other aspects of the enterprise. Despite the moral failure of the "holy experiment," Pennsylvania was a great economic success.

FINANCIAL RETURNS FOR PENN

This promising condition and optimistic outlook did not mean that the colonists were ready to assume the responsibility of providing William Penn with a financial return equal to his expectations.

Penn was always two persons to the colonists of Pennsylvania: he was a kindly governor and spiritual leader who helped them establish a vigorous state and a virtuous society; and he was a feudal overlord and financial oppressor who demanded payment of quitrents and taxes. Never had Penn's peculiar situation been more apparent to the colonists than it was during the two years when he returned to live among them once again. He was active as a minister among Friends and shared fully in the Quaker community. He cooperated with the legislators in reorganizing the laws and granted a constitution which met with general satisfaction. But Penn returned to Pennsylvania weighted down with the indebtedness which Philip Ford had fraudulently foisted on him, and he was determined to obtain as much money from the colonists as possible. Penn expected to sell land at higher prices than before along both the Delaware and Susquehanna rivers, to lighten his financial burden. He was in no mood to deal gently with attempts by the colonists to escape their feudal obligations to him, and he refused to modify his land policy in answer to the petition of the Assembly in September, 1701.

Penn's financial entanglement has been described. By 1699 the Governor had surrendered his proprietary rights in Pennsylvania to Ford and was forced to lease them back for an annual fee. In addition, Penn owed his wily creditor more than £11,000. Young Philip Ford came to the colony while Penn was there, and Isaac Norris was asked by the elder Ford to observe the actions of the Governor and report to him. Truly, William Penn was surrounded.[34]

Penn had invested more than £20,000 in Pennsylvania, and with interest added the figure would be doubled, yet he had received virtually nothing in return.[35] During his absence Penn had written innumerable letters to the political leaders directing them to enact laws in the government for the collection of taxes to lessen the financial burden of the colony, and they did nothing. He had been equally insistent in his correspondence with the men in charge of gathering his quitrents, and the result was just as frustrating. Penn had discovered to his sorrow that it was virtually impossible for an absentee Governor and Proprietor to profit from the prosperous plantation. Now he was determined to find out whether he could collect any money while he was in the colony.

Penn discussed his financial situation with some of the colonial leaders, although he did not disclose his humiliating obligation to Philip Ford. The provincial men of affairs were sympathetic and began to look for a way to assist him. They did not wish to discourage the legislature from appropriating more taxes, nor did they wish to set a precedent by granting an outright gift. They hit on the idea of purchasing land on the Susquehanna as a means of aiding their governor in an unobtrusive manner.[36]

Apparently some other freemen were not as understanding as these men, for on April 1, 1700, Penn said in Council, "Some say I come to gett monie & be gone, phapps they that say so wish itt so. I hope I or mine shall be wt you, while I or they Live." [37] The Governor was unable to keep that promise but his decision to return home was forced upon him by pressures beyond his control.

Penn's attempt to obtain money from the government was successful financially but left resentment in the hearts of many of the colonists. Years later James Logan described the situation to John, Thomas, and Richard Penn in these words:

Your father with whom I came over in 1699 being extreamly pinch'd by his Debt to fford, wch was Kept entirely Secret, had hopes on his Arrival of raising a considerable Sum here, which was not then easily practicable, therefore during the first year here, to the great dissatisfaction of his friends who had recvd him with transports of joy he was hard to the People, and thereby lost the affection of many who had almost adored him. the next year convinced of his former mistake, he gave all that was desired of him & more, yet at his departure left a powerful faction agst his Interest which continued several years.[38]

In response to requests from the Governor, a law was passed in June, 1700, which granted him duties on various imports including liquor, and the legislators said that it would provide him with an income of £1,000 annually. Penn thought it would bring in no more than one-half that amount and wrote, it "will not defray half of my house keeping." [39] Other observers in the colony agreed with this estimate. The Governor pressed for larger appropriations when the General Assembly convened in October, 1700, at New Castle. Three money bills were included in the 104 laws enacted at the session. The first of these renewed the law signed in June, after it had been amended. A duty of twenty shillings on the importation of Negro slaves over sixteen years of age was included, as well as a duty of forty shillings on every £100 worth of goods exported from the colony. A small tax on the retailing of alcoholic beverages such as cider, beer, ale, wine, and rum, was provided for in the law.

The second of the tax bills was drawn up to enforce the collection of the assessments laid in 1699 under Markham's rule. This act, like others in the 1690s, exacted one penny per pound worth of property, with a six shilling minimum. Those who had already paid their taxes were exempt under the new law but apparently most freemen were delinquent. The third and most important law provided £2,000 for William Penn. The members of the Assembly had little difficulty agreeing on the amount, but were unable to determine how the money would be secured. It was finally decided to give each county a quota to raise, and leave it to the local governments to secure the money.[40] A minimum of four shillings for each male over sixteen years of age was stated in the law, and the remainder of the money was to be collected from the property holders. The assessments were to be paid to William Penn in two installments, the first in May, 1701, and the second in December.[41]

Many people were not pleased with the third appropriation bill, although it had been passed unanimously in the Assembly. Norris heard rumors that some freemen would try to escape paying the assessments.[42] William Penn had been granted practically nothing in nineteen years, and now that the colony was prosperous enough to pay him something it had grown so independent that it resented any attempt to have it pay.

While he was in the colony Penn made plans for the sale of more property in the Delaware valley, but he was more interested in opening up the land on the banks of the Susquehanna. He traveled in the virgin territory along the course of the river on his way to visit among Friends in Maryland, and he began to revive the 1690 project for the establishment of a second community in what was then western Pennsylvania. As has been seen, several colonial leaders were willing to invest money in the new settlement. Penn was followed home to England by an optimistic report on finances from his commissioners of property, Edward Shippen, Griffith Owen, Thomas Story, and Logan. They estimated that he would receive £21,700 Pennsylvania money in the next three years. Much of that was to come from the sale of lands and nearly £1,000 was expected for land to be sold in East Jersey. Unfortunately, Penn never received more than a fraction of the receipts prophesied.[43]

Although Penn had some difficulty with the colonists in regard to the government and the payment of taxes, he had far more trouble attempting to defend his prerogatives as Proprietor. The conflict over the collection of quitrents was described in an earlier chapter. The disagreement between Penn and the landowners continued after he returned to the colony, and in fact, continued well into the eighteenth century. The tide turned at this time however, in favor of the Proprietor. Penn, who seemed to have a remarkable ability for choosing unqualified persons to fill positions in Pennsylvania, made an exception to the general rule when he named James Logan Receiver General and Secretary. Probably no single act during these two years proved more beneficial to the Penn family than the appointment of Logan. For more than a generation he served William Penn and his heirs in a most capable fashion. The successful collection of quitrents in later years must be largely attributed to his ability and diligence. Always loyal to the Proprietary, he was consequently frequently unpopular in the colony.

CHAPTER FOURTEEN

PREPARATIONS FOR THE FUTURE

WHEN WILLIAM PENN decided late in August, 1701, to return to England to defend his right to govern Pennsylvania, he determined to convene the General Assembly and make one last attempt to settle the issues still pending. There were three major problems which faced Penn and his colonists. First, several disputes about property were disturbing the tranquillity of Pennsylvania. Secondly, many persons in Delaware and Pennsylvania desired a separation of the two sections from one another. Finally, he hoped that it would be possible to reach an agreement in regard to a new constitution for the colony.

With the approbation of his Council, Penn issued writs calling for a new election of assemblymen on September 4 and ordered the body to meet September 15. This was the fifth and final General Assembly to convene during Penn's stay in the colony. On the appointed day William Penn delivered an address which had been written out in full, perhaps in deference to the Assembly.[1] He urged the legislators to reach agreement quickly so that he could return to England as soon as possible. "Enemies of the prosperity of this Country . . . taking the advantage of my absence, . . . have attempted by false or unreasonable Charges to undermine our Govmt, and thereby the true value of our Labours & Property: Governmt having been our first Encouragement." He expressed his reluctance at leaving them, and promised to return with his family as soon as convenient but, "I can at this time best serve you and myself on that side of the water." He added that he would go even though the winter season would soon begin and his wife Hannah, his

daughter Letitia, and his infant son John, might suffer during
the voyage.

He implored the members of the two houses to reconcile
their differences. "Think, therefore, since all men are mortal,
of some suitable expedient and Provision for your safety, as
well in your Privileges as Property, and you will find me ready
to Comply with whatsoever may render us happy, by a nearer
Union of our Interest.

"Review again your Laws, propose new ones that may better
your Circumstances, and what you do, do it quickly, remembering that the Parliament sitts the end of the next month, and
that the sooner I am there the safer." He closed with one more
plea for unanimity and speed, for their own sakes, and because
it would "much Contribute to the Disappointment of those
that too long have taught the ruine of our young Country."

After Growdon had again been chosen Speaker the Assembly
drew up an answer to Penn in which the members expressed
"a deep Sense of Sorrow" at learning that their Governor
needed to return to England. In consideration of Penn's
"peternal Regards of us and our Posterity," and his promises
to reach agreement with them on the problems which faced the
government, the members, *"in much Humility, and as a Token
of our Gratitude, render unto thee the unfeigned Thanks of
this House."* The Assembly then settled down to six weeks of
hard work. It was interrupted only once, when the Yearly Meeting was in session late in September and the affairs of state were
laid aside while the Quakers met for several days of worship
and business.

Penn urged the representatives of the freemen to suggest a
formula for ending the controversies over property. The Assembly appointed a committee to consider proposals which
should be sent to the Governor and made a sincere attempt to
put the grievances of the freemen into writing. The inhabitants
of Philadelphia drew up a petition in regard to property which
was also discussed by the legislators. The report of the committee was debated on the floor of the house, and on September
20 the final form of the document was agreed on. Speaker

Growdon, who read the report to Penn and the Council, feared that the petition was too presumptuous and begged the Governor's indulgence. He said that the Assembly had taken courage from Penn's fair promises to cooperate in reaching agreement, and added that some of the extravagant demands included in the address had originated with the freemen of Philadelphia.

There were twenty-one articles in the petition from the Assembly. The points which were included in this address indicated two things: the landowners felt insecure in their estates with Penn about to return to England and wanted to erect as many protective devices as possible; they wished to obtain a number of concessions from the Proprietor while he was among them and were even willing to take advantage of him if the opportunity arose. The Governor was requested to name persons of integrity to represent him in property matters during his absence. He was called upon to grant an instrument to the property owners which would secure them in their estates forever, and to hasten the confirmation of their patents. The freemen expressed a desire that records be kept in a proper fashion and in a safe place, and asked that the machinery for the regulation of property be modeled on that provided for in the laws of Jamaica. Penn was petitioned to guarantee that the freemen would not be examined in regard to their estates by the governor and Council, but only by the courts. He was asked to leave the licensing of ordinaries and drinking houses in the hands of the justices in the counties, and to settle the boundary dispute between Chester and New Castle counties.

The address requested William Penn to grant extensive common land to the two large towns, Philadelphia and New Castle, and to continue to sell land at the rate which was customary in 1682. He was petitioned to allow the inhabitants to "purchase off their Quitrents as formerly promised." [2]

Penn replied that several of the articles did not concern the Assembly, but he promised to consider the entire address and give his answer. For several days nothing was accomplished; most of the legislators were absent attending the Yearly Meet-

ing of Friends. Saturday, September 27, the Assembly sent a
messenger to inquire whether Penn was prepared to answer
the petition. Penn was not prepared. When two members were
sent to ask him the following Monday morning if his reply was
ready, he said with exasperation that he took it "hard the
House does not proceed to other Business, or to consider the
other Parts of his Speech."

Late that afternoon Penn called the Assembly into his presence and answered the petition of the lower chamber point by
point. He responded favorably to the requests related to procedure, and seemed anxious to join with the legislators in establishing a satisfactory system for administering property. He
agreed to confirm some other requests from the Assembly. But
where he sensed the freemen were attempting to expand the
concessions already granted or were attacking his fundamental
proprietary rights, he adamantly refused to concede anything.

Two articles of the petition were inserted into the Charter
of Privileges with the Governor's approval: one referred to the
licensing of ordinaries and the other prohibited the governor
and Council from examining freemen in regard to property
matters. Penn reminded the Assembly that the Proprietor (who
was also governor) did have a right to examine those who held
land from him under feudal contract.

Penn agreed that records should be properly kept, and added
that the papers of Philadelphia County were "in so great Disorder, by Razures, Blots, and Interlineations, that you would
do well to use some Method in Time for their Rectification."
He said that as the Jamaica law would increase his fees he was
willing to adopt it, if it would also improve the administration
of property.

Penn refused to grant large common lands, especially the
marsh lands and islands, to the two towns, but confirmed his
earlier promise of 1,000 acres to New castle. He declined to sell
land at the old rates and asked why his property should not
increase in value along with that belonging to other landowners. He used the complaint that the colony had never repaid him for the expense of defending the Delaware boundary

from the pretensions of Lord Baltimore in the 1680s as a further reason for his refusal. The Governor flatly vetoed the suggestion that he should allow the colonists to buy up their
quitrents, and reminded the freemen that if he lost the government to the Crown the yearly rents would be his sole source of
income.

The Assembly did not rest content with the Governor's answer to the original petition, but appointed Jasper Yeates and
John Swift to consider an appropriate reply. This was discussed
on the floor and presented to Penn and his Council on October 10.[3] The members of the Assembly thanked the Governor for the concessions which he had made and humbly
agreed to accept his rejection of certain petitions, but they
pressed him to reconsider his other answers. While Penn spent
several days at Pennsbury closing his affairs there, the Assembly
incorporated some of the proposals in regard to property in a
document entitled, "The Proposal and Concessions of the Proprietary and Governor, for the more Expeditious Settlement
of the Freeholders of this Province, and Territories, and their
Lands and Tenements," commonly called the Bill of Property.

One provision of this document became the center of a bitter
argument between the Proprietor and the Assembly. Among
the laws enacted in the fall of 1700 was one which provided for
resurveying plots of land when it was suspected that the original
survey was in error. The law stated that when a man had received more land than was stipulated in his deed he should be
allowed six per cent over his original purchase on the assumption that he would lose that much land for roads, barren areas,
and other worthless soil. Penn agreed to grant an additional
four per cent to such persons. This meant that if a man had
purchased 1,000 acres, and the resurvey indicated that he
really had received 1,200 acres, he would be granted 100 acres
free, but that he would either purchase the second 100 acres
or allow it to revert to the Proprietor.

The Assembly decided that all purchasers should receive a
bonus of ten per cent of the land they held if those involved in
resurveys were to be favored in this fashion, and they incorpo-

rated such a provision into the Bill of Property. Penn refused to admit the validity of the claim, although he eventually agreed to grant an additional six per cent to all purchasers. The Assembly rejected this offer and refused to enact the charter without the proviso for a ten per cent dividend. This disagreement continued up to the last day of the General Assembly, when Penn made a strong but unsuccessful plea to the Assembly to accept his offer.

After Penn was on board the *Dalmahoy* some of the colonial leaders appeared with a document probably prepared by David Lloyd, entitled the Charter of Property, and Penn was induced to sign it. However, the Governor left orders that the document was not to be endorsed with the Great Seal and become effective until six months had elapsed, and he reserved the right to withdraw his approval within that time. The following April, just before the time limit expired, Penn rescinded his previous approval and the agreement in regard to property did not become law.[4]

During the two years Penn spent in Pennsylvania he successfully defended his proprietary prerogatives. While he practiced justice in handling land questions he did not allow the colonists to take undue liberties. He refused to surrender the right to collect quitrents and he rejected attempts to obtain land from him gratis. Penn never reaped large profits from Pennsylvania, but his heirs had strong reason to be grateful to him for establishing the province and successfully defending his rights as a feudal overlord.

When the Assembly took up the question of approving the laws enacted at New Castle in October, 1700, it was discovered that only 69 of the 104 laws passed at that time had been forwarded to England, and the Assembly attempted to discover the reason for omitting the others. The discussion of this disclosure however, was soon overshadowed by a more important issue. Several of the officers and magistrates of Philadelphia County petitioned the Council to re-enact the laws which had been agreed upon at New Castle. It was almost impossible to collect the taxes and duties provided for therein, for the people were saying that they did not have to obey the laws passed outside of Pennsylvania. The members from the lower counties were insulted by the petition and when the matter came before the Assembly they argued vigorously against repassing the laws. When they found that they would be outvoted the Delaware Assemblymen, who felt that the honor of their province was at stake, walked out of the body.

The decision of the Delaware men to leave the Assembly was not the result of a sudden pique, nor was it caused entirely by political controversy. There were basic differences between the older part of the colony and the area which had been populated since 1682. Delaware had watched anxiously as she saw herself outdistanced in population and wealth in a few short years. She was predominantly Lutheran and Calvinist, while Pennsylvania was overwhelmingly Quaker. Delaware was Dutch and Swedish in background while Pennsylvania was largely English. The exposed colony believed in the necessity of defense, while the inland province was pacifist. The southern counties produced tobacco and the northern ones largely raised grain.

Most of the sessions of the General Assembly were held in Philadelphia and the executive branch of the government, whether a council, commission, or deputy governor, resided in that town. More officials were named from the inhabitants of Pennsylvania than from Delaware. The Lower Counties felt like the older, unwanted half-brother of the vigorous, growing Pennsylvania.

The connection between Pennsylvania and Delaware had always been tenuous. It has already been stated that James, Duke of York, had no legal title to Delaware when he granted it to Penn and for that reason Penn's hold on the Lower Counties was always precarious. The claim made by Lord Baltimore was settled in 1685 but was not followed by a more permanent grant to Penn, although James II was in the midst of drawing up such papers when he fled from England in 1688. There was no mention of government in the papers which gave Delaware to Penn and his political control over the three lower counties rested on an Act of Union passed by the Assembly in December, 1682, which united the new province with the old counties.[5] Since all laws enacted under William Penn fell when Governor Fletcher arrived in Pennsylvania in 1693, presumably the Act of Union became null and void. A number of old laws were re-enacted under Fletcher's supervision but the Act of Union was not one of them.

The citizens of Delaware had a precedent for separate rule, for just before Fletcher's arrival Penn allowed Markham to govern Delaware while Thomas Lloyd governed Pennsylvania. However, during that period there was a single General Assembly for all six counties. Fuel was added to the flame already burning in the hearts of many of the freemen in Delaware by the surveyor general of customs for the English government, Edward Randolph, who kept telling the settlers that Penn had no legal right to rule them. He wrote the same thing to the Board of Trade, saying, Penn rules "upon an imaginary title, grounded upon a Sham law of his owne contriving." [6]

This undercurrent of feeling and questioning came to the surface while Penn was again living in the colony, and it became apparent to the Governor before he left that the two peoples must be allowed to separate. A new campaign of non-cooperation began the spring before Penn arrived, when New Castle County refused to choose members for the General Assembly. Sheriff Wessell Alrichs wrote to Markham that great crowds collected for the election, "but all their Cry was they would not Make Choyse of Any." [7] However when Penn issued writs for an election in that county in January, 1700, the freemen chose representatives and continued to do so while he was in the colony. As an effort to make amends for one of the just grievances of the citizens of Delaware, the meeting of the General Assembly in October, 1700, was at New Castle. Since the work of the session was largely centered around compiling a new code of laws, the men from the lower counties decided to challenge the validity of the old Act of Union.

Thus on Monday, November 4, 1700, the members of the Assembly from the Lower Counties proposed, "That the Union shall be confirmed on Condition, that at no Time hereafter the number of Representatives of the People in Legislation in the Province, shall exceed them of the annexed Counties; but if hereafter more Counties be made in the Province, and thereby more Representatives be added, that then the Union shall cease." [8] The provincial members flatly refused to accept such a proposition, but it was agreed to submit the whole question to Governor Penn.

When the legislators met Penn in the afternoon he stated that the Act of Union was still in force; however to give the people of Delaware more security, he suggested adopting a new law as an amendment to the old act, as follows: "That in all Matters and Things whatsoever, wherein the Territories are, or shall be particularly concerned, in Interest or Privilege, distinct from the Province; then, and in that Case, no Act, Law, or Ordinance, in any wise shall pass in any Assembly in this Province, and Territories, unless two Parts in Three of the Members of the said Territories, and the Majority of the Members of the Province concur therein; & e converso." [9]

The following day the members from the Lower Counties stated that while the Act of Union was null and void in their estimation they could agree to cooperate in the government, resolved "that this House have full Power to act in Legislation," and agreed to leave a settlement to the subsequent General Assembly.[10]

Neither side in this controversy was approaching the problem objectively. The Pennsylvanians argued that the tax laws enacted at New Castle in 1700 were null and void while the Act of Union of 1682 was still in effect. The Delaware men resented the fact that Pennsylvanians questioned the validity of laws passed at New Castle but they denounced the law agreed on at Chester.

To go back to the troubles in 1701, the men who had withdrawn from the Assembly October 10 appealed to Penn in Council four days later in regard to the re-enactment of all laws passed the previous year at New Castle. The Governor, trying to pass off the quarrel as a matter of little significance, replied that laws were frequently re-enacted and reminded the men that Magna Charta had been confirmed at least fifty times. He admitted that he could see little reason for the resentment of the Delaware men and felt that it reflected on himself. The representatives denied this.

Failing to postpone the crisis between Delaware and Pennsylvania by a casual attitude, Penn decided later the same day to grant the separation many on both sides wished. His decision was influenced by his desire to conclude his affairs in Pennsylvania and sail for England as soon as possible. At the same time, he realized that the differences between the citizens of the upper and lower counties were of long duration, and many of them fundamental in nature. His legal grounds for holding and governing the people of Delaware were not strong enough to bear investigation by the Crown. He insisted that the separation "must be upon amicable Terms and a good understanding. They must first Resolve to settle the Laws, and as the Interest of the Province and those lower Counties would be inseparably the same, they should both use a Conduct to each other consistent with that Relation."

During the early weeks of the session, with several issues still pending, the atmosphere was very tense. Norris wrote to a friend, "Our Assembly Still Sitts and Little done but tueing and tugging. for ye Philistins be upon us still[.] they are now worse yn Ever believing ym selves Cocksure of ye Governmts Change—their Endeavours are (I mean the Low County Members & our Malecontents here) to Leave us if possible wthout Laws or Liberties." [11] However after William Penn gave his promise that Delaware might secede from Pennsylvania if she wished the last two weeks of the General Assembly were relatively peaceful. The Governor and his assemblymen had little difficulty reaching agreement on the Charter of Privileges, which was the matter of greatest importance. The debate over the Charter of Property continued until the last day. Norris lamented on October 25, "yet for my part I cannot Yet tell whether any thing will be pfected. Such unhappy misunderstandings and oppositions seem to arise." [12]

Penn allowed two paragraphs to be attached to the Charter of Privileges in answer to the requests from Delaware. The first made provisions for the separation of Delaware from Pennsylvania, and the second guaranteed to the inhabitants of the lower counties all the "Liberties, Privileges and Benefits, granted jointly."[13] Two years later Delaware took advantage of these provisions and separated itself from Pennsylvania. One Governor continued to rule both colonies, but each had its own legislature and exclusive control over the local government.

The matter ostensibly at the bottom of the quarrel between the two sections, the re-enactment of the laws approved at Newcastle in 1700, was concluded in a satisfactory manner. The statutes were re-enacted, but with a statement which did not hurt the feelings of the legislators from the lower counties. It said in part that the laws had been passed again to "prevent all further objections that may hereafter arise concerning them," without referring to specific objections from Pennsylvania.[14]

Nine other laws were placed on the statute books during this session of the General Assembly, and a few of them are of interest. The former enactment designed to prevent the sale of rum and other strong liquors to the Indians was unsatisfactory and a new law was approved. A bill to enlarge fire fighting equipment and to strengthen the provisions for fire prevention in the large towns was enacted. One law provided bounties for killing blackbirds and crows; three pence a dozen for the former, and three pence for each of the latter.

Discussion of proposed legislation was sometimes tempestuous. Norris wrote early in the session, "his [Penn's] & friends Enemies are as Violent as Ever and nothing more in their heads now yn a King's Govr[.] they Improve Strain or Misconstrue Everything[.] I see patience is an Exelent Virtue If wee Can Reach & keep it."[15] Some of the proposed legislation which failed to gain general concurrence was probably the cause of a few disputes. A bill was introduced which would have given the freemen the right to bring court action against the governor, his lieutenants, and other officials. The Assembly approved it but it was buried in the Council, and repeated questions failed to bring any satisfactory answer as to its whereabouts. In response to the petition of more than 100 Philadelphians, a bill was introduced which called for the dropping of the impost on liquors. Penn agreed to approve the bill if the Assembly would find him some other source for the same amount of money. The Assembly answered that it was too late to initiate new legislation.

The final law passed by the General Assembly, "An Act for Establishing Courts of Judicature in This Province and Counties Annexed," was the most important one of all. This bill was probably prepared by someone who was not a member of the Assembly or Council, presumably David Lloyd.[16] The law was a long, technical definition of the machinery, power, and jurisdiction of the courts of quarter sessions of the counties, of the provincial court including the circuit court, and of the orphans court held by the justices in the counties. A technical definition of the machinery of appeals was presented. Sample writs were included in the law for the use of the officials in the counties. It was only with the passage of this law "that the provincial court and the other tribunals were firmly established, and their jurisdiction defined." [17]

William Penn felt only one more task needed to be completed before he could begin the hazardous voyage to England. He was anxious to reach agreement with the legislators on a constitution for the colony.

The General Assembly which met in May, 1700, had been chosen according to the provisions of the Charter of 1683. While the members had expressed dissatisfaction with that constitution they could not agree on a new one to replace it, but they did unite in returning the Second Frame to Penn.[18] For the next sixteen months Penn ruled the colony without a constitution. This was not to Penn's liking, and he made a fruitless attempt to reach agreement with the legislators at the long session which convened in October, 1700. As long as Penn was in Pennsylvania the absence of a charter was not very important, for the Governor and the Assembly respected one another and the government operated smoothly without a formal frame. However as he prepared to sail for England, leaving the executive powers in the hands of a deputy, Penn felt it imperative that agreement be reached regarding a constitution.

Little is known about the debate of the new constitution in the Assembly and Council, for the minutes rarely recorded the speeches or comments of individual members. It is apparent from the infrequent mention of the Charter of Privileges in the minutes of the two houses that the new constitution produced less controversy than either the proposed document concerning property or the proposed laws. The charter had been discussed at length the previous year during the session at New Castle, and once Penn agreed to the separation of Delaware the debate over the new frame proceeded smoothly. On October 23 the new charter received the approval of all concerned and was sent to be engrossed. Four days later the Assembly requested Penn to add a paragraph which would guarantee to the freemen of Delaware, if they withdrew, the same rights and privileges they enjoyed as citizens of the combined plantation. As has been seen, Penn acceded to that request.

The Assembly met at 3 o'clock in the morning on October 28 and did not adjourn until eleven that night.[19] Presumably the Council kept more genteel hours. Most of the day was devoted to further debate of certain provisions of the Bill of Property. When that ended in a stalemate the laws approved were signed and sealed and the Charter of Privileges was also signed and sealed. The General Assembly was dismissed and Penn went to his ship.

The Charter of Privileges was a short document in comparison with the other two which received Penn's approbation. It consisted of an introduction, nine articles in the body of the constitution, and two paragraphs attached at the end. It remained in force until the American Revolution.[20] William Penn signed the Charter, Growdon "Signed on Behalf, and by Order of the Assembly," and six members of the Council also signed.

The charter contained little that was new. The first article was largely taken out of the laws enacted in the past, beginning with chapters I and II approved at Chester in 1682. Most of the other articles too were based on articles in previous charters or on old laws or customs. A great deal of nonsense has been written about this document.[21] It has been acclaimed as a great democratic instrument which granted the citizens of Pennsylvania all the freedom they could desire. Writers and orators have praised William Penn for granting this democratic constitution.

To be sure, the new constitution granted extensive powers to the Assembly and allowed it to initiate legislation. But the Council lost its former right to introduce bills. Furthermore the Assembly had been given that privilege by Governor Fletcher in 1693 during the royal interlude. As the document stated, the Assembly had been granted what was usual "in any of the King's Plantations in America." The Assembly, chosen by a limited suffrage, was allowed to "prepare Bills, in order to pass into Laws," but the proposed legislation became law only if it met with the approval of an hereditary governor or his deputy.

One striking difference between this frame and former charters was the fact that the Council, which was mentioned twice in the document, was no longer chosen by the freemen. Since June, 1700, Penn had been appointing the members of his council. This procedure, which was practiced in the royal colonies, met with his approval and was incorporated into the Pennsylvania government permanently when the Charter of Privileges was written. Formerly the Council contained men elected by the freemen, who often did not agree with the Governor. Under the new plan the governor would always be advised by men who were in sympathy with his ideas and proposals.

Scarcely less important, under this charter the governor was no longer responsible to an elected Council for his every act. The Charters of 1683 and 1696 provided that the Governor "shall att no time therein perform anie publick act of State whatsoever that shall or may relate unto the Justice, Trade,

Treasurie or Safetie of the Province and Territories aforesaid, but by and with the advice and consent of the Provincial Council thereof." The omission of this phrase allowed the governor considerably more freedom than before.

Under the new charter William Penn gave up one of his fondest concepts of lawmaking, in which the Council chosen by the freemen drew up the bills, and the Assembly elected by the citizens assented to or rejected the proposed legislation. However Penn did not lose any of his prerogatives by granting the Assembly the right to initiate legislation, for the power to propose laws had always rested in the hands of elected men. Furthermore, Penn's veto power remained unchallenged.

Other articles in the Charter of Privileges were designed to preserve liberty of conscience in Pennsylvania, to protect freemen from arbitrary attacks on their property by the Governor, to guarantee local regulation of public houses, to protect for the survivors the estate of a person who died a violent death, and to preserve the rights of those accused of crimes. These provisions were not aimed at William Penn for most of them were already accepted in Pennsylvania, but they were embodied in the new charter because the Crown was threatening to seize the government.[22] The freemen joined with Penn in the hope that the presence of these safeguards in the constitution would make it possible to maintain them under an unfriendly royal governor.

The Charter of Privileges granted more power to the Assembly than it previously held and contained several guarantees of the rights and privileges of the freemen. At the same time it reserved considerable power for the Proprietor and governor. In the years which followed the acceptance of this constitution there were times when both the Assembly and William Penn desired to alter it.[23] However it weathered all such stormy periods and had become a revered document by the time of the American Revolution, when it was replaced by the Constitution of 1776.

CHAPTER FIFTEEN

CONCLUSION: INHERITANCE FROM

THE "HOLY EXPERIMENT"

WHEN WILLIAM PENN left Pennsylvania in 1701 it was for the last time, despite his oft-repeated desire to return to die in his plantation. His departure marked a milestone in the history of the colony. William Penn was unquestionably the dominant figure in Pennsylvania during the two decades studied in this volume, even though he was in residence for less than four years. To him must go the credit for launching the "holy experiment." He deserved commendation for his enlightened leadership during the two years that he lived among the freemen at the turn of the century. While some of his influence was negative, he stands as the chief personage in these two decades.

However, during the years after his embarkation for England in 1701 Penn was frequently overshadowed by two men, James Logan and David Lloyd. Both of them became increasingly influential in the colony, while Penn's power decreased when Pennsylvania no longer needed its founder.

What did William Penn leave behind him in the plantation, what had been lost and what had been achieved in two decades? One important consequence of the twenty years was that Pennsylvania had failed to achieve the high level of life envisoned when the colony was launched as a "holy experiment." The responsibility for this failure cannot be placed on any one man or group of men. The colonists in Pennsylvania who might have made the utopian dream a reality must be assigned a large share of the responsibility, but they by no means deserve all of it. Certainly William Penn, who has been granted an important place in history as the founder of the colony, bears at the same time a portion of the blame for the failure of the "holy experiment." External forces had a share in causing the breakdown of the hopes and desires of the founders. In the summary of these three forces which follows no attempt has been made to assess their relative importance.

William Penn had expected the colony to be pervaded with a spirit of dedication to the Will of God and a desire to obey and fulfill the highest teachings of the Scriptures. That Pennsylvania found it impossible to realize the expectations of the founder was a prime reason for the failure of the "holy experiment." The intangible uplifting quality which had been manifest among the harassed Quakers in England was all too often missing where they lived in freedom in Pennsylvania. This spiritual deficiency influenced everything else.

The failure of the colonists to accept their responsibilities in the plantation was an example of this spiritual weakness. Penn had no sooner set sail for England on the *Endeavour* in 1684 than it became apparent that the freemen were unwilling to contribute their time, energy, and thought to making the new experiment succeed. They refused to participate in the government and complained of their responsibilities. They ignored repeated demands that the quitrents be paid, and fell back on any excuse to escape contributing money to the government. They lacked the spirit of cooperation which Penn considered fundamental to the attainment of the utopian goals to which they aspired.[1]

The colonists were motivated by a spirit of independence which often made it difficult to cooperate with William Penn. As Quakers they respected the omnipotence of God, but they had grown skeptical about obedience to earthly authorities. As Whigs they had learned to defend their rights and privileges against those who held jurisdiction over them. As colonists who were making a success of their venture they had developed a financial independence which boded no good for a feudal proprietor. These people could scarcely be described as meek.

The independence manifest in Pennsylvania was admirable in many ways, but the pugnacious spirit which accompanied it was deplorable. Even the Society of Friends was split by the Keithian Schism. Pennsylvania was aligned against Delaware on several occasions. The Council constantly disputed with the Assembly, and throughout the period a thread of faction was evident in connection with every issue in the colony. The wrangling grieved William Penn, as it did all true followers of the principles of Quakerism, for George Fox and his adherents had always stressed the value of peace and concord. Yet, the quarrelsome spirit was present constantly during these years and encompassed nearly everyone in the colony, even as fine a person as Thomas Lloyd. Unfortunately, the contentious spirit which sprang into being in the first decade continued long after 1701.

There was a greater disregard for law and order in Pennsylvania than might have been expected from a Quaker colony dedicated to a "holy experiment." The colonists rather openly countenanced the violation of the laws against illegal trade and piracy. They were not operating as illicit traders and pirates but they trafficked with such persons. The courts were not a good example to the settlers. Penn wrote about the magistrates, "How can offenses be well punished by offenders? or the Exalted teach the people Subjection? or the Quarrelsome by reconcilers, as all true Justices of the Peace ought to be? If Magistrates draw themselves into Contempt by a mean Behaviour, they can never exercise Power honourably nor successfully." [2] Frequently the non-Quakers protested that justice was not done in the courts. The deliberate deception of William Penn in 1687, about the installation of the new government under the commissioners of state, deserved condemnation.

In addition, there was apparently a good deal of lawbreaking by individuals. From the time that the Council dealt with a counterfeiter in the spring of 1683 until the end of this period, there was a steady growth of crime. Drunkenness was frequently condemned. Robert Turner wrote, "wickedness growes—& wine to much Raignes in ye grocest manner to ye sorrow & Reproach of gods people . . . To many scandolas Tipling houses ye sinks of sinn." [3] This contributed to the failure of the "holy experiment," and at the same time was the result of its failure. The colony was scarcely as virtuous as has been generally supposed.

William Penn contributed to the downfall of his "holy experiment" in many ways, for the most part unconsciously. The fact that he was absent for fifteen years during this period made it difficult to maintain a cordial and beneficial relationship between himself and his people, which should have been the cornerstone of a successful experiment. I believe that he could have come to Pennsylvania before 1699 if he had really wanted to return. Penn constantly harped on money matters and demanded that the freemen send him what was owed to him. Misunderstandings over financial matters occur easily and are difficult to mend. Penn adopted a paternalistic and patronizing tone in his letters, which must have been infuriating at times. Further, Penn did not follow a consistent policy. He frequently vacillated between a firm line of action and a loving, generous one. The most striking example of this characteristic is found in the contradictory letters which Penn sent to Blackwell and to the men in the Pennsylvania government about the appointment of Blackwell in 1688.

William Penn was a great man, and he possessed in large measure the spirit which he hoped to find in his colony. When he was present in Pennsylvania most affairs ran smoothly. However, as an absentee governor and Proprietor, he left much to be desired. Undoubtedly his prolonged absence made the failure of the "holy experiment" inevitable.

The other group of forces which contributed to the frustration of the utopian dream may be collectively labelled external forces. Perhaps the most important of these influences was the fact that Pennsylvania was in the English empire at a time of war with France. At the same time, this was a period when the Crown was attempting to tighten control over proprietary establishments. The issues between Quaker beliefs and imperial demands were brought into open conflict during the rule of Governor Fletcher. This was the beginning of the struggle between the testimonies of Friends and the demands of Mammon, which ended in victory for the latter in the 1750s. In addition, the denunciation of Pennsylvania and Quakers by neighboring colonies, royal officials, and Anglicans, did nothing to aid the "holy experiment," and probably injured it.

One is tempted to ask why anyone thought the "holy experiment" had any chance of survival. The answer is found in the faith and optimism of William Penn and a few like spirits, who believed all things possible if man is virtuous and relies on divine assistance. Unfortunately, we will never know whether Penn was right or not, for man failed to keep his half of the bargain and the "holy experiment" failed.

FRUITS OF THE "HOLY EXPERIMENT"

Such a portrayal of the failure of the "holy experiment" creates the impression that Pennsylvania was not a very desirable or attractive community. Actually that was not the case, for the accomplishments of the first two decades of Pennsylvania history far outweigh the failures. The colony fell short of the goal of perfectibility which had been held before it, but in terms of the experience in other provinces in their formative years or in comparison with contemporary neighboring colonies, Pennsylvania was not a failure.

Prosperity came to the plantation in the last years of the century. The discomforts of the early years were largely behind the settlers and a better way of life was available at least for some. Many of the farmers were enjoying more prosperity than would have been possible in England, and the merchant class in the towns was achieving an enviable position. Philadelphia had enjoyed unparalleled growth. The economic success constantly attracted new settlers and had long aroused the jealousy of neighboring provinces. Since Penn's return in 1699, the colony had largely lived down the bad reputation gained late in the seventeenth century, and it was once again believed that Pennsylvania was a virtuous community.

While there had been many conflicts over government during these two decades, the end result of the incessant controversy was a frame of government which endured with minor changes for three-quarters of a century.[4]

Penn had given up his utopian ideas about a two house General Assembly with the smaller body proposing the laws and the larger one approving or rejecting them. Under the Constitution of 1701 the elected Assembly was granted the powers usual in such legislative bodies at this time. The Council, appointed by the governor as was customary in neighboring colonies, performed the duties of such a select, appointive group. Thus Pennsylvania no longer had a unique legislative system. But the colony did continue to enjoy unusual suffrage privileges. With virtually no religious requirements and with modest property restrictions on voting, more freemen participated in the government through elected representatives than in many other colonies. Later in the eighteenth century the three original counties refused to allow proportional representation to the new western counties, but no such problem existed in 1701.

After 1701 the executive branch of the government resembled what was customary in the English settlements. During the first two decades William Penn had placed the executive power in the hands of elected members of the Council on several occasions. This was not only most unusual, but proved to be unworkable, for the elected representatives would not devote the time needed to make this plan effective. Penn was forced to resort to appointing deputy governors to maintain law and order and to represent his interests. While it seems likely that Penn did not have a veto power under the first two constitutions which he granted the colonists, he assumed that power during his absence and did not relinquish it under the Charter of Privileges of 1701. Penn did grant to his freemen certain safeguards against an arbitrary governor which did not exist in other colonies. However he claimed some powers as Proprietor which he relinquished as governor.

While the administration of justice had sometimes been haphazard in the early years, under the judicial act of 1701 a logical and fair system of courts was established. With James Logan and strong deputy governors present, there were few occasions to complain about the courts in the years which followed. The laws were not as harsh in Pennsylvania as in some of the neighboring colonies, and capital offenses were kept to a minimum until 1718. The Quaker emphasis on settling disputes peacefully without going to court had been practiced faithfully by the Friends during the first two decades, and continued to be the custom.

Thus it is evident that solid foundations for the future government of the colony had evolved from these two turbulent decades. The citizens of Pennsylvania were ready to move forward in the new century. The controversies which swept over the province from time to time became acrimonious but did not lead to the overthrow of the constitution or to any major change in the government.

William Penn had new reason for feeling hopeful about the future of Pennsylvania a few weeks before he departed for England, when members of the Society of Friends issued a statement which promised cooperation with the government and denounced the tempestuous political wrangling of the past. This assurance from his fellow religionists made it easier for Penn to leave the plantation.

The Quakers protested their loyalty in these words: "We have now for many Years approved our Selves Peaceable Subjects to them whom God by his Providence hath Set over us; First to the King as Supreme, & next to those in Authority under him." They continued however, by denouncing members of the Society of Friends who:

have been too Factious and Troublesome in the Governments, . . . And have by their Seditious Words, Insinuations & Practices, disquieted the Minds of others, to the making of Parties & Disturbances; and some under the Fair Colours of Law & Priviledges, have promoted their Sinister Ends, when indeed it was but to take Vengeance, against those whom they had taken Disgust against; And this we cannot but declare our Just abhorrence of; that any Should Sacrifice the Peace of a Province to Private Revenge; Warning all to beware of such: And wherever they find them, forthwith to deal with them, and to Aquit our Holy Profession of them in a Gospell Way.[5]

William Penn hoped that the official statement from Friends would prevent members of the Society from engaging in political quarrels in the future.[6] He was doomed to disappointment, for there was a wide gap between what Quakers said they believed regarding political matters and the way they behaved. The Society of Friends officially deplored political machinations, factions, and all that goes with participation in government. Actually, the leaders of the Yearly Meeting were the leaders of the government.[7] The Quakers shared actively in the political dissension which frequently disrupted Pennsylvania after William Penn departed, despite the official disapproval of the Yearly Meeting.

Although the colonists failed to live up to the high ideals of the "holy experiment," there survived a rich inheritance from the attempt to establish a utopian community. Several of the results may be isolated and examined, but there is a vast intangible heritage which cannot be portrayed in words. Religious toleration is the best known legacy from the "holy experiment," but there were many others. There was opposition to war, humane treatment of the Indians, and the virtual abolition of capital punishment.

Religious toleration was accepted in Pennsylvania from the very beginning and was incorporated in the Charter of Privileges. The Anglicans were occasionally given reason to doubt that the Quakers were as tolerant as Penn would have wished, but all faiths were admitted to Pennsylvania and most persons were allowed to share in the government. Pennsylvania went beyond toleration and became a haven for the oppressed everywhere. The plantation grew rapidly in the eighteenth century because it welcomed the Germans, Scots-Irish, and others who filled the back country of the Quaker province and of other colonies as well. The willingness of the Pennsylvanians to accept non-English immigrants was in contrast to the cool reception which such settlers received in many plantations. The refusal of the old settlers to grant political equality to the new colonists partially nullified the spirit of toleration.

Although Pennsylvania compromised the principles of the "holy experiment" by making contributions toward the expense of defending the colonies from the French and the Indians during the first two decades, no one doubted that the Quakers had a strong testimony against war. For the next fifty years Pennsylvania refused to erect defenses against attack, opposed attempts to force the colony to fight for the empire, and contributed money for wars with great reluctance. Friends believed that war was evil and were determined to have no part of it. In the twentieth century all men agree that war is evil, but have found no way to avoid it. Pennsylvania did escape direct participation in war for the next half-century.

The decision to treat the Indians of Pennsylvania with justice originated in the ideals of the "holy experiment." The same principles guided the handling of relations between the whites and the aborigines for several decades after the Proprietor returned to England, and as long as the policies of William Penn were followed there was peace between the two races.

In a period of history when capital punishment was meted out for a great many crimes, the "holy experiment" envisaged a society where wilful murder was the sole offense punishable by death. This progressive ideal was enacted into law and capital punishment was nearly nonexistent in the colony until 1718, when the English criminal code was adopted.[8] During the nearly forty years in which this new attitude was held a precedent was established for later generations of humanitarians.

The "holy experiment" left its mark on other facets of life in Pennsylvania. The early attitude toward education was continued in later years, and the Quaker testimony against taking oaths was maintained. Perhaps the opposition of Friends to slavery had origins in the "holy experiment," although that is open to question. Certainly the spirit of William Penn and the idealism of the early years of Pennsylvania's history influenced the province in later generations.

Shortly before taking his leave in 1701, Penn wrote to a friend, "We are an approved experiment what sobriety and industry can do in a wilderness against heats, colds, wants and dangers." [9] The colony had made remarkable progress in the twenty years and Penn had little reason to be ashamed, even though it failed to measure up to his expectations as a "holy experiment." A strong nucleus of dedicated Friends remained in Pennsylvania despite the buffetings of the first twenty years; they appreciated William Penn, and longed to have him live among them. Norris described the feelings of these Quakers in the following words: [10]

him [Penn] we shall want tho Unhappy Missunderstandings In Some & unwarrantable Opposition in Others has been a block to our Plenary Comforts In him & his own Quiet, but these things are Externals only—our Communion In ye Church Sweetens all, & our Inward waitings & worships together has often been a Generall Cumfort & Consolation, & In this I take a degree of satisfaction after all yt we part In love, and Some of his last words In Our Meeting yesterday was that he lookt over all Infirmitys & outwards & had an Eye to ye Regions of Spirits, wherein was our Surest tye[,] and in true Love there he took leave of us.

APPENDIX

The Charter has been printed in many places, and it has been discussed at length in other volumes. For the purposes of this study it is only necessary to outline briefly some sections which are fundamental to the establishment of the government in the new colony, and to quote a few passages in full.[1]

The land was granted to William Penn, his heirs and assignees as "true and absolute Proprietaries," to hold the land in "free and common Socage by fealty only for all services." The right of government was granted as well:

Know yee therefore, that wee reposing speciall trust and Confidence in the fidelitie, wisdome, Justice, and provident circumspeccon of the said William Penn, . . . Doe grant free, full and absolute power, . . . to him and his heires, . . . for the good and happy government of the said Countrey, to ordeyne, make, Enact and under his and their Seales to publish any Lawes whatsoever, for the raising of money for the publick use of the said province, or for any other End apperteyning either unto the publick state, peace, or safety of the said Countrey, . . . by and with the advice, assent and approbacon of the freemen of the said Countrey, . . . And wee doe likewise give and grant unto the said William Penn, and his heires, . . . such power and authoritie to appoint and establish any Judges, and Justices, Magistrates and Officers whatsoever, for what Causes soever, for the probates of will and for the granting of Administracons within the precincts aforesaid, and with what power soever, and in such forme as to the said William Penn, or his heires, shall seeme most convenient.

The Charter required that the laws "bee not repugnant or contrarie, but as neare as conveniently may bee agreeable to the Lawes, Statutes and rights of this our Kingdome of England, And Saveing and reserving to us, Our heires and Successors" the right to hear appeals from Pennsylvania to the Crown. While appeals from Pennsylvania were allowed, Penn exercised very considerable judicial power, and was given the right to grant pardons and reprieves in all cases excepting "Treason and wilful and malicious Murder," and he was to be able to exercise the power of reprieve even in these two crimes.

The King granted Penn the privilege of issuing ordinances which would have the effect of law, and would be obeyed as law. He hedged this power by providing that it would only be used when it was inconvenient to call together representatives of the freemen, that ordinances should be made public, that they should be in agreement with the laws of England, and that they should not be of "any sort to bind, charge or take away the right or Interest of any person or persons, for or in their life, members, freehold, goods or Chattells." Further, Charles II demanded that all laws published in the province be submitted to the Privy Council within five years. Within six months after they were delivered to that body, it might declare such laws null and void if they were "inconsistent with the sovereignety or lawfull prerogative of us, our heirs or successors, or contrary to the faith and allegiance due by the legall Government of this Realme, from the said William Penn."

Penn was given complete control in local affairs, the establishing of local government, the establishing of ports and harbors, the collecting of duties. He was guaranteed the right to establish manors, with manor courts. He was given the power to raise troops and pursue enemies of the province, even outside of the province, both on land and sea. Penn in turn promised to allow members of the Church of England to worship freely, with a minister chosen by the Bishop of London as their leader, if as many as twenty persons in the colony requested it. He was required to maintain a representative, "an Attorney or Agent," at London to appear to "Answer for any misdemeanors that shall be comitted, or by any wilfull default or neglect pmitted by the said William penn."

THE FIRST FRAME OF GOVERNMENT OF PENNSYLVANIA, 1682 [2]

The introduction, which followed the long preamble, included the following words: "Now know ye, that for the well-being and government of the said province, and for the encouragement of all the freemen and planters that may be therein concerned . . . I the said William Penn . . . do declare, grant and confirm unto all the freemen, planters and adventurers, of, in and to the said province, these liberties, franchises, and properties, to be held, enjoyed and kept by the freemen, planters and inhabitants of the said province of Pennsylvania for ever."

The first chapter announced "that the government of this province shall, according to the powers of the patent, consist of the Governor and freemen of the said province, in form of a Provincial Council and General Assembly, by whom all laws shall be made, officers chosen, and publick affairs transacted, as is hereafter respectively declared."

The following twelve chapters described the Council and its powers and responsibilities. It was to be made up of seventy-two persons elected by the freemen to serve three years, and after the first year, twenty-four were elected each year. No member would be eligible to re-election after two terms of service until a year had elapsed. In important matters, two-thirds of the membership was needed for a quorum, and a two-thirds majority was needed to approve such issues. In lesser affairs, one-third was a quorum, with a simple majority vote necessary to carry a motion. Further, the governor or his deputy would have three votes in the Council, but there was no mention of a veto. The governor and Council were to prepare all bills, and publish them thirty days before the meeting of the General Assembly, to give ample time for discussion. The governor and Council were to execute laws, statutes, and ordinances; be responsible for the peace and safety of the province; establish cities, ports, market towns, roads and highways; inspect the public treasury; erect public schools, and "encourage and reward the authors of useful sciences and laudable inventions in the said province." To accomplish these various ends the Council was to be divided into four committees, namely: Plantations; Justice and Safety; Trade and Treasury; and Manners, Education and Arts.

The fourteenth chapter provided for the General Assembly. The freemen were annually to choose 200 assemblymen. They were to meet for eight days to discuss the promulgated bills; during which time they might consult with a committee from the Council, and vote on the ninth day to approve or reject the proposed legislation. It was necessary to have two-thirds of their number present for a quorum. The fifteenth chapter stated that laws approved by the Assembly were to be enrolled "with this stile: *By the Governor, with the assent and approbation of the freemen in Provincial Council and General Assembly.*" The next chapter allowed the enlargement of the General Assembly as the increase of population warranted it.

The two following chapters provided for the choice of officials in the province, including those in the counties. The Council was to nominate two candidates for judges, treasurers, masters of rolls; and the Assembly two candidates for sheriffs, justices of the peace, and coroners; the governor or his deputy were to select officers from those nominated. However, in the beginning, Penn stated that he would name persons to fill the positions, to serve during good behavior. The replacements of such appointees would be chosen by the method described above.

The nineteenth chapter mentioned that the Assembly had the power of impeachment, but this power was not spelled out. It also stated that the Council had control over the meeting and adjourning of the Assembly. The following chapter called for the use of the ballot in all elections and votes, and added that the Council should not vote on matters of business on the same day that they were introduced, except in unusual cases.

The twenty-first chapter provided machinery for choosing a guardian and deputy governor when the governor was a minor, and when the father of the child had not provided for the emergency before death. The next part stated that when elections or meetings of the legislative bodies fell on Sunday, they were to be held over until the following day. The final chapter provided for amendment of the constitution by a six-sevenths vote of the "freemen in Provincial Council, and General Assembly."

LAWS PASSED IN THE EARLY YEARS, 1682 TO 1684 [3]

THE FIFTEEN FUNDAMENTAL LAWS

The first of these protected liberty of conscience, and opened the colony to all who believed in one Almighty God; guaranteed complete freedom of worship; and provided for punishment of any who derided the religion of others. The law contained a paragraph which called for putting aside the Sabbath as a day of rest. A second fundamental law required that marriages be performed after the manner of Friends, with penalties for other marriages. However, this arbitrary ruling was modified in 1684. Two laws required the erection of an Enrollment Office for the registry of charters, gifts, grants, bills, bonds, and deeds; and a special registry for births, marriages, burials, wills, and the names of executors, guardians, trustees, and letters of administration. One fundamental law provided that taxes could only be laid with the consent of the freemen and that tax laws were to continue for only one year at a time. The act for naturalizing the former inhabitants of the province and territories was declared fundamental. A law which established property qualifications for voting, and which demanded a declaration of fidelity from office-holders was so classified, as was one which called for penalties against those found guilty of corruption in elections.

Seven other fundamental laws had to do with courts and trials. Freemen were guaranteed trial by jury and the protection of the laws of the land. They were further guaranteed that all courts of law would be open to them, and that they could be released on bail, except in cases involving capital offenses. Speedy trial was guaranteed in all cases involving forty shillings or less. One law provided rules for witnesses and punishment for perjury, another established rules for juries, and a third demanded that jurors be chosen by drawing lots in criminal and capital cases.

EXAMPLES OF OTHER LAWS

One law established fees for the entire province: the governor's secretary, the master of the rolls, the treasurer, the provincial secretary, the coroners, the clerk of the county court, the constable, the register, the justices of the peace and the sheriff. A few examples might be of interest: the master of the rolls was to receive one-half penny for every line of the laws and statutes of the province he wrote upon parchment "in a fair, easy and Close hand," the public to furnish the parchment; the coroner was to have ten shillings for viewing a dead body; the clerk of the county court was to have seven and one-half pence for entering cattle's ear and brand marks; the register received six pence for registering a birth, one shilling for a marriage, and three shillings for registering a will; the sheriff received two shillings six pence when a prisoner was taken into his jail, and the same amount when the prisoner was released.

One chapter provided that fines should be moderate, and not so severe as to impair a man's ability to earn a livelihood. A law was passed to end primogeniture by providing that at least one-third of a man's estate was to go to his widow on his death, and one-third to his children. Two laws dealt with the question of indentured servants. One promised that if a servant had no indenture he could only be forced to work for five years, or if he was less than seventeen years of age, until the age of twenty-two. The other provided that the master or mistress was to appear in court within three months after the arrival of the servant. He was to promise to furnish the servant, when his time for freedom arrived, with an outfit of clothing, ten bushels of wheat or fourteen bushels of Indian corn, an axe, two hoes, and a formal discharge from service.

The legislators took four statutes to deal with various kinds of swearing, cursing, and profanity, and the punishment was generally several days of imprisonment at hard labor, on bread and water. Sex offences were mentioned, including fornication, incest, sodomy, rape, and bigamy, with punishment for first offenders ranging from public whipping and a year's imprisonment to life imprisonment, but all second offenders were to be imprisoned for life.

Persons who proposed healths "which may provoke people to unnecessary and excessive Drinking," were to be fined five shillings, and public officials who became drunk were to pay double the penalty for other persons. No one was to sell strong liquor to the Indians. Dueling was frowned upon, and both parties were to pay five pounds and serve three months at hard labor. Persons who were "Clamorous, Scolding, & Railing with their tounges," were punished according to one law with three days at hard labor, but a later law provided that those convicted for "Rayling or Scolding; Shall Stand one whole hour in the most public place, where Such offence was Committed, with a Gagg in their mouth or pay five shillings."

Prices were fixed to the extent that strong beer and ale was not to be sold for more than two pence sterling a quart if made of barley malt. Half that price was to be charged for a drink made from molasses. Prices for meals in an ordinary or tavern were established at seven and one-half pence, if they consisted of beef or pork "or such like produce of the Countrie, and Small beer." The ordinary keeper might charge a man on foot two pence for a bed, but if a man had his horse cared for at six pence he was entitled to a free bed. Prices went up, for in 1684 the price of beer made of barley malt was allowed to rise to three pence.

PENN'S INSTRUCTIONS TO BLACKWELL, 1688 [4]

I. THAT things be transacted in my name, by the style of my patent only, viz. *Absolute Proprietary of Pennsylvania*, &c. if not contrary to the charter and laws of the Province, as I suppose not.

II. That Commissions signed and sealed by me here shall be sufficient warrants and directions to pass them under the great seal.

III. To collect the laws, that are in being, and send them over to me, in a stitched book, by the very first opportunity; which I have hitherto often, and so much, in vain, desired.

IV. To be careful that speedy, as well as thorough and impartial justice be done; and virtue, in all, cherished, and vice, in all, punished.

V. That fines be in proportion, both to the fault and ability of the party, that so they may be paid.

VI. That feuds between perswasions, or nations, or countries, be suppressed and extinguished, if any be; and, if none, that by a good conduct, they may be prevented.

VII. That the widow, orphan, and absent may be particularly regarded, in their rights; for their cry will be loudest in all ears; but by absent, I mean such as are so of necessity.

VIII. To countenance the Commissioners of property, where land is unseated, or people are unruly in their settlements, or comply not with reasonable obligations, about bounds, banks, timber, &c. For though we come to a wilderness, it was not that we should continue it so.

IX. That the Sheriffs of their respective counties be charged with the receipt of my rents, fines, &c. as they do in *England,* and give security to the Receiver General, for the same.

X. To have a special care, that Sheriffs and clerks of the peace impose not upon the people; and that the magistrates live peaceably and soberly;—for I could not endure one loose, or litigious person in authority.—Let them be men having some fear of God, and hating covetousness, whatever be their perswasion: to employ others is to prophane an ordinance of God.

XI. That care be taken of the roads, and high-ways, in the country; that they may be straight and commodious for travellers; for I understand, they are turned about by the planters; which is a mischief, that must not be endured.

XII. Consider by what means, or methods, the good and prosperity of the plantation may be promoted; what laws, in being, are unnecessary, or defective, and what are wanting; and in each particular hereof, let me have advice as distinctly, and as speedily as may be.

XIII. Rule the meek meekly; and those that will not be ruled, rule with authority; and God Almighty prosper all honest and prudent endeavours.

THE CHARTER OF PRIVILEGES OF 1701 [5]

The introduction to the Charter of Privileges reviewed the grant of Pennsylvania to William Penn by Charles II, in 1681, and the bestowal of the Territories by James in 1682. Penn's concessions to the "Freemen, Planters and Adventurers" in the Charter of 1683 were also briefly mentioned, as was the return of that document to him in 1700. The introduction concluded with this promise:

Know ye therefore, That . . . I the said *William Penn* do declare, grant and confirm, until all the Freemen, Planters, and Adventurers, and other inhabitants in this Province and Territories, these following Liberties, Franchises, and Privileges, so far as in me lieth, to be held, enjoyed, and kept, by the Freemen, Planters and Adventurers, and other Inhabitants of and in the said Province, and Territories thereunto annexed for ever.

The first article supplemented the initial chapter in the laws of 1700 regarding Liberty of Conscience. It guaranteed civil liberties to all who believed in God. The second paragraph limited officeholding to those who professed a belief in Jesus Christ and would take the attests provided for in Chapter thirty-three of the laws passed in 1700. A paragraph in the eighth article stated: "That the first Article of this Charter relating to Liberty of Conscience, and every Part and Clause therein, according to the true Intent and Meaning thereof, shall be kept and remain, without any Alteration, inviolably for ever."

The second article provided for an Assembly to be chosen yearly by the freemen, and referred to chapter twenty-eight of the laws enacted in 1700 for instructions in regard to elections. This Assembly was to have power, "to chuse a Speaker and other their Officers; and shall be Judges of the Qualifications and Elections of their own Members; sit upon their own Adjournments; appoint Committees; prepare Bills, in order to pass into Laws; impeach Criminals, and redress Grievances; and shall have all other Powers and Privileges of an Assembly, according to the Rights of the Freeborn Subjects of *England,* and as is usual in any of the King's Plantations in *America.*"

The third article referred to the choice of the officials in the counties, such as sheriffs and coroners, and was similar to that in the Charter of 1683 except that the men were to serve for three years. The fourth article, as in 1696, stated that laws would be enacted in the following style: "By the Governor, with the Consent and Approbation of the Freemen in General Assembly met." The fifth article stated: "THAT all Criminals shall have the same Privileges of Witnesses and Council as their Prosecutors."

The sixth and seventh articles, drawn up in reply to the initial address of the Assembly in regard to property, provided first, "THAT no Person or Persons, shall, or may, at any Time hereafter, be obliged to answer any Complaint, Matter or Thing, whatsoever relating to Property, before the Governor and Council, or in any other Place, but in ordinary Course of Justice, unless Appeals thereunto shall be hereafter by Law appointed." The other article guaranteed that the governor would not license an ordinary, tavern, or house of public entertainment until the licensing had been recommended to him by the justices of the county in which the establishment was located. It further ordered the justices to keep such places under surveillance and to suppress those guilty of misbehavior.

The eighth article guaranteed that the estates of men who committed suicide or were killed in any violent manner should descend to the widow and children with no forfeiture to the governor. As in 1683, provision was made for amendment of the charter by the consent of the governor and six-sevenths of the Assembly, except as mentioned in connection with article one above.

The final article, in the words used in the charters of 1682 and 1683, promised that Penn, his heirs, and assigns would do nothing "whereby the Liberties in this Charter contained and expressed, nor any Part thereof, shall be infringed or broken; And if any Thing shall be procured or done, by any Person or Persons, contrary to these Presents, it shall be held of no Force or Effect."

The two paragraphs attached at the end of the document were discussed in chapter fourteen in connection with the dispute between the freemen of Pennsylvania and Delaware. The first paragraph, in addition to providing for the withdrawal of the lower counties, stated that in such an eventuality, to prevent the Assembly in Pennsylvania from becoming too small, "the Inhabitants of each of the Three Counties of this Province, shall not have less than Eight Persons to represent them in Assembly for the Province; and the inhabitants of the Town of *Philadelphia* (when the said Town is incorporated) Two Persons to represent them in Assembly; and the Inhabitants of each County in the Territories, shall have as many Persons to represent them, in a distinct Assembly for the Territories, as shall be by them requested as aforesaid."

NOTES

ABBREVIATIONS USED IN NOTES

Amer. Phil. Soc.	American Philosophical Society
Charter and Laws of Penna.	*Charter to William Penn, and Laws of the Province of Pennsylvania Passed between the Years 1682 and 1700 . . .*
Col. Rec.	*Minutes of the Provincial Council of Pennsylvania*
Col. Series	*Calendar of State Papers, Colonial Series, America and West Indies*
Hazard's *Register*	*The Register of Philadelphia. Samuel Hazard, editor*
HSP	Historical Society of Pennsylvania. All manuscript material used in this study is from the HSP unless indicated otherwise. Items used for the first time will be marked HSP
Journal, B of T	Board of Trade Journals, 1675–1782 (HSP)
N.Y. Documents	*Documents Relative to the Colonial History of the State of New York*
Penn and Logan Correspondence	*Correspondence between William Penn and James Logan . . . with notes by Deborah Logan*
Penn Letters	Dreer Collection, Letters and Papers of William Penn (HSP)
Penn MSS, Domestic	Penn Manuscripts, Domestic and Miscellaneous Letters (HSP)
PMHB	*Pennsylvania Magazine of History and Biography*
PMOC	Penn Manuscripts, Official Correspondence (HSP)
Phila. Y.M.	Philadelphia Yearly Meeting, Department of Records
Proprieties	Board of Trade Papers—Proprieties 1697–1776 (HSP)
Society Misc. Coll.	Society Miscellaneous Collection (HSP)
Votes	*Votes and Proceedings of the House of Representatives of the Province of Pennsylvania, 1682–1776*

CHAPTER ONE: THE BACKGROUND OF THE "HOLY EXPERIMENT"

1. William Penn to James Harrison. August 25, 1681. Robert Proud, *The History of Pennsylvania . . .* (Philadelphia, 1797), I, 169. The original manuscript copy of the letter begins, "for my country, I eyed the lord in ye obtaineing of it, . . ." and later reads, "I have so obtained it & desire

that I may not be unworthy." However, the edges of the page have frayed and it is impossible to read the entire passage in the original. Penn MSS, Domestic. HSP.

2. *A Journal or Historical Account of the Life, Travels, Sufferings,* . . . , *of George Fox* (Cambridge Bi-centenary Edition, 1891), I, 8.

3. Proud, *History of Pennsylvania,* I, 305–07.

4. (New York, 1939), 24. See also, Mary Maples, "William Penn, Classical Republican," *PMHB,* LXXXI (1957), 138–56.

5. Original broadside, Quaker Collection. Haverford College.

6. Original pamphlet, Quaker Collection. Haverford College.

7. Staughton George, etc., *Charter and Laws of Penna.,* (Harrisburg, 1879), pp. 91–93.

8. *Romans* 13: 1–2.

9. *Journal,* I, 68, 69. See also, Vernon Noble, *The Man in Leather Breeches. The Life and Times of George Fox* (New York, 1953).

10. *Memoirs,* Historical Society of Pennsylvania (Philadelphia, 1826), I, Part 1, 204.

11. William C. Braithwaite, *The Second Period of Quakerism* (London, 1919), p. 9.

12. Braithwaite, *The Beginnings of Quakerism* (London, 1912), p. 451. A recent interpretive study of the Society of Friends sheds some light on this period. Howard Brinton, *Friends for 300 Years: The History and Beliefs of the Society of Friends* (New York, 1952).

13. *The Second Period of Quakerism,* pp. 114, 115. See also, John E. Pomfret, "The First Purchasers of Pennsylvania, 1681–1700," *PMHB,* LXXX (1956), 139.

14. Frederick B. Tolles, *Meeting House and Counting House: The Quaker Merchants of Colonial Philadelphia, 1682–1763* (Chapel Hill, 1948), pp. 34–37.

15. *Ibid.*

16. Rufus M. Jones, *The Quakers in the American Colonies* (London, 1911), xiv, 73.

17. *Ibid.,* Book I, "The Quakers in New England."

18. See a map of most of the Fox itinerary in James Bowden, *The History of the Society of Friends in America* (London, 1850), facing I, p. 338.

19. Jones, *The Quakers in the American Colonies,* p. 361.

20. *The History of the Society of Friends in America,* I, 390.

21. A new study of West New Jersey has been made by John E. Pomfret, *The Province of West New Jersey, 1609–1702* (Princeton, 1956).

22. *The Beginnings of Quakerism,* pp. 466, 467. G. P. Gooch, *English Democratic Ideas in the Seventeenth Century* (Cambridge, 1927), describes the political actions and beliefs of the primitive Friends from a non-Quaker viewpoint, pp. 228–38.

23. Braithwaite, *The Beginnings of Quakerism,* p. 481.

24. *Ibid.,* p. 484.

25. *Authority in Church and State* (London, 1928), pp. 111, 112.

26. *Quaker Social History, 1669–1738* (London, 1950), pp. 80–89.

27. *Ibid.,* pp. 90–92.
28. Braithwaite, *The Second Period of Quakerism,* pp. 604, 605.
29. William Penn to Thomas Lloyd and others. August 15, 1685. Penn MSS. Domestic.

CHAPTER TWO: PRELIMINARIES OF COLONIZING

1. A new study of the problem has recently been published, too late to be consulted during the writing of this volume. Vincent Buranelli, *The King and the Quaker* (Philadelphia, 1962).
2. Samuel Hazard, *Annals of Pennsylvania, from the Discovery of the Delaware* (Philadelphia, 1850), p. 474. A copy of a fragment of Penn's petition to the King, introduced into court in 1735, makes mention of a debt of £11,000, and perhaps interest and other items brought it up to £16,000. In a letter Penn wrote to Robert Harley, dated February 9, 1704, he said that there was a debt of "16,000 £, of money lent by my father for the victualling of the navy 1667." *The Manuscripts of the Duke of Portland,* Historical Manuscripts Commission (London, 1894–1901), IV, 81.
3. *Charter and Laws of Penna.,* pp. 81–90.
4. *The Colonial Period of American History* (New Haven, 1937), III, 281.
5. Fulmer Mood, in "William Penn and English Politics in 1680–81," *Journal* of the Friends Historical Society (London), XXXII (1935), 3–19, has proposed an interesting theory in regard to the grant of Pennsylvania to Penn. He has suggested that Charles II was gratified at having been given this opportunity to provide for the withdrawal from England of the Quakers, who were strong supporters of the Whig movement. He was especially pleased to see the removal from the political scene of that arch agitator who had done so much in the campaigns of Algernon Sydney, William Penn. William I. Hull, *William Penn A Topical Biography* (New York, 1937), agreed with the idea, at least in part. Andrews, *The Colonial Period in American History,* was quite skeptical of the whole theory, and denied that there were facts to support it.
6. March 5, 1681. Hazard, *Annals,* p. 500.
7. *Ibid.,* p. 502.
8. April 8, 1681. Penn Letters. Hazard, *Annals,* pp. 502, 503.
9. Hazard, *Annals,* pp. 503, 504.
10. The following quotations are from Albert Cook Myers, *Narratives of Early Pennsylvania, West Jersey, and Delaware* (New York, 1912), pp. 202–15.
11. October 10, 1681. Society Misc. Coll.
12. August 21, 1681. *Ibid.*
13. February 19, 1682. Penn MSS, Domestic.
14. "An account of the Grant of Pennsylvania . . . with an account of the Sales . . ." Penn Papers, Friends House, London. Photostats at HSP. Some authorities suggest these figures are too large. See John E. Pomfret,

"The First Purchasers of Pennsylvania, 1681–1700," *PMHB,* LXXX (1956), 137–63.

15. Samuel Hazard, editor. *Pennsylvania Archives,* First Series (Philadelphia, 1852), I, 40–46.

Men who were prominent in the colony who purchased 5,000 acres or more included Nicholas More, James Claypoole, Griffith Jones, William Markham, Christopher Taylor, Joseph Growdon, John Simcock, James Harrison, Robert Turner, Thomas Holme, and Samuel Carpenter.

16. Tolles, *Meeting House and Counting House,* p. 43, gives several examples among the wealthier merchants.

17. August 21, 1681. Society Misc. Coll.

18. April 12, 1681. *Memoirs,* HSP, I, Part 1, 202, 203.

19. Penn Papers, Charters and Frame of Government. HSP.

20. Some writers have made much of the liberal Concessions and Agreements of West Jersey as compared with the more conservative First Frame, and speculate about the change which swept over Penn in the interim. Pomfret suggests a positive answer to the query, namely that Penn did not write the Concessions. He quotes a letter written by Thomas Budd and Samuel Jennings, in 1685, in which they say that it was "of his [Edward Byllynge's] preparing." Byllynge was one of the original proprietors of West Jersey, and managed to continue his grasp of the government, even though giving control of his land to Penn, Gawen Lawrie, and Nicholas Lucas. *The Province of West New Jersey,* p. 93.

21. Alex. Charles Ewald, *Algernon Sydney* (London, 1873), II, 197–203.

22. Two of the recent studies of Penn review this matter in a competent fashion: Beatty, *William Penn as Social Philosopher,* pp. 16–29; Hull, *William Penn,* pp. 227–33. Both credit Penn with the Concessions.

23. *Charter and Laws of Penna.,* pp. 91–99.

24. Hazard, *Annals,* pp. 589, 592.

25. Penn MSS, Domestic.

CHAPTER THREE: THE BIRTH OF THE "HOLY EXPERIMENT"

1. March 17, 1683. Penn Letterbooks, I. Amer. Phil. Soc.

2. To the Lord of Dartmouth. July 28, 1683. Jonah Thompson Collection, II. HSP.

3. To Lord North. July 24, 1683. *Memoirs,* HSP.. I, Part 2, 412.

4. October 19, 1683. Library Company Manuscripts, 1660–1855. Library Company of Philadelphia.

5. To the Lord Deputy of Ireland. January 9, 1684. Penn Papers, Friends House, London. Photostats, HSP.

6. *Minutes of the Provincial Council of Pennsylvania* (Philadelphia, 1852), I, 79, 80.

7. September 30, 1681. Pennsylvania Miscellaneous Papers, Penn & Baltimore. HSP.

8. *Votes. Pennsylvania Archives,* Eighth Series (Harrisburg, 1931–1935), I, 1–13.

9. Sister Joan de Lourdes Leonard, "The Organization and Procedure of the Pennsylvania Assembly 1682–1776," *PMHB*, LXXII (1948), p. 226.

10. The number of laws passed has long remained a mystery. Phineas Pemberton's "Abridgement of Laws of Pennsylvania," a notebook compiled in 1684, listed sixty "Laws passed at Chester, 6 10 mo. [December], 1682." HSP.

A manuscript copy of the Laws of Pennsylvania among the Penn papers purchased in 1874, listed sixty-two laws for the year 1682. HSP. Marvin W. Schlegel, in his article "The Text of the Great Law of 1682," *Pennsylvania History*, XI (1944), No. 4, 276–83, reported that there were seventy-one laws passed at Chester, and he published the ten missing laws. These were discovered in a manuscript in the Pennsylvania State Library.

11. All these laws may be found in the *Charter and Laws of Penna.*, pp. 108–75.

12. *Col. Rec.*, I, 91.

13. Library Company MSS. Library Company of Philadelphia.

14. May 30, 1684. Norris Papers, Family Letters. I. HSP. The signers included Robert Turner, William Frampton, John Songhurst, John Jones, James Claypoole, Thomas Wynne, Patrick Robinson, John Test, and Samuel Carpenter. In the address at the head of the letter, James Harrison and Griffith Jones were included, but they did not sign.

15. Penn Letters.   16. *Col. Rec.*, I, 58.

17. For the Council: John Moll, Francis Whitwell, William Clarke, James Harrison, William Clayton, and Thomas Holme. For the Assembly: James Walliams, Benony Bishop, Luke Watson, Thomas Fitchwater, Dennis Rochford, and Thomas Wynne. *Col. Rec.*, I, 69.

18. *Votes.*, I, 19.   19. *Ibid.*, 42.   20. *Col. Rec.*, I, 72.

21. *Charter and Laws of Penna.*, 155–61.

22. In the introduction, the powers granted to William Penn were repeated briefly, and in listing the powers in Delaware, no mention was made of governing powers. They are quoted as follows: for Pennsylvania, "Divers great powers, preheminencies, royalties, jurisdictions and authorities, necessary for the well being and government thereof;" and for Delaware, "Together with all royalties, franchises, duties, jurisdictions, liberties and privileges thereunto belonging."

23. The numbering of the chapters in the two frames differed because of omissions and combinations. Only where there were differences between the two documents has mention been made of it.

The period for the promulgation of bills, before the Assembly met, was shortened from thirty to twenty days. The four committees of the upper house named in the earlier constitution were abolished, and instead it was provided that all provincial matters would be settled by the new, smaller Council.

It was stated that thereafter joint meetings, sessions, acts and proceedings of the Governor, Council and Assembly were to be called: "*The meeting sessions acts and proceedings of the General Assembly of the Province of Pennsylvania and Territories thereunto belonging.*" Provisions were made for enlarging representation in the two houses of the General Assembly as it became necessary.

The new constitution stated that estates of unnaturalized aliens should descend to the wife and children despite custom to the contrary, and the right to hunt and fish was guaranteed to the inhabitants.

24. *Votes,* I, 14–19.

25. To [Jasper Yeates] Chester, February 5, 1683. *PMHB,* VI (1882), 469.

26. *Col. Rec.,* I, 59.

27. *Ibid.,* 109. January 16, 1684. Anthony Weston was condemned to a public whipping, on three successive Market Days, for his "presumption and Contempt of this Government and authority." *Ibid.,* 92.

28. *Votes,* I, 46.

29. Thomas Holme, Christopher Taylor, Edmund Cantwell, Edward Southern, William Clayton, and John Richardson were named. Of these, Holme and Taylor were the most faithful, but two other members, William Clark and Lacy Cock, were frequent attenders although not specially named.

30. A member proposed that all men should be forced to marry by a certain age, and another that all persons should be limited to two sorts of clothing, one for winter and one for summer wear. *Col. Rec.,* I, 93.

31. *Proprietary Government in Pennsylvania* (New York, 1896), p. 373.

32. *Charter and Laws of Penna.,* p. 83.

33. *Ibid.,* p. 168.

34. Nicholas More, William Welch, William Wood, Robert Turner, and John Eckley. *Col. Rec.,* I, 121.

35. Society Misc. Coll.   36. *Col. Rec.,* I, 157.

37. The first rule provided that whenever the court was in session, the sheriff or his deputy, the clerk, the crier, and one constable were to be in attendance at all times, unless given permission to leave. The second stated that no person could speak without leave, under the penalty of a fine. The third rule provided that the plaintiffs and defendants were to speak to the point, put their pleas into writing, forbear reflections and discriminations on the court, jury, or one another, under penalty of a fine. The fourth point, was that fines should be levied on the goods of those fined, and that executions should be signed in open court while still sitting. n.d., Penn Letterbooks, I, Amer. Phil. Soc.

38. *Votes,* I, 47.

39. *Charter and Laws of Penna.,* pp. 92, 93.

CHAPTER FOUR: THE COLONISTS AND THE LAND

1. A brief survey of early meetinghouses in Philadelphia may be found in *Historic Philadelphia,* edited by Luther P. Eisenhart. Edwin B. Bronner, "Quaker Landmarks in Early Philadelphia," Volume 43, Part I, *Transactions,* of the American Philosophical Society (1953), 210–16.

2. Epistle to London Yearly Meeting, 1696. Minutes of the Yearly Meeting. Phila. Y.M.

3. William Wistar Comfort, "Quaker Marriage Certificates," *Bulletin,* Friends Historical Association, Vol. 40 (1951), Number 2, 67–80.

4. February 28, 1701. Miscellaneous Papers of Philadelphia Monthly Meeting, 1682–1737. Phila. Y.M.

5. *Publications* of the Genealogical Society of Pennsylvania, I, II, IV, VI, (1895–1917), contain printed copies of the Minutes of Philadelphia Monthly Meeting up to and including 1701. VI, 74, 76.

6. September 2, 1686. Misc. Papers of Philadelphia Monthly Meeting. Phila. Y.M.

7. October 16, 1700. *Ibid.*

8. September 14–18, 1700. Minutes of the Yearly Meeting. Phila. Y.M.

9. September 16–19, 1694. *Ibid.*

10. Proud Papers, Item 175. HSP.   11. *Ibid.*

12. March 7, 1696. Minutes of the Yearly Meeting, and General Spring Meeting of Ministers, 1686–1719. Phila. Y.M.

13. *A Journal of the Life of Thomas Story* (Newcastle, England, 1747).

14. March 2, 1685. Minutes of Philadelphia Quarterly Meeting, 1683–1711. Phila. Y.M.

15. March 4, 1700. *Ibid.*

16. To friends. August 19, 1685. Logan Papers, I, 8. HSP.

17. July 26, 1685. Penn Letters.

18. Penn to ————. October 21, 1687. Penn MSS, Domestic.

19. For the story of the various groups who settled Pennsylvania, see Sydney G. Fisher, *The Making of Pennsylvania* (Philadelphia, 1896); the appropriate chapters in Wayland F. Dunaway, *A History of Pennsylvania* (New York, 1946).

20. To T. Lloyd. October 2, 1685. Penn MSS, Domestic.

21. To James Harrison. April 24, 1686. *Ibid.*

22. To the Council. July 13, 1685. *Ibid.*

23. See the first chapter of the excellent study, Thomas E. Drake, *Quakers and Slavery in America* (New Haven, 1950).

24. September 23, 1696. Minutes of the Yearly Meeting. Phila. Y.M.

25. *The Negro in Pennsylvania* (Washington, 1911), p. 15.

26. January 13, 1690. Society Misc. Coll.

27. Viola F. Barnes, in her article, "Land Tenure in English Colonial Charters of the Seventeenth Century," pp. 4–10, in *Essays in Colonial History Presented to Charles McLean Andrews by His Students* (New Haven, 1931), discusses this matter in some detail, and points out that the land was held as of the Castle of Windsor to escape the responsibilities of holding directly of the Crown, as tenants-in-chief.

28. John E. Pomfret, "The First Purchasers of Pennsylvania, 1681–1700," *PMHB,* LXXX, 149–50. This article also contains some interesting material about the origins, social status and occupations of many of the first purchasers.

29. *Votes,* I, xli–xlv. See also: Nicholas B. Wainwright, "Plan of Philadelphia," *PMHB,* LXXX (1956), 164–226.

30. September 30, 1681. Pennsylvania Miscellaneous Papers, Penn and Baltimore.

31. July 14, 1682. *PMHB*, X (1886), 196, 197.

32. Joseph S. Davis, *Essays in the Earlier History of American Corpo-rations* (Cambridge, Mass., 1917), pp. 41–45.

33. Shaw Livermore, *Early American Land Companies* . . . (New York, 1939).

34. Pomfret, "The First Purchasers of Pennsylvania, 1681–1700," *PMHB*, LXXX, 137–63.

35. Rayner W. Kelsey, *Friends and the Indians* (Philadelphia, 1917), p. 48.

36. In *A Further Account of the Province of Pennsylvania*, published in 1685, Penn reported, "I have made seven Purchases, and in Pay and Presents they have received at least twelve hundred pounds of me. Our humanity has obliged them so far, they generally leave their guns at home, when they come to our settlements; they offer us no affront, not so much as to one of our Dogs; and if any of them break our Laws, they submit to be punisht by them: and to this they have tyed themselves by an obligation under their hands. We leave not the least indignity to them un-rebukt, nor wrong unsatisfied." Myers, *Narratives of Early Pennsylvania*, p. 276.

37. *Votes*, I, lxvi.   38. *Ibid.*, I, lxviii.

39. April 12, 1681. *Memoirs*, HSP, I, Part 1, 202, 203.

40. A good discussion of this point may be found in Shepherd, *Proprietary Government in Pennsylvania*, pp. 117–32. See also: Nicholas B. Wainwright, "The Missing Evidence: Penn vs. Baltimore," *PMHB*, LXXX (1956), 227–35.

41. Richard S. Rodney, "Early Relations of Delaware and Pennsylvania," *PMHB*, LIV (1930), 209 ff.

42. September 16, 1681. *Col. Series*. 1681–1702 (London, 1898–1912), 1681–85, No. 437, II.

43. April 2, 1684. Society Misc. Coll. (Photostat of letter from Delaware Archives).

44. October 7, 1684. Penn MSS, Domestic.

45. March 17, 1685. Proud Catalog, 3. Proud Papers.

46. Journal, B of T. Transcribed from the original manuscript volumes in the Public Record Office of England for the Historical Society of Pennsylvania.

47. Hazard's *Register*. X(1832), 92. The figure was from Thomas Lloyd's letter to Dolobran Quarterly Meeting, November 2, 1684. Howland Collection. Quaker Collection. Haverford College.

48. *History of Pennsylvania*, I, 288–90.

CHAPTER FIVE: ECONOMIC CONDITIONS OF PENN AND THE COLONY

1. *Memoirs*, HSP. (1836), III, Part 2, 103.

2. In a letter to James Logan, September 14, 1705, Penn blamed Thomas Lloyd for the loss of the impost, but Penn should share at least equal responsibility. *Penn and Logan Correspondence*, II, 70, 71.

3. July 11, 1685. Penn MSS, Domestic.

4. To James Harrison. November 7, 1685. *Ibid.* To Thomas Lloyd. September 21, 1686. "William Penn on Public and Private Affairs, 1686: An Important New Letter," edited by Frederick B. Tolles, *PMHB,* LXXX (1956), 246.

5. To James Harrison. n.d. Penn MSS, Domestic, p. 27. . .

6. September 21, 1686. *PMHB,* LXXX, 243.

7. To Harrison. January 28, 1687. Penn MSS, Domestic.

8. February 1, 1687. Society Misc. Coll., Philadelphia County. HSP.

9. To Harrison. October 22, 1687. Penn MSS, Domestic.

10. To Commissioners of State. March 28, 1688. Penn Letters.

11. September 18, 1688. *Ibid.*

12. To Penn. April 9, 1689. Gratz Collection, Governors. HSP.

13. To Phineas Pemberton. October 12, 1689. Library Company MSS, 1660–1855. Library Company of Philadelphia.

14. To Arthur Cook and others. November 5, 1695. Gratz Collection, Governors.

15. December 25, 1696. Penn Letters.   16. June 26, 1697. *Ibid.*

17. April 27, 1698. *PMHB,* XXXVI (1912), 123.

18. To Logan. February 7, 1706. *Penn and Logan Correspondence,* II, 101.

19. *Proprietary Government in Pennsylvania,* pp. 183–98.

20. March 6, 1701. Norris Letterbook. HSP.

21. Carl Bridenbaugh, *Cities in the Wilderness* (New York, 1938), p. 6.

22. To Edward Claypoole. December 2, 1683. James Claypoole Letterbook, 1681–84. HSP.

23. Hazard's *Register,* VI (1830), 198.

24. February 4, 1687. *PMHB,* XXIX (1905), 102–5.

25. February 18, 1685. Etting Collection, Pemberton. HSP.

26. *Col. Rec.,* I, 162.   27. *Ibid.,* 180.

28. July 18, 1685. Penn MSS, Domestic.

29. August 9, 1685. *Ibid.*

30. To Harrison. April 24, 1686. *Ibid.*

31. Robert Turner to ———. October 15, 1686. *PMHB,* IV (1880), 451, 452.

32. Curtis Nettels, "The Economic Relations of Boston, Philadelphia and New York, 1680–1715," *Journal of Economic and Business History,* III, No. 2, February, 1931.

33. To Francis Dove and others. February 4, 1687. *PMHB,* XXIX, 102–5.

34. To ———. July 13, 1685. *Journal,* Friends Historical Society (London), VI (1909), 173, 174.

35. To Edward Claypoole. December 2, 1683. Claypoole Letterbook.

36. February 1, 1687. Society Misc. Coll. Philadelphia County.

37. James Claypoole to Edward Haistwell. April 4, 1684. Claypoole Letterbook.

38. To Gawen Lawrie. February 24, 1684. *Ibid.*

39. November 17, 1686. *Historical Magazine,* III (1859), 105.
40. To Thomas Lloyd. October 2, 1685. Penn MSS, Domestic.
41. To ———. September 17, 1687. *Ibid.* The controversy over building the Center Square Meetinghouse, under construction at this time, rested in part on a shortage of money, and in part on the unwillingness of the settlers to cooperate in Penn's project to develop a group of public buildings on the Center Square. See: Edwin B. Bronner, "The Center Square Meetinghouse," *Bulletin,* Friends Historical Association, Vol. 44 (1955), 67–73.
42. *Charter and Laws of Penna.,* pp. 145, 162.
43. May 31, 1684, and November 6, 1685. Etting Collection, Provincial Council. HSP.
44. September 26, 1686. Pemberton Papers, I. HSP.
45. May 14, 1688. Pennsylvania Miscellaneous Papers, Penn and Baltimore.
46. August 2, 1688. Early Letters from Bristol, England, and Philadelphia. HSP.
47. January 25, 1689. Society Misc. Coll.
48. October 14, 1690. *PMHB,* IV (1880), 199.
49. To ———. December 12, 1690. *Ibid.,* 200.
50. October 4, 1689. Penn Letters.

CHAPTER SIX: POLITICAL DIFFICULTIES, 1684 TO 1688

1. November 2, 1684. Howland Collection. Quaker Collection. Haverford College.
2. These statements are based upon a study of *Col. Rec.,* I, 119–229.
3. To Harrison. January 28, 1687. Penn MSS, Domestic.
4. February 8, 1687. Etting Collection, Early Quakers and the Penn Family. HSP.
5. August 19, 1685. Logan Papers, I.
6. Phineas Pemberton to Penn. April 3, 1687. Etting Collection, Pemberton.
7. To the Council. September 18, 1688. Penn Letters. While there was difference of opinion concerning the position of the Assembly and the Council which was not settled until many years later, I will refer to the upper and lower houses from time to time, both as a convenience and to avoid repetition.
8. *Col. Rec.,* I, 183.
9. The 1685 proceedings of the General Assembly may be found in *Votes,* I, 58–71; and *Col. Rec.,* I, 132–41.
10. *Votes,* I, 70, 71. Italicized in the original.
11. The 1686 session of the General Assembly may be found in *Votes,* I, 71–77; *Col. Rec.,* I, 176–85.
12. The brief 1687 proceedings are found in *Votes,* I, 78–82; *Col. Rec.,* I, 202–6.
13. To Harrison. July 11, 1685. Penn MSS, Domestic.

14. September 21, 1686. *PMHB*, LXXX, 240.

15. To the Council. September 25, 1686. Penn Letters.

16. September 21, 1686. *PMHB*, LXXX, 241.

17. Penn, in the so-called Penn-Mead Trial, had helped to establish a precedent against the intimidation of juries by justices.

18. *Col. Rec.*, I, 135–37. The action of the Assembly can be followed in *Votes*, I, 65–69.

19. July 13, 1685. Penn MSS, Domestic.

20. September 20, 1686. Penn MSS, Assembly & Provincial Council of Pennsylvania. HSP. The men were Arthur Cook, John Simcock, and James Harrison.

21. October 3, 1686. Etting Collection, Pemberton.

22. December 21, 1687. Penn MSS, Domestic.

23. July 13, 1685. *Ibid.*   24. *Col. Rec.*, I, 148.

25. Penn to Pemberton. October 26, 1685. *William Penn, 1644–1718.* The Blumhaven Library (Philadelphia, 1950).

26. June 6, 1687. Penn MSS, Domestic.

27. September 21, 1686. *PMHB*, LXXX, 241, 242.

28. *Col. Rec.*, I, 198.

29. To the Council. July 13, 1685. Penn MSS, Domestic.

30. To Harrison. January 28, 1687. *Ibid.*

31. November 7, 1686. Parrish Collection, Proud Papers (copy). HSP.

32. November 20, 1686. Penn MSS, Domestic. Joran Keen or Kyn was one of the early settlers at Upland.

33. Proud, *History of Pennsylvania*, I, 305–7. A letter to Thomas Lloyd, written the same day confirms the authenticity. It may be found in Penn MSS, Domestic. These men were Thomas Lloyd, Nicholas More, James Claypoole, Robert Turner, and John Eckley.

34. February 8, 1687. Etting Collection, Early Quakers and the Penn family.

35. [Philadelphia, 1687.]   36. *Col. Rec.*, I, 212.

37. August 4, 1687. Penn Letterbooks, I. Amer. Phil. Soc.; also Dreer Collection, Governors in the Colonies. HSP.

38. Penn MSS, Domestic. Harrison died before the letter arrived.

39. *Ibid.* Claypoole was dead.

40. Parrish Collection. Proud Papers.

41. December 21, 1687. Penn MSS, Domestic.

42. Parrish Collection, Proud Papers.

43. June 6, 1687. Penn MSS, Domestic.

44. The proceedings of the 1688 General Assembly may be found in *Votes*, I, 82–93; *Col. Rec.*, I, 221–27.

45. Penn to T. Lloyd. March 28, 1688. Penn MSS, Domestic.

CHAPTER SEVEN: PENN'S ADMISSION OF FAILURE: GOVERNOR BLACKWELL

1. December 27, 1687. Parrish Collection, Proud Papers (copy).

2. January 13, 1690. Society Misc. Coll.

3. Penn Letters.

4. Proud, *History of Pennsylvania*, I, 339. This was checked against a manuscript copy in Penn MSS, Forbes Papers, I, 10. HSP.

5. The exception was found in the first chapter. Penn asked Blackwell to act in the name of the "Absolute Proprietary of Pennsylvania," while the Second Frame stated that the laws were to be put in effect *"By the Governour with the assent and approbation of the freemen in Provinciall Council and Assemblie mett."* The same constitution also stated: "the Governour or his Deputie . . . shall att no time therein perform anie publick act of State whatsoever that shall or may relate unto the Justice, Trade, Treasurie or Safetie of the Province and Territories aforesaid, but by and with the advice and consent of the Provinciall Council thereof."

6. Nicholas B. Wainwright, "Governor John Blackwell," *PMHB,* LXXIV (1950), 457–72. This is an excellent summary of Blackwell's year at Philadelphia.

7. January 25, 1689. Blackwell Papers. HSP. *Pennsylvania Archives*, I, 106–7. The original of the second letter is in the Roberts Collection. Haverford College.

8. This narrative is from a letter to Penn dated January 25, 1689. Society Misc. Coll.

9. T. Lloyd was Keeper of the Great Seal.

10. September 24, 1688. Penn Letters.

11. In Philadelphia County apparently four of the justices named refused to serve, for eight signed the back of the commission and four did not. The four who refused to serve were John Goodson, Samuel Carpenter, Samuel Richardson, and Griffith Owen. January 12, 1689. Penn Letterbooks, III. Amer. Phil. Soc.

12. *Col. Rec.,* I, 237.   13. *Ibid.,* 250.   14. *Ibid.,* 255.

15. *Ibid.,* 245.   16. *Ibid.,* 256, 257.

17. January 25, 1689. Society Misc. Coll.

18. April 2, 1689. Penn MSS, Blackwell Papers. HSP.

19. This material is from the *Colonial Records,* and the letter to Penn dated January 25, 1689. Society Misc. Coll.

20. April 2, 1689. Penn MSS, Blackwell Papers.

21. *Col. Rec.,* I, 270–72.

22. *Ibid.,* 273, 274.

23. William Bradford was the only printer within several hundred miles of Philadelphia.

24. Blackwell dismissed Richardson after their quarrel and called for the election of a successor to him from Philadelphia County.

25. *Col. Rec.,* I, 277–83.

26. April 8, 1689. Etting Collection, Pemberton.

27. PMOC, I.

The seven signers were Joseph Growdon, Bartholemew Coppock, John Simcock, William Yardley, John Curtis, Samuel Carpenter, and William Stockdale.

28. To Penn. April 9, 1689. Gratz Collection, Governors.

29. The proceedings of the General Assembly in May, 1689, may be followed in *Votes*, I, 94–110; *Col. Rec.*, I, 284–94.

30. There had been an unofficial report to the Council February 24, by Zachariah Whitpain, and perhaps letters arrived by May.

31. This speech may be found in *Col. Rec.*, I, 286–89; *Votes*, I, 98–102.

32. May 23, 1689. Etting Collection, Governors. HSP. Also, *Col. Rec.* I, 296, 297.

33. June 4, 1689. Society Misc. Coll.

34. *Votes*, I, 106–8. This remonstrance was printed in italics.

35. *Col. Rec.*, I, 294.   36. *Ibid.*, 301.

37. *PMHB*, VI, 363, 364.   38. *Col. Rec.*, I, 298–301.

39. *Ibid.*, 302–11.   40. *Ibid.*, 312–15.   41. *Ibid.*, 315–17.

42. January 13, 1690. Society Misc. Coll.

43. Edward Roberts to Blackwell. September 20, 1689. Penn Letters (copy).

CHAPTER EIGHT: CONFLICT AND CHAOS, 1690 TO 1693

1. August 12, 1689. Penn Letters.

2. December 30, 1689. *Proud Catalog*, 14, Proud Papers.

3. *Ibid.*

4. September 6, 1689. Etting Collection, Pemberton.

5. *Col. Rec.*, I, 317–20.

6. *Ibid.*, 322–33.

7. Box 2, Proud Papers. This answer is dated April 22, two days before the Council met, according to the minutes, and is not signed by the same men who are listed as present April 24. There is no record of an April 22 session.

8. Lacy Cock, an old settler along the Delaware, knew the Indian language. *Col. Rec.*, I, 334, 335.

9. The Minutes for the May, 1690, session of the General Assembly may be found in *Votes*, I, 110–17; *Col. Rec.*, I, 335–40.

10. *Charter and Laws of Penna.*, 182–88.

11. *Col. Rec.*, I, 344, 345.

The months which followed, from with December, 1690, to April 26, 1693, might be described as the Dark Ages of Pennsylvania history. The printed *Minutes of the Provincial Council* are blank for that period, there are no laws recorded in the *Charter and Laws of Pennsylvania*, and there is no record of the meeting of the Assembly in 1691, in the *Votes and Proceedings of the House of Representatives*, although the 1692 session is recorded. There are some manuscript minutes of the Provincial Council available at the Historical Society of Pennsylvania, but they are very scattered, very brief, and some at least, appear to have been written after the fact, and not by a secretary actually in attendance. The student is forced to depend on these minutes, on official and personal correspondence sometimes reprinted in Proud, *History of Pennsylvania*, and on rare notices of Pennsylvania events in the printed archives of neighboring provinces, in attempting to portray what was happening in these twenty-nine months. With the arrival of Governor Benjamin Fletcher with a royal commission, the task of the historian is made easier.

A list of manuscript minutes of the Provincial Council follows. Those which are starred (*) may be found in the Penn MSS, Assembly and Provincial Council, and the remainder in the Society Miscellaneous Collection, Provincial Council of Pennsylvania. HSP.

March 30, 31; April 1, 2, 1691.*

April 2, 3, 10, 11, 18; May 11, 12, 13, 19, 20, 1691.

April 4, 5, 7; May 19; September 20, 1692.*

12. November 26, 1690. Box 2, Proud Papers.

13. November 11–17, 1690. Society Misc. Coll.

14. Penn MSS, Assembly and Provincial Council of Pennsylvania.

15. Proud, *History of Pennsylvania*, I, 355, 356. The original is in Penn MSS, Three Lower Counties. HSP.

16. April 2, 1691. Society Misc. Coll., Provincial Council of Pennsylvania.

17. *Ibid.*

18. Proud, *History of Pennsylvania*, I, 356n.

19. April 6, 1691. Penn MSS, Three Lower Counties.

20. April 11, 1691. Penn MSS, Beaver Skins, etc. HSP.

21. May 18, 1691. Ibid.

22. May 19, 1691. Society Misc. Coll., Provincial Council of Pennsylvania.

23. May 23, 1691. Penn Letters.

In one peculiar paragraph, Turner wrote as if the Council still governed, and the Lower Counties had remained in the government, and urged Penn to prevent the naming of a single deputy governor. At the same time, he clearly stated that Thomas Lloyd was deputy governor in another part of the communication.

24. September 11, 1691. Penn Letters.

25. September 30, 1691. *Bulletin* of the Friends Historical Society (Philadelphia), II (1908), 72, 73.

26. September 10, 1691. Norris Papers, Family Letters, I.

27. Proud, *History of Pennsylvania*, I, 357. In a letter dated June 29, 1692, Penn mentioned this decision.

28. Penn MSS, Assembly and Provincial Council.

29. Proud Papers, Box 2.

30. *Votes*, I, 118–27. While four bills were mentioned in the letter to William Penn, the minutes of the Assembly stated that there were five acts. The petition is found in *PMHB*, XXXVIII (1914), 495–501.

31. June 15, 1692. Penn Letters.

32. February 4, 1693. Penn Letters. Printed by Samuel M. Janney, *The Life of William Penn* (Philadelphia, 1852), pp. 379, 380.

33. n.d. *N.Y. Documents*, IV, 35.

34. August 21, 1691. Gratz Collection, Governors.

35. March 27, 1693. *N.Y. Documents*, IV, 35.

36. The Keithian movement gained some following in the Jerseys as well as in Pennsylvania.

37. Ethyn Williams Kirby, *George Keith* (New York, 1942). This is a very competent biography of Keith, and the schism is described in detail. The book contains some erroneous statements about the political situation in Pennsylvania in these years. This volume has been the principal source for this discussion of the schism.

38. Two non-Quakers, Lacy Cock and John Holmes, proclaimed this whole question a Quaker matter, and refused to join their fellow justices in signing the proclamation. The signers were: Arthur Cook, Samuel Jennings, Samuel Richardson, Humphrey Murrey, Anthony Morris, and Robert Ewen. *Ibid.*, pp. 74, 78, 79.

39. Penn Letterbooks, I. Amer. Phil. Soc.

40. December 9, 1700. Penn Mottled Letterbook. HSP.

41. Photostatic Copy in the Quaker Collection. Haverford College.

CHAPTER NINE: ROYAL INTERLUDE, 1693 TO 1695

1. Hull, *William Penn*, p. 266.

2. *Manuscripts of the Duke of Portland*, III, 403.

3. To Harrison. n.d. [1686] Penn MSS, Domestic, 27.

4. Hull, *William Penn*, 255. The previous paragraphs are largely based on this volume.

5. December 5, 1692. *Col. Series,* 1693–96. No. 397.

6. November 29, 1692. Penn MSS, J. Francis Fisher Copies. HSP.

7. To ———. n.d. *Col. Series,* 1689–92. No. 2667.

8. Proud, *History of Pennsylvania*, I, 380.

9. *Col. Rec.*, I, 364.

10. Fletcher to Earl of Nottingham. August 18, 1693. *Col. Series,* 1693–96. No. 507.

11. The Governor named William Markham, Patrick Robinson, Robert Turner, Andrew Robeson, Lacy Cock, William Salway, John Cann, William Clark, and George Forman. He later added Charles Sanders, Griffith Jones, and John Donaldson. *Col. Rec.*, I, 365–75, 449, 472.

12. *Ibid.*, 352–57.   13. *Ibid.*, 372, 373.

14. Proud, *History of Pennsylvania*, I, 383, 384. Signers were Joseph Growdon, John Bristow, John Delavall, John Simcock, Hugh Roberts, Samuel Lewis, and Richard Hough.

15. The proceedings of this General Assembly are to be found in *Col. Rec.*, I, 398–433; *Votes*, I, 127–54.

16. *Col. Rec.*, I, 370–75.

17. Growdon's address to the Governor closed with these words, "it was a great Charge & trust, & more then he Could Conceive himself capable of; Therfor moved that his Excell. wold Command the representatives to return to their house and choose some fitter person." *Col. Rec.*, I, 399.

18. 192–241.

19. June 12, 1693. *N.Y. Documents*, IV, 32.

20. *Col. Series,* 1693–96. No. 386.

21. June 12, and August 15, 1693. *N.Y. Documents,* IV, 31, 32, 37.

22. August 18, 1693. *Col. Series,* 1693–96. No. 507.

23. September 15, 1693. Penn MSS, Domestic.

24. December 21, 1693. Parrish Collection, Proud Papers (copy).

25. January 18, 1694. *Ibid.* The signers were Arthur Cook, John Simcock, Samuel Richardson, James Fox, George Murrie, and Samuel Carpenter.

26. Quaker Collection. Haverford College.

27. *A Collection of Memorials Concerning Divers Deceased Ministers . . .* (Philadelphia, 1787), pp. 23, 24.

28. January 25, 1694. Penn Letterbooks, I. Amer. Phil. Soc.

29. *Col. Rec.,* I, 453–58; *Votes,* I, 154–58.

30. The proceedings of the May 22, 1694, session of the General Assembly may be found in *Col. Rec.,* I, 458–72; *Votes,* I, 158–77.

31. At a meeting of the Council, June 11, Fletcher reported that he had been told that Saturday night, June 9, "after the dissolution of the Assemblie, David Loyd, with the Representatives, returned to the place of their sessions, and david Loyd assumed the Chair, and said they wer not dissolved until they had dissolved themselves also, and caused some minute to be entred upon record." The Assembly clerk reported, however, that Lloyd had said, since the Governor dissolved this house, it is dissolved. *Col. Rec.,* I, 445. See also the new biography by Roy N. Lokken, *David Lloyd, Colonial Lawmaker.* (Seattle, 1959).

32. Penn Letterbooks, I. Amer. Phil. Soc.

33. July 13, 1694. Journal, B of T.

34. *Ibid.*   35. *Ibid.*

36. *Col. Series,* 1693–96. No. 1213.

37. November 24, 1694. Penn Letterbooks, I. Amer. Phil. Soc.

CHAPTER TEN: GOVERNMENT UNDER WILLIAM MARKHAM, 1695 TO 1699

1. May 26, 1696. *Col. Series,* 1696–97. No. 27 xi.

2. Proud, *History of Pennsylvania,* I, 407, 408. The election day was April 10.

3. The proceedings of this legislative session of the Council may be found in *Col. Rec.,* I, 482–88.

4. Penn Letterbooks, II. Amer. Phil. Soc.

5. Pennsylvania was called upon to furnish eighty men with their officers plus provisions for one year, or a monetary grant of equal value. The force of men was to include one captain, two lieutenants, four sergeants, four corporals, and two drummers.

6. April 15, 1695. Etting Collection, Governors. June 12, 1695. Penn Letterbooks, II. Amer. Phil. Soc.. September 3, 1695. *Ibid.*

7. The proceedings of the General Assembly of 1695 can be found in *Col. Rec.,* I, 488–95; *Votes,* I, 177–84.

8. No copy of the proposed Act of Settlement of 1695 has been found.

9. Whitehall, April 20, 1696. Penn Letterbooks, II. Amer. Phil. Soc.

10. May 26, 1696. *Col. Series*, 1696–97. No. 27 xi.

11. The five non-Quakers were Jasper Yeates, Richard Halliwell, John Brinkloe, John Hill, and Patrick Robinson, secretary. John Donaldson and William Clark were added later. *Col. Rec.*, I, 495–98.

12. The proceedings of the General Assembly of 1696 can be found in *Col. Rec.*, I, 502–9; *Votes*, I, 185–94. This remonstrance is also in Penn Letterbooks, II. Amer. Phil. Soc.

13. Another commission was produced which named both Cook and Samuel Jennings, if Carpenter also refused to serve.

14. *Charter and Laws of Penna.*, pp. 245–60.

15. The Organization and Procedure of the Pennsylvania Assembly, 1682–1776. (Unpublished Doctoral Dissertation, University of Pennsylvania, 1947), pp. 19, 32, 33.

16. There are three copies of this petition extant, one in the Society Miscellaneous Collection, Philadelphia Petitions. HSP; and the other two in Penn Letterbooks, II, III. Amer. Phil. Soc.

17. *Proprietary Government in Pennsylvania*, p. 284.

18. Goodson retired from office before the discussion of the new frame began.

19. April 9, 1697. Penn MSS, Additional Miscellaneous Letters, I. HSP.

20. Penn MSS, Forbes Papers, II.

21. November 5, 1695. Gratz Collection, Governors.

22. Quaker Collection. Haverford College.

23. Proprieties, II, B 3.19. Transcribed from the original manuscript volumes in the Public Record Office of England for the Historical Society of Pennsylvania.

24. November 28, 1696. *Ibid.*, B 3.20.

25. For the Council: Arthur Cook, Samuel and Joshua Carpenter. For the Assembly: Robert Turner, Joseph Fisher, Joseph Wilcox, Joseph Ashton, Toby Leech, and Andrew Barikson.

26. Edward Shippen, etc., to Penn. May 25, 1697. Fallon Scrap Book. HSP.

27. April 15, 1697. Penn Letters.   28. *Ibid.*

29. May 26, 1698. Penn Letterbooks, III. Amer. Phil. Soc.

30. December 25, 1696. Penn Letters.   31. Proprieties, II, B 3.12.

32. The Minutes of the General Assembly in 1697 can be found in *Col. Rec.*, I, 516–26; *Votes*, I, 194–97 (includes only the minutes of the first three days).

33. An investigation into the collection of the tax laid upon the population in 1696 revealed that little more than half of the money had been collected, and that collectors had been lax in making reports and keeping records. Some citizens refused to pay the tax. A law was enacted to aid in the collection of the money.

34. May 25, 1697. Fallon Scrap Book.

35. December 1, 1697. Quaker Collection. Haverford College.

36. September 5, 1697. Penn Letters.   37. *Col. Rec.*, I, 528–33.

38. The Minutes of the General Assembly in 1698 can be found in *Col. Rec.*, I, 546–55; and *Votes*, I, 201–14.

39. *Charter and Laws of Penna.*, 268–77.

40. December 19, 1698. Journal, B of T.

41. The Minutes of the General Assembly in 1699 can be found in *Col. Rec.*, I, 567–72; *Votes*, I, 214–21.

42. *Charter and Laws of Penna.*, 278–90.

CHAPTER ELEVEN: PENNSYLVANIA DENOUNCED, 1682 TO 1701

1. August 3, 1685. Penn MSS, Domestic.

2. *Col. Series*, 1685–88. Nos. 1160, 1250. May 18, 1687. Journal, B of T. Other complaints must have been made at the same time for Penn wrote June 6, 1687, that because of that "which is real, and that malice in your neighbours of some governments invent, we have much ado to keep our heads above water here." Penn MSS, Domestic.

3. *Col. Series*, 1689–92. No. 1691. February 8, 1693, Journal, B of T.

4. October 18, 1695. *Archives of Maryland* (Baltimore, 1883–1911), XX, 328, 329.

5. September 3, 1689. Minutes of the Ministers. Phila. Y.M.

6. *Col. Series*, 1689–92. Nos. 690, 1246, 1302.

7. *Ibid.*, No. 2472. September 19, 1692. Journal, B of T.

8. *The American Colonies in the Eighteenth Century* (New York, 1924), I, 55, 56.
Some sense of Pennsylvania's size in the eyes of the English government can be gained by examining the list of men required from each colony to aid New York in its fight against the French: Massachusetts Bay, 350; Rhode Island, 48; Virginia, 240; Maryland, 106; Connecticut, 120; the Jerseys, 700; and Pennsylvania, 80. April 13, 1694. Journal, B of T.

9. To Samuel Carpenter and others. December 1, 1697. Haverford MSS, Quaker Collection. Haverford College.

10. *Col. Series*, 1685–88. No. 1898.

11. *Col. Series*, 1689–92. No. 2344. See Leonidas Dodson, "Pennsylvania Through the Eyes of a Royal Governor," *Pennsylvania History*, III (1936), 89–97.

12. *Col. Series*, 1693–96. No. 1897.

13. Osgood, *The American Colonies in the Eighteenth Century*, I, 177, 178.

14. Andrews, *The Colonial Period in American History*, III, 279.

15. G. H. Guttridge, *The Colonial Policy of William III*, etc. (Cambridge, 1922), pp. 11, 12.

16. May 16, 1689. Journal, B of T.

17. July 29, 1696. Journal, B of T.

18. For the Delaware Bay area the following were named: Robert Quary, judge; Edward Chilton, advocate; William Rodney, register; and Robert Webb, marshal. Winfred T. Root, *The Relations of Pennsylvania*

with the British Government, 1696–1765 (New York, 1912), pp. 94, 95. This book was extremely useful in connection with this chapter.

19. September 16, 1698. Proprieties, II, B 35.
20. June 1, 1699. Proprieties, III, C 30.
21. To the Earl of Bridgewater, August 30, 1698. Proprieties, II, B 30.
22. September 6, 1698. Proprieties, II, B 34.
23. October 20, 1698. Proprieties, II, B 40.
24. October 20, 1699. Proprieties, V, E 24.
25. August 8, 1698. Proprieties, III, C 26.2. See Robert N. Toppan, *Edward Randolph* (Boston, 1898). A new biography has recently been published which has not been consulted. Michael G. Hall, *Edward Randolph and the American Colonies, 1676–1703* (Chapel Hill, 1960).
26. *Col. Series,* 1697–98. No. 451, I.
27. June 26, 1697. Penn Letters.
28. April 21, 1698. Proprieties, II, B 18.9.
29. *Charter and Laws of Penna.,* pp. 268–74.
30. December 19, 1698. Proprieties, II, B 38.
31. *Manuscripts of the Duke of Portland,* III, 601, 602.
32. March 1, 1699. Proprieties, III, C 16.
33. To Board of Trade. June 6, 1699. Proprieties, III, C 31.
34. May 30, 1698. Proprieties, II, B 18.1. (Erroneously listed as April 30).
35. May 18, 1699. Proud Papers, Box 2.
36. To Penn. April 24, 1697. Proprieties, II, B 3.11.
37. February 2, 1694. Journal, B of T.
38. *Acts of the Privy Council of England. Colonial Series* (Hereford, 1910), 1680–1720. No. 609.
39. November 20, 1698. *PMHB,* XIII (1889), 216–18.
40. April 25, 1698. Proprieties, II, B 14.
41. January 28, 1701. Proprieties, 6 1, G 12.
42. October 27, 1701. Proprieties, 6 2, I 2.
43. *Penn & Logan Correspondence,* I, 29, 30.
44. October, 1700. Penn Mottled Letterbook.
45. n.d. *Manuscripts of the Duke of Portland,* IV, 31, 32.
46. December 31, 1700. Journal, B of T.
47. June 20, 1700. Proprieties, V, F 60. This is a copy of the commission to the sheriff of Philadelphia County, Thomas Farmer.
48. November 14, 1700. Proprieties, V, 57, 58, 64.10.
49. December 13, 1700. Journal, B of T. December 10, 1700. Proprieties, 6 1, G 40.
50. March 24, 1701. Proprieties, 6 1, G 3.
51. August 26, 1701. Proprieties, 6 1, G 39.
52. The Duke of Devonshire, the Marquis of Normanby, the Duke of Somerset, Lord Jefferys, Lord Powlett, the Earl of Dorset, Sir Heneage Finch, Lord Romney, Robert Harley, and the Honorable John Hone. Most of these letters may be found in the Penn Mottled Letterbook.
53. September 7, 1701. Penn MSS, Granville Penn Book. HSP.

CHAPTER TWELVE: PENN'S RETURN TO PENNSYLVANIA, 1699

1. To Friends. September 5, 1697. Penn Letters.

2. Hazard's *Register*, X(1832), 92. Isaac Norris to Jonathan Dickinson. December 5, 1699. Norris Letterbook.

3. To William Penn, Jr. September 25, 1700. *Penn and Logan Correspondence*, I, 17.

4. To John Askew. December 30, 1699. Norris Letterbook.

5. To Philip Ford. December 30, 1699. *Ibid.*

6. To Askew. March 31, 1700. *Ibid.*

7. To William Penn, Jr. September 25, 1700. *Penn and Logan Correspondence*, I, 17.

8. Lords Justice to Penn. September 12, 1699. PMOC, I.

9. April 28, 1700. Proprieties, V, F 26. Many students of this period feel that this action by Penn against Lloyd was the event which made the latter the implacable enemy of the Proprietor for many years. See Burton A. Konkle, "David Lloyd and the First Half-Century of Pennsylvania," (Unpublished manuscript, Friends Library, Swarthmore College). Lokken is not as positive on this question as Konkle. *David Lloyd*, pp. 87, 88.

10. Proprieties, V. F 24.   11. *Votes*, I, 228.

12. Proprieties, V, F 25.   13. March 6, 1700. Proprieties, V, F 5.

14. Proprieties, V, F 25.   15. April 28, 1700. Proprieties, V, F 26.

16. To Lord Summers. October 22, 1700. Penn Mottled Letterbook.

17. August 23, 1700. *Col. Series*, 1700. No. 734.

18. *Col. Rec.*, I, 574.

19. Minutes for this session of the General Assembly may be found in *Col. Rec.*, I, 589–95; *Votes*, I, 221–33. There is a gap here between *Charter and Laws* and the *Statutes at Large*, and no record of the laws for the first two sessions of 1700 are extant.

20. *Col. Rec.*, I, 573–74.   21. *Ibid.*, 595–600.

22. Griffith Jones, who had refused to serve in the General Assembly unless under the Charter of 1683, had his wish gratified and took a seat in the Assembly as a delegate from Kent County.

23. Phineas Pemberton proved himself a poor prophet by writing to his wife Alice, early in the session, that though "Things go heavily on here about our publick affairs wich makes my Stay uneasie; but doubt it will be Long ere I come home for we have done little as yet." May 10, 1700. Etting Collection, Pemberton.

24. Minutes for the session of the General Assembly which convened May 10, 1700, may be found in *Col. Rec.*, I, 600–14. The minutes in *Votes*, I, 233–42, are blank from May 16 to June 1.

25. The other eight were: Edward Shippen, Samuel Carpenter, John Moll, Robert Turner, Griffith Owen, William Clark, Caleb Pusey, and Joseph Growdon. Humphrey Morrie was added later. *Col. Rec.*, I, 580–89.

26. Minutes of the session of the General Assembly which met October 14, 1700, may be found in *Col. Rec.*, I, 614–24; *Votes*, I, 243–77.

27. Gratz Collection, Quakers. HSP. Pemberton, who was named to the

Council after this letter was written, was nearly as busy in that capacity as he would have been had he been elected to the Assembly.

28. December 10, 1700. Norris Letterbook.

29. December 8, 1700. *Ibid.*

30. To Thomas Lloyd, son of Thomas Lloyd. March 6, 1701. *Ibid.*

31. The final General Assembly will be discussed in the next chapter.

32. The King's letter to Penn, January 19, 1701, may be found in Penn MSS, Additional Misc. Letters, I.

33. The minutes of the August, 1701, session of the General Assembly may be found in *Col. Rec.,* II, 27–32; *Votes,* I, 277–81.

34. *Col. Rec.,* I, 615.

35. James T. Mitchell and Henry Flanders (Commissioners), *The Statutes at Large of Pennsylvania, 1682–1801* (Harrisburg, 1896), II, 3–141.

36. February 27, 1700. Proprieties, V, F 23.3.

37. December 30, 1700. Penn Mottled Letterbook.

38. *Ibid.*   39. February 27, 1700. *Ibid.*

40. December 31, 1700. *Ibid.*   41. *Ibid.*

CHAPTER THIRTEEN: A FLOURISHING PLANTATION, 1690 TO 1701

1. In 1697 Penn reported to the Board of Trade that there were 1,500 houses in Philadelphia, and that the population was 12,000. This figure is undoubtedly too large. Penn must have been referring to the entire Philadelphia County. The best estimate places the figure at 5,000. E. B. Greene and Virginia D. Harrington, *American Population Before the Federal Census of 1790* (New York, 1932), pp. 117, 118.

2. Penn to Sir John Lowther, August 16, 1701. Historical Manuscripts Commission, *The Manuscripts of the Earl of Lonsdale* (London, 1893), p. 246.

3. March 10, 1700. Proprieties, V, F 5.

4. Quary to Board of Trade. September 22, 1697. *Col. Series,* 1696–97. No. 1338.

5. Francis Brown to Penn. November 13, 1697. Proprieties, II, B 3.

6. To Robert Harley. n.d. *Manuscripts of the Duke of Portland,* IV, 32.

7. To Ezekiell Gomersall. September 6, 1700; and to Anthony Major, June 25, 1700. Dickinson Letterbook. HSP.

8. To Jeffery Pinnell. November 18, 1699. Norris Letterbook.

9. February 22, 1697. Proprieties, II, B 3.16.

10. One law was enacted during Penn's first visit to Pennsylvania which provided for duties on commerce, but it was set aside before it became effective.

11. September 21, 1698. Yearly Meeting Minutes. Phila. Y.M.

12. To Rip Van Dam, etc., July 28, 1699. Norris Letterbook.

13. Horatio Gates Jones, "Historical Sketch of the Rittenhouse Paper-Mill; the First Erected in America, A.D., 1690." *PMHB,* XX (1896), 315–33.

14. December 27, 1693. Journal, B of T.

15. To Pinnell. July 1, 1699. Norris Letterbook.

16. Nettels, "The Economic Relations of Boston, Philadelphia and New York, 1680–1715." *Journal of Economic and Business History*, III, No. 2, February, 1931, 211, 212.

17. *N.Y. Documents*, IV, 159.

18. *The Manuscripts of the House of Lords*, New Series (London, 1903, 1912), IV, 446, 447.

19. *Col. Rec.*, I, 481.

20. Dickinson to James Pinnuck. April 21, 1698. Dickinson Letterbook.

21. To James Mills. September 1, 1699. Norris Letterbook.

22. Penn to Lord Bellomont. December 9, 1700. Penn Mottled Letterbook.

23. To John Hance. June 16, 1699. Norris Letterbook.

24. To Alexander Perris. April 8, 1700. *Ibid.*

25. To Pinnell. May 6, 1700. *Ibid.*

On the other hand, Edward Shippen sent gold valued at fifty pounds sterling to England in 1699 for the poor among Friends, and offered more. James Backhouse, *The Life and Correspondence of William and Alice Ellis* (Philadelphia, 1850), 176. See Frederick B. Tolles, "The Transatlantic Quaker Community in the Seventeenth Century," *Huntington Library Quarterly*, XIV (1951), 239–58.

26. To Pinnell. April 23, 1700. Norris Letterbook.

27. n.d. *Ibid.*

28. To Joshua Willson. December 11, 1700. *Ibid.*

29. To Robert Elliott. July 11, 1700. *Ibid.*

30. *Col. Series*, 1696–97. No. 717.   31. *Col. Series*, 1700. No. 812.

32. March 6, 1701. Proprieties, 6 [1], G 12.

33. To the Board of Trade. July 2, 1701. Proprieties, 6 [1] G 31.

34. In justice to the Philadelphia merchant a few lines from his answer are quoted: "Thine of the 30th I perceive Requires more yn I am at psent able to Answr. I would Carry my Dish even & Endeavr To give no offence, it being a New thing for a private pson to Give acct of the business of great Men & more especially ought wee be Carefull where they are great & Good. Therefore, as I shall from time to Time answr thy Requests of ys Kind I shall depend on thy Discrecon that it may not be to my disadvantage." May 3, 1700. Norris Letterbook.

35. Penn to Lord Romney. September 6, 1701. Penn MSS, Granville Penn Book.

36. Norris to Ford. July 10, 1700. Norris Letterbook.

37. *Col. Rec.*, I, 597.

38. November 14, 1731. PMOC, II.

39. To Lord Summers. October 22, 1700. Penn Mottled Letterbook.

40. The quotas in pounds for the counties were: Philadelphia, 1,025; Chester, 325; and Bucks, 225; or a total of 1,575; New Castle, 180; Kent, 139; and Sussex, 106; or a total of 425. These figures, more than anything else, speak eloquently of the difference between the three upper and the

three lower counties in 1700. Yet the members from Delaware demanded equal representation in the new frame of government. *Votes,* I, 275.

41. *Statutes at Large of Pennsylvania,* II, 105–18.

42. To Zachary. March 6, 1701. Norris Letterbook.

43. December 2, 1701. Logan Papers, I, 36.

44. Logan, in describing why he decided to remain in Pennsylvania in 1701, wrote, "I was wrought on by Several Inducemts, of wch a generous Resentmt at ye unkind usage he [Penn] mett wth here was not ye least." To ———. November 25, 1727. Logan Letterbook, IV. HSP. A new biography of Logan has recently been published. Frederick B. Tolles, *James Logan and the Culture of America* (Boston, 1957).

CHAPTER FOURTEEN: PREPARATIONS FOR THE FUTURE

1. Minutes for the September, 1701, session of the General Assembly may be found in *Col. Rec.,* II, 34–56; *Votes,* I, 281–327.

2. *Votes,* I, 287–89.

3. The minutes of the Council indicate September 30, but the records of the Assembly clearly show that the remonstrance was not drawn up until October 9. *Votes,* I, 303–5.

4. *Col. Rec.,* II, 62.

The Charter of Property has never been published, and was lost for 250 years. However in 1957 a representative of the Pennsylvania Historical and Museum Commission found the second and third sheets of this document while examining the archives of the Bureau of Land Records, in the custody of the Department of Internal Affairs, Commonwealth of Pennsylvania. A major part of what must have been on the first sheet is extant in an earlier draft written on paper, at the Historical Society of Pennsylvania, in the Penn Manuscripts, Assembly and Provincial Council of Pennsylvania. There is a gap between the draft at the HSP and the two parchment sheets in Harrisburg. These two parts were published with an introduction by Edwin B. Bronner in *Pennsylvania History,* XXIV (1957), 267–92, under the title, "Penn's Charter of Property of 1701."

5. Richard S. Rodney, "Early Relations of Delaware and Pennsylvania," *PMHB,* LIV (1930), 209–40, expressed the suspicion that Penn was responsible for the "spontaneous" request for an Act of Union by the assemblymen from Delaware.

6. February 19, 1701. Proprieties, V, F 69.

7. May 2, 1699. Penn Letterbook, II. Amer. Phil. Soc.

8. *Votes,* I, 258. Original in italics.

9. *Ibid.,* 259. Original in italics. 10. *Ibid.,* 260. Original in italics.

11. To Daniel Zachary. October 3, 1701. Norris Letterbook.

12. To Thomas Lloyd, Jr. *Ibid.* 13. *Votes,* I, 392.

14. *Statutes at Large of Pennsylvania,* II, 142–70.

15. To Thomas Lloyd, Jr. September 16, 1701. Norris Letterbook.

16. The minutes of both the Council and Assembly contain references

to an outsider as the author of the bill, and the Assembly authorized two payments to him, one for fifty pounds, and the other for twenty pieces of eight.

17. Shepherd, *Proprietary Government in Pennsylvania,* p. 373.

18. See Chapter 12.

19. Norris to John Askew. October 28, 1701. Norris Letterbook.

20. *Votes,* I, 387–93.

21. For example, Isaac Sharpless wrote of "The Charter of 1701 which embodied the final triumph of radical democratic principles." *A Quaker Experiment in Government* (Philadelphia, 1902), I, 64.

22. Penn to Roger Mompesson. February 17, 1705. *Penn and Logan Correspondence,* I, 373. Penn said in part, "The charter I granted was intended to shelter them against a violent or arbitrary governor imposed on us."

23. Sister Joan de Lourdes Leonard, "The Organization and Procedure of the Pennsylvania Assembly, 1682–1776" (Unpublished Dissertation), 27.

CHAPTER FIFTEEN: INHERITANCE FROM THE "HOLY EXPERIMENT"

1. No attempt will be made to repeat in this chapter the explanations and justifications of some of these failures if they have been discussed in previous chapters.

2. To Thomas Lloyd. February 1, 1687. Penn MSS, Domestic.

3. December 9, 1697. Penn Letters. Turner wrote to Penn in this vein on many occasions.

The Indians joined in this revelry, for it was reported that they "go Reeling and bawling in the streets, Especially at night." A petition to the government. May 21, 1695. Hazard's *Register* V (1830), 8.

Another petition of the same year complained of the unseemly activity in the streets by the settlers. See: Edwin B. Bronner, "An Early Example of Political Action by Women, 1695," *Bulletin,* Friends Historical Association, Vol. 43 (1954), 29–32.

The records of the court of quarter sessions and common pleas of Philadelphia County, for six months of the year 1695, recorded the following: twelve persons were accused of selling liquor without a license; nine persons were tried for various forms of abuse and assault; six were accused of fornication and bastardy; three persons were accused of profanity; and one each was accused of lying in court, stealing, drunkenness, and keeping a disorderly house. See: Edwin B. Bronner, "Philadelphia County Court of Quarter Sessions and Common Pleas, 1695." *PMHB,* LXXVIII (1953), 457–80. Only the minutes of the Court of Quarter Sessions are printed in this article. The complete record has been printed in *The American Journal of Legal History,* beginning, I (1957), 79.

4. Unfortunately, Penn was forced to consent to the eventual separation of Delaware from Pennsylvania in order to maintain peace between the citizens of the two areas.

5. Epistle to Quarterly and Monthly Meetings from the Yearly Meeting at Philadelphia, September, 1701. Manuscript Yearly Meeting Minutes. Phila. Y.M.

6. There had been a minor uprising in East Jersey earlier that year, and this statement was directed in part towards any who were involved in that disturbance, but it also applied to the difficulties which had plagued Pennsylvania.

7. Phineas Pemberton, who was Clerk of the Friends business meetings during most of these years, and Samuel Carpenter who replaced him in 1699, were very active in the government. Thomas Lloyd had been a leading figure, as was David Lloyd at the time the letter was written. Samuel Jennings, Edward Shippen, John Simcock, and many others were prominent in both groups.

8. Harry E. Barnes, *The Evolution of Penology in Pennsylvania* (Indianapolis, 1927), pp. 27, ff. See also, Herbert W. K. Fitzroy, "The Punishment of Crime in Provincial Pennsylvania," *PMHB*, LX (1936), 242–69, especially 242–50.

9. To Sir John Lowther. August 16, 1701. *The Manuscripts of the Earl of Lonsdale*, p. 246.

10. To Joseph Pinnell. October 27, 1701. Norris Letterbook.

APPENDIX

Hazard, *Annals,* pp. 488–99. Proud, *History of Pennsylvania,* I, 171–87. The quotations from the Charter are from the copy in the *Charter and Laws of Penna.,* pp. 81–90. Where "v" was used in place of "u," the "u" has been substituted.

2. *Charter and Laws of Penna.,* pp. 91–99.
3. *Charter and Laws of Penna.,* pp. 108–75.
4. Proud, *History of Pennsylvania,* I, 339.
5. *Votes,* I, 387–93.

BIBLIOGRAPHY

All students of Pennsylvania history are deeply indebted to Norman B. Wilkinson, who compiled the *Bibliography of Pennsylvania History*, and to the Pennsylvania Historical and Museum Commission, publishers of this comprehensive work, which first appeared under a slightly different title in 1946, and was published in an enlarged form in 1957.

PRIMARY SOURCES

MANUSCRIPTS

American Philosophical Society
  Penn Letters and Ancient Documents
Haverford College Library, Treasure Room
  Quaker Collection
  Roberts Collection
Historical Society of Pennsylvania
  Blackwell Papers, Compiled by Brinton Coxe
  Board of Trade Journals, 1675–1782 (Transcribed from the original manuscript volumes in the Public Record Office of England for the HSP, 1681–1702.)
  Board of Trade Papers, Proprieties, 1697–1776 (Transcribed from the original manuscript volumes in the Public Record Office of England for the HSP, 1697–1702.)
  Claypoole, James, Letterbook, 1681–1684
  Court of Common Pleas, Philadelphia County, 1695
  Dickinson, Jonathan, Letterbook, 1698–1701
  Dreer Collection: Governors In the Colonies; Letters and Papers of William Penn
  Early Letters from Bristol England and Philadelphia
  Etting Collection: Early Quakers and the Penn Family; Governors; Pemberton; Provincial Council
  Fallon Scrap Book
  Gratz Collection: Governors; Quakers
  Logan Letterbooks, III, IV
  Logan Papers, I, III
  Norris Papers: Family Letters, I; Isaac Norris Letterbook, 1699–1702
  Parrish Collection, Robert Proud Papers
  Pemberton's Abridgement of the Laws of Pennsylvania, 1684

Pemberton Papers, I, II
Penn Manuscripts: Additional Miscellaneous Letters, I; Assembly and
    Provincial Council of Pennsylvania; Beaver Skins, etc.; Blackwell
    Manuscripts; Domestic and Miscellaneous Letters; Granville Penn
    Book; J. Francis Fisher Copies; Forbes Papers; Official Correspond-
    ence, I, II; Three Lower Counties; William Penn Letterbook, 1699–
    1703 (sometimes called Mottled Letterbook)
Penn Papers, Charters and Frame of Government
Penn Papers from Friends House, London. (Photostats)
Pennsylvania Miscellaneous Papers, Penn and Baltimore
Proud Papers
Society Miscellaneous Collection: Philadelphia County; Philadelphia
    Petitions; Provincial Council of Pennsylvania
Thompson, Jonah, Collection, II
Library Company of Philadelphia
Library Company Manuscripts, 1660–1855
Pennsylvania Historical and Museum Commission
The Charter of Property, 1701
Philadelphia Yearly Meeting, Department of Records, 302 Arch Street,
    Philadelphia
Minutes of Philadelphia Quarterly Meeting of Friends
Minutes of the Yearly Meeting
Minutes of the Yearly Meeting and General Spring Meeting of Ministers
Miscellaneous Papers of Philadelphia Monthly Meeting

                          PRINTED SOURCES

Acts of the Privy Council of England. Colonial Series. 1680–1720. W. L.
    Grant, etc., editors. Hereford, 1910.
Archives of Maryland. Maryland Historical Society. Baltimore, 1883–1911.
Armstrong, Edward. *Correspondence between William Penn and James
    Logan . . . with notes by Deborah Logan.* Philadelphia, 1870.
Calendar of State Papers, Colonial Series, America and West Indies. J. W.
    Fortescue, editor. London, 1898–1912.
A Collection of Memorials Concerning Divers Deceased Ministers. Phila-
    delphia, 1787.
*Documents Relative to the Colonial History of the State of New York; Pro-
    cured in Holland, England and France.* London Documents 1614–1706.
    John R. Brodhead, Agent. Albany, 1853, 1854.
George, Staughton, etc., *Charter to William Penn, and Laws of the Prov-
    ince of Pennsylvania, passed between the years 1682 and 1700, . . .*
    Harrisburg, 1879. Commonly called *Charter and Laws of Penna.*
Hazard, Samuel. *Annals of Pennsylvania, . . .* Philadelphia, 1850.
Historical Manuscripts Commission. *The Manuscripts of the Earl of Lons-
    dale.* London, 1893.
Historical Manuscripts Commission. *The Manuscripts of the House of
    Lords.* (New Series) London, 1903, 1912.

Historical Manuscripts Commission. *The Manuscripts of the Duke of Portland.* London, 1894–1901.

A Journal of the Life of Thomas Story. Newcastle, England, 1747.

A Journal or Historical Account of the Life, Travels, Sufferings, . . . of George Fox. Cambridge, England, 1891.

Leeds, Daniel. *News of a Strumpet Co-habiting in the Wilderness or, A brief Abstract of the Spiritual & Carnal Whoredoms & Adulteries of the Quakers in America.* New York, 1701.

Memoirs of the Historical Society of Pennsylvania, I, II, III, IV. Philadelphia, 1826–1850.

Minutes of the Provincial Council of Pennsylvania, I, II. Philadelphia, 1852. Commonly called *Colonial Records.*

Mitchell, James T., and Flanders, Henry. *The Statutes at Large of Pennsylvania. 1682–1801.* II. Harrisburg, 1896.

Myers, Albert Cook. *Narratives of Early Pennsylvania, West Jersey and Delaware.* New York, 1912.

Penn, William. *An Address to the Protestants upon the Present Conjuncture.* 1679.

—— *England's Great Interest in the Choice of this New Parliament.* Probably 1679.

—— *The Excellent Priviledge of Liberty and Property Being the Birthright of the Free-born Subjects of England.* [Philadelphia, 1687.]

—— *One Project for the Good of England: That is, our Civil Union is Our Civil Safety.* 1679.

—— *Some Proposals For a Second Settlement in the Province of Pennsylvania.* London, 1690.

Pennsylvania Archives (First Series). Samuel Hazard, editor. Philadelphia, 1852.

Pennsylvania Archives, Series VIII, *Votes & Proceedings of the House of Representatives.* I. Harrisburg, 1931–1935. Commonly called *Votes.*

Proud, Robert. *The History of Pennsylvania in North America, . . .* I, II. Philadelphia, 1797.

Smith, Samuel. *History of the Province of Pennsylvania.* William M. Mervine, editor. Philadelphia, 1913.

Thomas, Gabriel. *An Historical and Geographical Account of the Province and Country of Pennsylvania.* London, 1698.

Tolles, Frederick B., and Alderfer, E. Gordon, editors. *The Witness of William Penn.* New York, 1957.

William Penn, 1644–1718. The Blumhaven Library. Philadelphia, 1950.

SECONDARY SOURCES

Andrews, Charles M. *The Colonial Period of American History.* New Haven, 1937.

Armour, William C. *Lives of the Governors of Pennsylvania.* Norwich, Conn., 1874.

Backhouse, James. *The Life and Correspondence of William and Alice Ellis*. Philadelphia, 1850.
Barnes, Harry E. *The Evolution of Penology in Pennsylvania*. Indianapolis, 1927.
Beatty, Edward C. O. *William Penn as Social Philosopher*. New York, 1939.
Belasco, Philip S. *Authority in Church and State*. London, 1928.
Bond, Beverley W., Jr. *The Quit-Rent System in the American Colonies*. New Haven, 1919.
Bowden, James. *History of the Society of Friends in America*. London, 1850–1854.
Braithwaite, William C. *The Beginnings of Quakerism*. London, 1912.
—— *The Second Period of Quakerism*. London, 1919.
Bridenbaugh, Carl. *Cities in the Wilderness*. New York, 1938.
Brinton, Howard. *Friends for 300 Years, The History and Beliefs of the Society of Friends*. New York, 1952.
Bronner, Edwin B. "Quaker Landmarks in Early Philadelphia," *Historic Philadelphia*, Luther P. Eisenhart, editor. Philadelphia, 1953. Also published as Vol. 43, Part I, *Transactions* of the American Philosophical Society.
—— "The Failure of the 'Holy Experiment' in Pennsylvania, 1684–1699," *Pennsylvania History*, XXI, 93–108.
—— "The Center Square Meetinghouse," *Bulletin*, Friends Historical Association, Vol. 44, 67–73.
Buell, A. C. *William Penn as the Founder of Two Commonwealths*. New York, 1904.
Cadbury, Henry J. "Hannah Callowhill and Penn's Second Marriage," *Pennsylvania Magazine of History and Biography*, LXXXI, 76–82.
Channing, Edward. *History of the United States*, II. New York, 1908.
Clarkson, Thomas. *Memoirs of the Private and Public Life of William Penn*. London, 1813.
Comfort, W. W. "Quaker Marriage Certificates," *Bulletin*, Friends Historical Association, Vol. 40, 67–80.
—— *William Penn, 1644–1718: A Tercentenary Estimate*. Philadelphia, 1944.
Cooper, Irma Jane. *Life and Public Services of James Logan*. New York, 1921.
Davis, Joseph S. *Essays in the Earlier History of American Corporations*. Cambridge, Mass., 1917.
Dobree, Bonamy. *William Penn: Quaker and Pioneer*. New York, 1932.
Dodson, Leonidas. "Pennsylvania through the eyes of a Royal Governor," *Pennsylvania History*, III, 89–97.
Dorfman, Joseph. "Captain John Blackwell: a Bibliographical Note," *Pennsylvania Magazine of History and Biography*, LXIX, 233–237.
Drake, Thomas E. *Quakers and Slavery in America*. New Haven, 1950.
Drinker, Sophie H. *Hannah Penn and the Proprietorship of Pennsylvania*. Philadelphia, 1958.
Dunaway, Wayland F. *A History of Pennsylvania*. New York, 1948.

Eshleman, H. Frank. "The Struggle and Rise of Popular Power in Pennsylvania's First Two Decades (1682–1701)," *Pennsylvania Magazine of History and Biography*, XXXIV, 129–161.

Essays in Colonial History Presented to Charles McLean Andrews by his Students. New Haven, 1931.

Ewald, Alex. Charles. *Algernon Sydney.* London, 1873.

Fisher, Sydney George. *The Making of Pennsylvania.* Philadelphia, 1896.

Fiske, John. *The Dutch and Quaker Colonies in America.* New York, 1899.

Fitzroy, Herbert W. K. "The Punishment of Crime in Provincial Pennsylvania," *Pennsylvania Magazine of History and Biography*, LX, 242–269.

Gooch, George P. *English Democratic Ideas in the Seventeenth Century.* H. J. Laski, editor. Cambridge, England, 1927.

Gordon, Thomas. *The History of Pennsylvania . . . to 1776.* Philadelphia, 1829.

Guttridge, G. H. *The Colonial Policy of William III.* Cambridge, England, 1922.

Hershberger, Guy. "The Pennsylvania Quaker Experiment in Politics, 1682–1756," *The Mennonite Quarterly Review*, X, 187–221.

Hull, William I. *William Penn: A Topical Biography.* New York, 1937.

Janney, Samuel M. *The Life of William Penn.* Philadelphia, 1852.

Jenkins, Howard M., editor. *Pennsylvania Colonial and Federal.* Philadelphia, 1903.

Jones, Horatio Gates. "Historical Sketch of the Rittenhouse Papermill; The first Erected in America, A.D. 1690," *Pennsylvania Magazine of History and Biography*, XX, 315–333.

Jones, Rufus M. *Quakers in the American Colonies.* London, 1911.

Keith, Charles P. *Chronicles of Pennsylvania, 1688–1748.* Philadelphia, 1917.

Kelsey, Rayner W. *Friends and the Indians, 1655–1917.* Philadelphia, 1917.

Kirby, Ethyn Williams. *George Keith, 1638–1715.* New York, 1942.

Konkle, Burton A. "David Lloyd and the First Half Century of Pennsylvania." Unpublished manuscript, Friends Library, Swarthmore College.

Labaree, Leonard Woods. *Conservatism in Early American History.* New York, 1948.

Leonard, Sister Joan de Lourdes. "The Organization and Procedure of the Pennsylvania Assembly, 1682–1776." Unpublished Doctoral Dissertation at the University of Pennsylvania, 1947. A portion of it was published in the *Pennsylvania Magazine of History and Biography*, LXXII, under the same title.

Lloyd, Arnold. *Quaker Social History, 1669–1738.* London, 1950.

Lokken, Roy N. *David Lloyd, Colonial Lawmaker.* Seattle, 1959.

Maples, Mary. "William Penn, Classical Republican," *Pennsylvania Magazine of History and Biography*, LXXXI, 138–56.

Mervine, William M. "Pirates and Privateers in the Delaware Bay and River," *Pennsylvania Magazine of History and Biography*, XXXII, 459, ff.

Mood, Fulmer. "William Penn and English Politics in 1680–81," *Journal,* Friends Historical Society (London), XXXII, 3–19.

Nettels, Curtis. "The Economic Relations of Boston, Philadelphia and New York, 1680–1715," *Journal of Economic and Business History,* III, 185–215.

Noble, Vernon. *The Man in Leather Breeches. The Life and Times of George Fox.* New York, 1953.

Osgood, Herbert L. *American Colonies in the Eighteenth Century.* New York, 1924.

—— *American Colonies in the Seventeenth Century.* New York, 1904.

Peare, Catherine Owens. *William Penn, a Biography.* Philadelphia, 1957.

Pilcher, James E. *The Seal and Arms of Pennsylvania.* Harrisburg, 1902.

Pomfret, John E. "The First Purchasers of Pennsylvania, 1681–1700," *Pennsylvania Magazine of History and Biography,* LXXX, 137–163.

—— *The Province of West New Jersey, 1609–1702.* Princeton, 1956.

Rodney, Richard S. "Early Relations of Delaware and Pennsylvania," *Pennsylvania Magazine of History and Biography,* LIV, 209–240.

Root, Winfred T. *Relations of Pennsylvania with the British Government, 1696–1765.* New York, 1912.

Scharf, J. Thomas, and Westcott, Thomas. *History of Philadelphia, 1609–1884.* Philadelphia, 1884.

Schlegal, Marvin W. "The Text of the Great Law of 1682," *Pennsylvania History,* XI, 276–283.

Sharpless, Isaac. *A Quaker Experiment in Government.* Philadelphia, 1902.

—— *Political Leaders of Provincial Pennsylvania.* New York, 1919.

Shepherd, William R. *History of Proprietary Government in Pennsylvania.* New York, 1896.

Tolles, Frederick B. *Meeting House and Counting House.* Chapel Hill, 1948.

—— *James Logan and the Culture of Provincial America.* Boston, 1957.

Toppan, Robert N. *Edward Randolph.* Boston, 1898.

Turner, Edward R. *The Negro in Pennsylvania.* Washington, D. C., 1911.

Wainwright, Nicholas B. "Governor John Blackwell," *Pennsylvania Magazine of History and Biography,* LXXIV, 457–472.

—— "The Mystery of Pennsylvania's Royal Charter," *Pennsylvania Magazine of History and Biography,* LXXIII, 415–428.

—— "Plan of Philadelphia," *Pennsylvania Magazine of History and Biography,* LXXX, 164–226.

—— "The Missing Evidence: Penn vs. Baltimore," *Pennsylvania Magazine of History and Biography,* LXXX, 227–235.

Watson, John F. *Annals of Philadelphia.* Philadelphia, 1898.

Wertenbaker, Thomas J. *The Founding of American Civilization. The Middle Colonies.* New York, 1928.

Woody, Thomas. *Early Quaker Education in Pennsylvania.* New York, 1920.

INDEX